**Basics of Language for
Language Learners**
2ND EDITION

Basics of Language for Language Learners

2ND EDITION

Peter W. Culicover and Elizabeth V. Hume

THE OHIO STATE UNIVERSITY PRESS / COLUMBUS

Library of Congress Cataloging-in-Publication Data
Names: Culicover, Peter W., author. | Hume, Elizabeth V., 1956– author.
Title: Basics of language for language learners / Peter W. Culicover and Elizabeth V. Hume.
Description: Second edition. | Columbus : The Ohio State University Press, [2017] | Includes
    bibliographical references and index.
Identifiers: LCCN 2017015374 | ISBN 9780814254431 (pbk. ; alk. paper) | ISBN 0814254438
    (pbk. ; alk. paper)
Subjects: LCSH: Language and languages—Study and teaching.
Classification: LCC P51 .C78 2017 | DDC 418.0071—dc23
LC record available at https://lccn.loc.gov/2017015374

Cover design by Laurence Nozik
Text design by Jennifer Forsythe and Juliet Williams
Type set in Adobe Minion Pro

♾ The paper used in this publication meets the minimum requirements of the American
National Standard for Information Sciences—Permanence of Paper for Printed Library Materials. ANSI Z39.48-1992.

9   8   7   6   5   4   3   2   1

Contents

●●●●●●●●●●●●●●●●●

SECTION IV ACTING LIKE A NATIVE SPEAKER

Preface

Who This Book Is for

We wrote this book for the student of language who wants to understand better how language works. We assume that the student is a speaker of English, either a native speaker or someone who has learned English as a second language. The challenge for this student is to learn how to become a successful learner of other languages.

Our view is that you (the student) have had some exposure to learning a language. You have found certain parts of the activity to be relatively easy, and others to be very challenging, perhaps almost impossible. Our goals are to help you take advantage of the parts that you find easy and build on them and to find ways to deal more effectively with the parts that you find more challenging.

Language learning, like many other skilled activities that people engage in, does not come easy for the average person. Think of playing a sport at a very competitive level, or a musical instrument. Success in these activities, and in language learning, requires perseverance and practice for the average person (and that's most of us!). The truth is that there is no silver bullet, no magic potion, no super pill that will get us where we want to go without exerting the effort.

How Language Works

"OK," you say, "I understand that this is going to take work, I am willing to put in the effort." The approach that we are taking in this book is that the effort will pay off much more if you have an understanding of how language works. In learning a second language you have a tremendous advantage, which is that you have already learned at least one other language—your native language. You have an **intuitive** understanding of how language works, so that you will very likely recognize a lot about language if we illustrate it using your own language.

But most people have a very imperfect and sometimes mistaken **explicit** understanding of how language works. That is, they are not able to recognize aspects of language on their own, such as what the possible sounds are and how they are produced, and explain them to themselves and others. What we are aiming for in this book is a basic, explicit understanding of how language works that is **based on** one's own language and can be **applied to** thinking about the language to be learned. It is our belief that a conscious understanding of the workings of language is a very important tool in dealing with the challenge of learning another language. It does not substitute for perseverance and practice, but it should help you to make the best use of the effort that you are willing to make.

Here is one illustration. In order to be able to speak a language, you need to be able to make the sounds. You can try to imitate the sounds and get correction from an instructor, you can hire a tutor, you can work with tapes and software, and you can even go live in a country where the language is spoken. All of this is helpful, and if you work at it long enough, you will get better.

What this book contributes is an understanding of how the various parts of the mouth are used to make different sounds and how the sounds differ depending on how the parts of the mouth are used. It does not substitute for imitation and correction, for practice with tapes, and so on. Its goal is to provide you with a conscious understanding of what is going on in your mouth and in your mind as you are trying to produce the sounds of a language. We want you to understand why some sounds are easy for you and some are hard, what kinds of mistakes you make and why those, and how to fix them most efficiently.

We have the same kinds of goals in your understanding of grammar, of how language is used in social settings and how language can be inadvertently misused. This book is not about theory; it is about practical understanding. Of course, there is a lot of theory behind what we have put in this book—we are not making it up. But your concern is not with understanding the theory of how language works; it is with understanding how language works.

So, with this in mind, we keep the technical terminology to a minimum. We introduce terms for things so that we can refer to them—the first sound in *boy* is a bilabial stop (we'll explain what that is soon), the word *boy* is a noun, and so on. Some of these terms are familiar to some readers, but not all are familiar to all. So check off what you already know, and pay close attention to what is new to you. Most importantly, the things that are most familiar to us in our own language reemerge in other languages in many different ways, some of which are familiar, and some of which are not. We are using the native language, and the terminology for main features of the native language, as a platform for looking at other languages that differ from it.

Just below we provide a more detailed overview of the four sections that make up this book:

I: Tools and Strategies for Learning a Language
II: Sounding like a Native Speaker
III: Thinking like a Native Speaker
IV: Acting like a Native Speaker

Section I of the book, "Tools and Strategies for Learning a Language," focuses on language learning and on learning more generally. We begin by considering how children learn a first language (e.g., developmental stages, types of mistakes children make) and how adults differ from children in terms of learning a language. This section, new to the second edition, includes a discussion of the advantages and disadvantages that the adult has in carrying out this task and how this information can help you approach the task of learning a language. We then explore the properties of language that make it not only challenging to learn but similar to other activities such as juggling, driving a car, playing the piano, and so forth. These include sequencing, precision, speed, and the active, ongoing, and coordinated involvement of the mind. With information about these properties as a basis, students are given advice on how to be more successful at learning a language or any new skill. The role of memory in learning a language is also discussed in this section. Topics include the difference between temporary vs. permanent memory and the goal of storing new information in permanent memory, effective techniques for memorizing elements of another language, the most common words in language, advantages and disadvantages of flash cards, and the role of chunking in memorization. We finish the section by giving some practical information on bilingual dictionaries, including discussion of what to look for in a dictionary and how to effectively use a bilingual dictionary, whether it be in print or on-line.

Section II, "Sounding like a Native Speaker," takes up the topic of foreign accent, one of the most noticeable aspects of foreign language learning. It is easy enough to spot a foreign accent in someone speaking English, but what does an "American" accent sound like in Spanish or Japanese? What do you do when you speak foreign words that make you sound, well, like a foreigner? Can you do anything to sound more like a native speaker of the language? In addressing these questions you will learn about making so-called exotic sounds as well as combining them to form new words. You will also learn how to avoid making the typical mistakes that may interfere with communication.

Section III, "Thinking like a Native Speaker," delves further into language structure, focusing on how words combine to form sentences. Every language has to provide its speakers with ways of carrying out the same basic human activities of expressing and communicating ideas, intentions, and desires. The way languages do this is by combining words and other linguistic elements into phrases and sentences in particular systematic ways. How a given language forms phrases and sentences is called its **structure** or its **grammar.**

But languages differ, sometimes subtly and sometimes dramatically. The structure of a language may be identical or very similar to English in certain respects, and very different in others. Being able to deal effectively with learning the grammar of another language involves having an understanding of how one's own language works and recognizing the similarities and differences.

As will become clear in section IV, "Acting like a Native Speaker," there is much more to learning a language than learning its structure. Language is a human phenomenon, and since an important part of how people define themselves is through culture, it is not surprising that language and culture are necessarily interwoven. In this section, we explore the link between language and culture in two ways. On the one hand, we introduce some of the roles that language plays in social interaction and examine how these roles can differ from one culture to another. One example relates to expressing emotions. Do all cultures express anger or insults in the same way? How about politeness? We will see that they do not. We'll also explore ways in which cultural ideas are reflected in language. One topic treated in relation to this concerns potential differences in how language is used by men and women in English as well as in other languages.

Changes to the Second Edition

In the second edition we have taken the opportunity to include additional chapters that should help the language learner. They form part of the new section I called "Tools and Strategies for Language Learning," which focuses on four new chapters: chapter 1, "Language Learning"; chapter 2, "Brain Training"; chapter 3, "Memory"; and chapter 4, "Using a Dictionary." In addition, the chapters in section III, "Thinking like a Native Speaker," have been modified to include more discussion of errors made by language learners, and the material in these chapters has been substantially reorganized. The chart on consonants at the end of the book has also been modified to follow that of the International Phonetic Association. Finally, we have corrected some minor errors and revised the wording in some places to enhance clarity.

Acknowledgments

We would like to express our appreciation to a number of individuals who played a role in the development of this book. These include Dan Culicover, Hope Dawson, Kathleen Currie Hall, Dan Humphries, Julie McGory, Jeff Mielke, and Bridget Smith. We are also grateful to Malcolm Litchfield and Tony Sanfilippo at The Ohio State University Press for their input and support of this project. In addition, we acknowledge our former colleague, Keith Johnson, who contributed to the writing of chapter 3, "Memory." We are also grateful to instructors, including Diana Archangeli, and our students over the years who provided us with valuable feedback. Many thanks to Sharon Rose for doing the index and to Pauline Welby for her juggling.

SECTION I

Tools and Strategies
for Language Learning

Language Learning

What Can We Learn from First Language Acquisition?

*T*he most distinctive fact about language learning is that children learn their first language completely naturally, apparently effortlessly, and without formal instruction. Moreover, they become competent native speakers in just a few years, in full command of the sounds and structures of their language,

> Pal franse pa di lespri pou sa.
> 'To speak French doesn't mean you are smart.'
>
> —HAITIAN PROVERB

although they continue to acquire vocabulary over many years as their understanding of the world develops. And they are indistinguishable from other native speakers in their ability to interact socially with the language. They **are** native speakers.

Contrast this situation with that of an adult learning a second language. For the vast majority of us, this learning does not feel entirely natural, it is certainly not effortless, and formal instruction appears to be quite necessary (although it is not sufficient). The adult second language learner typically has a foreign accent, makes frequent grammatical errors, does not have active control over the full vocabulary, has difficulty figuring out how to say even the most mundane things, and often does not understand what is being said. In many respects, the linguistic abilities of a second language learner are comparable to those of a very young child (say, two or three years old) who is learning a first language. The vast majority of adult second language learners never achieve the facility of native speakers.

These observations certainly do not come as news to anyone who has tried to learn a second language, yet they are worth revisiting. Focusing on the differences between first and second language learning, and on why first language learning appears to be so easy, will help us understand what we have to do in order to facilitate second language learning (although it will never be totally effortless).

This chapter looks first at some of the most salient characteristics of first language learning. We survey what particular tools children bring to the task of language learning that make them so successful. We also look at the learning environment in which the child typically acquires a first language. We sample some of the errors that children make in learning their first language, and take note of the major stages in first language development.

We then turn to second language learners (that is, us) and compare our situation to that of a first language learner. On the basis of this comparison, we make some observations about where we have to focus our attention and energies in learning a second language, and also about the ways in which as adults we have certain advantages over a first language learner that we should try to use when possible.

How Do Children Learn a First Language?

THE BASICS OF FIRST LANGUAGE LEARNING

From the study of first language learning by children, we have learned a number of interesting and sometimes surprising things. It is of course quite obvious that very young children are not exposed to formal language instruction of the sort that we experience in school. Yet by the time they begin formal schooling, they are already competent speakers of their language(s). And this fact raises a number of puzzling questions: Who taught them and how was it done? Where were the language lessons? How were their mistakes identified and corrected? And, come to think of it, who trained the teachers?

The answers to these questions are surprising. No one "teaches" children language. There are no language lessons. In general, and contrary to popular belief, children do not acquire their language as a consequence of the correction of mistakes by their parents and other adults (and older children) whom they interact with. Most of the mistakes that children make are not corrected by adults. When they are corrected, the children generally persist in making them in spite of the correction, sometimes for years. And, of course, since there are no language teachers for first language learners, there is no teacher training for first language acquisition.

Much of the evidence for these statements comes from detailed diary studies of children's language development and the analysis of transcripts of interactions between adults and children. Many of the materials are available to all researchers on the CHILDES database (the Child Language Data Exchange System at childes.psy.cmu.edu/; MacWhinney 2000).

As we think about the difference between first language learning by children and second language learning by adults, the disparities become ever more astonishing. How can it be that adults, who are so much more educated and knowledgeable about the world, have so much more difficulty in learning a language? There is an old joke about an American who goes to Paris, comes back to the United States, and says to his friends that the French kids must all be geniuses—they can all speak French like natives!

But obviously, the reason that they can all speak French like natives is that they **are** all natives. Learning a first language is what it means to be a native speaker. There is something special about the tools that the child brings to the task of language learning and the language learning environment that makes acquisition of native competence by the child the norm. And in the adult, there are critical differences that make the task much different, and in general more formidable.

WHAT ARE THE CAPACITIES OF THE FIRST LANGUAGE LEARNER?

All scientists who specialize in the study of learning believe that human beings are born with powerful abilities for extracting patterns from the world around them, associating patterns with one another and generalizing from particular instances to general rules. Many, but not all, believe that humans are born with specialized tools for learning language, exclusive of their ability to acquire other complex skills (like driving a car or playing basketball) and complex systems of knowledge (like chess or mathematics). We do not take a position on this issue here but simply note that whatever capacities humans are born with, these capacities make them extraordinarily adept at learning a first language.

Other creatures, regardless of what capacities they may have, cannot learn a language (nor for that matter can they drive a car, play basketball, play chess, or do mathematics). But other creatures, especially highly evolved creatures, are capable of communicating with one another, and they are also capable of some extraordinary feats by virtue of their biological makeup. And many are capable of acquiring certain simple aspects of very complex tasks. For example, some primates and birds can count to as high as 6 or 7, some dogs have been taught to distinguish between "left" and "right," some primates can do very simple arithmetic, and some primates have been able to acquire hand gestures that stand for objects and relations between objects. These species have impressive cognitive capacities, and the extent of these capacities has yet to be fully understood. But it is fair to say that they do not have the capacities that humans have.

The first language learner is exposed to spoken language from the moment it achieves consciousness in her mother's womb, prior to birth. The sounds of language can be perceived by the prenatal language learner, and experimental evidence shows that the prenatal learner has already developed a certain sensitivity to the sounds of the language that she will be learning. The ear develops in the third week after conception and becomes functional in the sixteenth week; the fetus begins active listening in the twenty-fourth week. Prior to birth the fetus responds distinctively to its mother's voice while still in the womb. Lecanuet et al. (1995) found that just prior to birth the fetus is able to discriminate reversals of vowel sounds, such as /babi/ versus /biba/. When the fetus hears the same sequence over a period of time, it becomes habituated to it (as

● ● ● ● ● ● ● ● ● ● ● ● ● ● ● ●

measured by heart rate); when the sequence changes, the heart rate decelerates briefly, indicating recognition of the distinctive properties of speech. Other experiments have shown the sensitivity of the fetus to music.

Adults talk to the newborn child even though it is clear that the child cannot possibly understand what is being said. As the child gets older, but still cannot speak the language, adults continue to interact with him/her. Here is a sample of an interaction between Stefan, aged fourteen months, and his mother and father (Feldman, CHILDES database). The child's utterances are notated as *STV, the mother's as *MOT, and the father's as *FAT. We've highlighted the child's utterances in boldface.

```
*FAT:   hi there.
*FAT:   woh.
*FAT:   yes.
*STV:   gee.
*FAT:   uh-huh.
*FAT:   is that your badada down
        there?
*FAT:   badada and your red
        balloon.
*FAT:   oh did you like that
        last night.
*MOT:   the body lotion?
*FAT:   oh, you wouldn't, when
        you were going down?
*MOT:   you know what?
*MOT:   you know why he likes
        this all of a sudden?
*FAT:   why's that?
*MOT:   because I take the lid
        off for him.
*FAT:   yeah, last night I
        opened it up.
*MOT:   right.
*FAT:   and he is just
        fascinated with that.
*FAT:   do you like that badada?
*FAT:   now, tell me Stef, is
        this a badada or is it a
        bottle?
*STV:   badada.
*FAT:   it's a badada.
*MOT:   it had Stef's body
        lotion in it.
```

```
*MOT:   right?
*MOT:   at one time.
*STV:   Dada.
*FAT:   yes, Stefan?
*MOT:   body lotion.
*FAT:   it's not a bottle.
*FAT:   it's a badada?
*STV:   badada.
*FAT:   ok.
*FAT:   absolutely sure.
*MOT:   and what's this?
*FAT:   no uncertainties.
*STV:   badada [× 4].
*MOT:   is this a badada or is
        this a bottle?
*FAT:   this is a bottle, right?
*STV:   badada.
*MOT:   there's an overlap
        there.
*FAT:   I guess there is!
*MOT:   clearly this has milk in
        it.
*FAT:   ah.
*STV:   baba.
*FAT:   yeah.
*MOT:   now he said baba for the
        body lotion.
*FAT:   yeah.
*MOT:   the empty one.
*FAT:   right.
*STV:   badada baba.
*MOT:   ok, thank you for
        clarifying things.
```

Notice that the child is exposed to a considerable amount of talk, although he is very limited in his ability to contribute to the conversation at this point.

For purposes of comparison, here is a brief excerpt from an interaction between Stefan and his parents about thirteen months later.

```
*FAT:   you got a budleyley with      *FAT:   wanna read this bookie?
        ya there, huh?                *MOT:   wake up Bob the puppet.
*MOT:   oh boy.                       *FAT:   got it, what does this
*MOT:   the budleyley's goin(g)               say Tadi, m o m mom?
        kaboomps too?                 *MOT:   what's m o m mom?
*STV:   no.                           *MOT:   oh, it does.
*STV:   budleyley stuck.              *FAT:   m o m mom!
*FAT:   oh.                           *FAT:   and with d a d.
*STV:   budleyley stuck.              *STV:   and Derek.
*FAT:   yeah.                         *FAT:   yeah, here's Derek.
*FAT:   whoops!                       *FAT:   and Derek.
*STV:   <xxx> [>].                     *STV:   Derek.
*MOT:   do you <you want> [<]          *MOT:   oh, and Bobbie.
        Bob the puppet or not,        *FAT:   here's Bobbie!
        Stefan?                       *FAT:   oh, hi Bobbie!
*FAT:   you want Bob the puppet?      *FAT:   oh, give Bobbie a big
*MOT:   do you wanna see Bob the              hug.
        puppet?                       *FAT:   oh.
*STV:   yeah.                          *MOT:   your friend, huh?
*MOT:   yeah, ok.                     *FAT:   yeah.
*FAT:   mama is gonna bring that      *MOT:   can I sit here?
        out.                          *STV:   I don't like you sitting
*MOT:   I am.                                 there.
*MOT:   and maybe Bob would like     *MOT:   in the car?
        to read the book too.         *STV:   yeah.
*FAT:   yeah.                         *MOT:   ok.
```

At this stage, the child gives the impression of being a more or less fully competent speaker of the language, although there are still childlike mannerisms, like *budleyley stuck* instead of *budleyley's stuck*. Particularly striking is the transition from being limited to producing utterances like *badada* at fourteen months to saying things like *I don't like you sitting there* just thirteen months later.

In order to be able to achieve native competence in the target language, the learner must be able to carry out the following tasks, among others.

Distinguish speech sounds. As a preliminary to learning words, the learner must be able to distinguish the sounds of a language from one another. These sounds may be very similar to one another, like 'th' and 's' in English, but distinguishing them is critical to understanding and being understood (consider the difference between *I thank my friends* and *I sank my friends*).

Correlate sound differences with meaning differences. Different languages distinguish different sounds, as we will discuss in chapters 4, 5, and 6. Sound differences that are meaningful in one language may not be in another. So it is not simply a matter of hearing that two sounds are different; it is also a matter of relating this difference to a difference in meaning. Being able to do this presupposes that the learner can link the sounds of the language to the meanings that are expressed. Of course, the sounds are not produced in isolation but are produced in words, and it is the words, with their particular forms, that have meaning and may differ in meaning.

Understand the intentions of other speakers. The learner must understand why it is that other people are making sounds. It is possible that the learner figures this out from the fact that the same sounds (that is, words and phrases) are being produced by others in the same kinds of contexts. For example, parents may say *dog* when there is a dog and point to the dog. But then the learner must be able to understand what communicative function the pointing is intended to perform. Tomasello (2003) argues that other animals, even higher primates, are not able to link the production of a symbol, such as a word, with pointing to an object, and understand that the speaker intends the symbol to be treated as the name or description of the object. Understanding these intentions, Tomasello argues, is a prerequisite to acquiring a language, and only humans have this capacity.

Understand what language is about. A word or a phrase may refer to an object, such as *book*. A word or a phrase may also refer to an object with a certain property, such as *big book,* to an event, such as *the World Cup* or *We ate the cake,* to a time, to a place, to an emotion, to an idea, and so on. In order to be able to understand what language is about, a learner must have an understanding of the world that the language refers to. The learner must have an understanding of things, properties, times, places, events, and so on, that may be guided by language but must at least in some respects precede language. In order to be able to learn that a linguistic expression has a particular meaning, the learner must have the meaning in some form already as a consequence of experience in the world.

Put words together. The learner must have the capacity to put words together to express complex ideas, as well as the understanding that this is what other speakers are doing when they speak. Again, it is not clear whether this is a specific capacity of human beings when they come into the world or whether it is something that we all learn to do through experience.

With this in place, let us consider in a little more detail the course of first language development.

WHAT IS THE COURSE OF FIRST LANGUAGE DEVELOPMENT?

There are traditionally four stages of language development. These stages do not have sharp boundaries; that is, we cannot see dramatic transitions between them from one day or week to the next. But if we step back and look at the entire course of language development, we can see that there are things that occur early that are lost, and things that do not occur early that are fully in place at some later point.

Babbling. When children begin to produce speech sounds, they "babble." That is, they do not produce words of the target language, or even nonsense that sounds like the target language, or even exclusively sounds of the target language. The babbling stage lasts until eight to ten months. Toward the end of the babbling stage, children's babbling begins to take on qualities of the target language. The sounds are those of the target language, but the babbling is still nonsense.

The one-word stage. At about one year of age, children begin to produce single word utterances. During the one-word stage children's vocabulary grows slowly. Comprehension typically exceeds production by a factor of about 10 to 1. A child typically produces on the order of twenty distinct words at one year, and about fifty at one and a half years of age.

The two-word stage. At around two years of age children begin to produce phrases. The first phrases consist by and large of two words; hence this is called the two-word stage. At around this time, the number of words that a child knows begins to grow significantly, as does the rate of increase in word learning. It is difficult to measure vocabulary size precisely, but it appears that at two years of age and beyond, a child is learning about ten words a day, and the vocabulary size of the typical high school student is 60,000 words.

Grammatical competence. After the two-word stage, there is not only a significant growth in vocabulary, but children begin to show evidence that they have acquired or are in the process of acquiring the rules and constructions of the grammar of a language (see Stefan's *I don't like you sitting there* at age twenty-six months.)

WHAT KINDS OF INFORMATION ARE CHILDREN EXPOSED TO?

In order to understand the differences between first and second language learning, we should think a bit about differences in the learning environments for the two types of learners. There are three main characteristics of the first language learner's environment to take note of.

Quantity. A first language learner is exposed to an extraordinary quantity of linguistic experience. In a typical transcript of an interaction between Stefan and his parents, the parents spoke ninety-five sentences in thirty-four minutes, or about three sentences per minute. Assuming that the child is awake and interacting with his parents ten hours per day between the ages of one and two, that makes approximately 650,000 sentences per year. If sentences spoken to young children average five words per sentence, that means that the child has heard around 3,250,000 word tokens (that is, individual words) during the first year of linguistic interaction. Over the first four years this would come to over two and half million sentences and thirteen million word tokens, even assuming an average of five words per sentence.

Cognition and concreteness. In general, the language spoken to children is about things that the children understand, especially when we are responding to what a child says or trying to get the child to do something. We typically do not talk to very young children about politics or philosophy, at least not with the intent of communicating. Nor do we talk extensively to children who have only a very minimal understanding of calculus or theoretical physics, or even about the future or possible future events. It is very likely that until children have the cognitive development to understand these matters, what we say to them is effectively meaningless, although they might assign some interpretation to it.

What we do talk to children about concerns objects in their experience, such as food, animals, and diapers. The properties that we talk about are more or less concrete: hot, cold, sharp, and pretty. The events that we talk about are also concrete: eating, bodily functions, sleeping, and playing.

At the same time, we talk about other things in the presence of the child, and sometimes to the child, not knowing exactly how much the child knows. When the child's understanding of the world grows, words that we use become meaningful to the child as they are connected to the context in which they are used.

Redundancy. While the number of sentences and words that the first language learner is exposed to is very large, there is a lot of redundancy in this experience. The same words and linguistic constructions are used over and over again. This is particularly the case when adults are talking to the child, rather than to one another in the presence of the child. Here is a sample interaction taken from a transcript with Stefan at approximately a year and a half.

```
*MOT:   he's gettin(g) hungry.          *STV:   baba [: bottle]
*FAT:   yeah.                                   [=! cries].
*MOT:   somebody I know # is            *STV:   baba [: bottle].
        gettin(g) hungry.               *MOT:   the water bottle.
*STV:   (h)a:tie.                       *FAT:   time?
*MOT:   oh, your ha:tie.                *MOT:   it's eleven forty.
*MOT:   (h)a:tie.                       *STV:   baba [: bottle]?
*STV:   babua [: bottle] dada?          *MOT:   yeah?
*MOT:   we're gonna go bye bye,         *STV:   bababa [: bottle].
        and we're gonna go on           *MOT:   you wanna drink from
        a walkie with dada very                 that?
        soon, right?                    *MOT:   ok.
*FAT:   that's right.                   *MOT:   uh uh uh uh uh.
*MOT:   take a nice walk, and           *MOT:   you thirsty?
        we haven't decided where        *FAT:   um:.
        yet.                            *FAT:   ah.
*STV:   baba [: bottle]?                *MOT:   is that good?
*MOT:   oh, yes, that's the baba        *MOT:   um:.
        [: bottle].                     *FAT:   oh, that's good, huh?
*MOT:   good.                           *MOT:   very good.
                                        *FAT:   whoops, whoopsie.
```

And for comparison, here is a portion of a transcript with Eve at eighteen months, also in the CHILDES database. Here, *CHI is the child.

```
*CHI:  more cookie.              *MOT:  here you go.
*MOT:  you xxx more cookies?     *CHI:  more cookie.
*MOT:  how about another graham  *MOT:  you have another cookie
       cracker?                         right on the table.
*MOT:  would that do just as     *CHI:  more juice?
       well?                     *MOT:  more juice?
*MOT:  here.                     *MOT:  would you like more
                                        grape juice?
```

Notice that when the parents talk to the child, they repeat what they say and what the child says, and sometimes add elaborations. Typically, the contexts for young children are very concrete, involving such things as food and drink.

WHAT KINDS OF MISTAKES DO CHILDREN MAKE, AND WHY?

Our intuition tells us that children learn language by imitating the language spoken around them. Examination of the transcripts shows that the adults speak like adults (unsurprisingly), while the children speak like children. In a way this is a puzzle: if children imitate adults, why don't they speak just like adults do?

A number of answers have been offered to explain this puzzle. They are not mutually incompatible, so they may all be right, at least to some extent. Here are some of the most plausible answers.

- **Memory**: Young children have limited memory. As a consequence, they are unable to remember the full form of a word and so truncate it. Similarly, they are unable to process long sentences and thus cannot learn complex constructions at the early stages of language learning.
- **Articulation**: Young children are unable to produce the more complex sounds and sound combinations that they hear and therefore produce approximations, such as *baba* instead of *bottle*.
- **Structure**: Young children do not have access to the full range of grammatical structures that occur in adult language and therefore are able only to acquire and produce a subset of these structures.
- **Generalization**: Young children do not have enough experience to recognize that certain forms are exceptional and have to be learned separately, so after they have learned a general rule, they tend to use it even when it is should not apply. Hence we get children's forms such as *goed* instead of *went*.
- **Cognition**: Young children have a very restricted mental representation of the world and little or no understanding of abstractions like time, emotion, and opinion. Therefore they are unable to understand talk about these things and unable to acquire the words and constructions that are used to express ideas about them.

Summary: The Essential Characteristics of First Language Learning

To summarize to this point, we have seen that young children are very good at learning language. While they do make mistakes, they are presented with an overwhelming amount of redundant information about how the language is supposed to be and therefore have a very good basis for correcting their mistakes. The amount of linguistic experience that children are exposed to may well make up for memory limitations that children may have, since repetition relieves the child of the burden of having to remember what was said. Moreover, language is a crucial aspect of the interactions between children and adults and allows children to get their basic needs met.

How Do Adult Second Language Learners Differ from Children in Terms of Language Learning?

Let us turn now to the situation of an adult second language learner by comparing it to that of the first language learner.

CRITICAL PERIOD

Perhaps the most salient property of first language learning, after the fact that it is accomplished naturally and quickly by all "normal" children without formal instruction, is that this property fades away as the child approaches adulthood. Some scientists have proposed that there is a "critical period" for language learning in which the parts of the brain devoted to language acquisition remain active, after which these parts turn off. It has been suggested that the end of the critical period correlates with the onset of puberty, which is one mark of the transition to adulthood.

Others have suggested that there is no critical period specific to language, but that as we age there is a gradual falling off of the capacity to learn complex skills naturally and accurately. On this view, the loss in our ability to acquire native competency in a language is paralleled by a loss in our ability to acquire expert facility in playing a musical instrument or a sport. As is the case with language, we are able to learn to do these things as adults but lack the deep intuitions that we develop when we begin to learn them as children.

Whatever the case may be for a specialized critical period for language, the fact remains that adults are not as adept at language learning as children. This means that we adults have to approach the task in a very different way than the child approaches it.

DISADVANTAGES

There are other ways in which adults are at a disadvantage in learning a language, besides the fact that they have passed out of the critical period.

Motivation. The first language learner has an extremely strong motivation to learn the language. This motivation may be in part biological and in part social. In any case, there is no conscious decision on the part of the child about whether to learn the language or what language to learn. The child simply **must** learn the language of the surrounding environment.

In order to be successful in learning a second language, an adult must seek the strongest possible motivation. In an academic setting, the motivation is in part external—there is a requirement to be satisfied, there is a grade to be assigned, and so on. But what is far stronger is a genuine desire to learn the language and a sense of enjoyment in doing so since the work involved is considerable, there is frequent failure, and it can be very tedious. In order for the effort to be successful, the learner must find a language to learn that is so attractive to study that putting forth the effort is itself appealing. A book cannot tell you what **your** motivation might be, but we strongly urge you to find a language to study where the motivation is strong.

Strong first language. As a consequence of having spent many years hearing and speaking our native language, we have developed very rapid mental computations for translating between sounds and meaning. When we hear something in our language, we know immediately what it means, and we typically understand the words and the intentions of the speaker as reflected in his or her use of particular phrasings, intonation, and style. We may have a good idea of the social group or groups that the speaker belongs to based on the speaker's speech patterns.

Similarly, when we want to say something, typically the words spring to our tongue to express the thoughts that we have. We do not have to remember the words or figure out how to pronounce them. We have been practicing the articulatory gestures that are necessary for us to be able to sound like a native speaker for years, perhaps dozens of years. No wonder that we are able to sound "just like" native speakers! This level of competence and this amount of practice is a good part of what it means to **be** a native speaker.

And we know exactly where to put the words in order to make our sentences grammatical. In English, the subject comes first, and when the subject is finished, we add the verb or sequence of verbs, and then there are the object and perhaps adverbs and other similar expressions. The ordering of words is different in other languages, but in each language, the speakers have been practicing putting the words where they are supposed to go for their entire lives.

Thus, the habits connected with the first language are very strong in the adult. In order to develop some level of competence in a second language, the habits of the first language must be identified and controlled. The situation is very similar to that in which American drivers and pedestrians find themselves when they go to the United Kingdom (UK) (and when the British go to parts of Europe or to the United States). In the United States, cars drive on the right; in the United Kingdom, cars drive on the left. After having

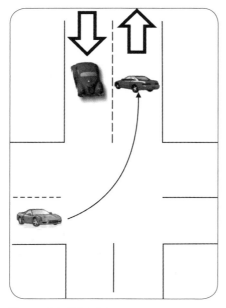

Figure 1.1. U.S. left turn

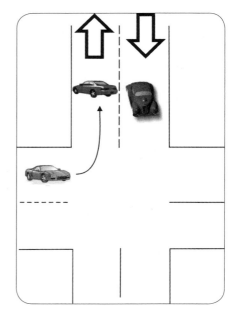

Figure 1.2. UK left turn

driven for many years in the United States, we have the habit of making a left turn into the right lane, as shown in figure 1.1. But in the United Kingdom, the left turn must be made as shown in figure 1.2.

It is very natural for someone with U.S. driving habits to make a left turn into the right lane, something that can be quite dangerous if there is oncoming traffic, as shown in figure 1.3. The solution here is to control and put aside U.S. driving habits while creating an equivalent British driving habit. Creating the British driving habit does not mean forgetting how to drive in the United States; it simply means becoming conscious of the old habit and learning how to suspend it while the new habit is being implemented. Learning a second language requires the same type of suspension of an old and very well learned habit.

Perceptual biases. Adults can have similar difficulty in distinguishing the sounds of a foreign language. Yet a very young child is more or less neutral with respect to the sounds of language, although he already has some preference for the sounds of the language in the environment. After ten or twenty years of being exposed only to the sounds of this language, the first language learner has become extremely adept at picking out very fine distinctions among sounds that signify differences in meaning. When an adult is exposed to the sounds of a new language, he naturally imposes the habits of hearing on the new language, even though the new language may have very different sounds and very different distinctions than does the old language.

Limited input; limited redundancy. The young child is exposed to a vast amount of information about a first language. In general, the adult second language learner, particularly in an academic setting, is exposed to dramatically less informa-

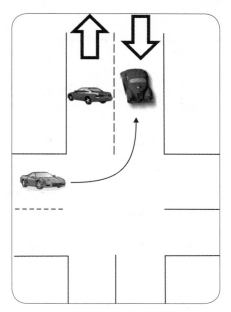

Figure 1.3. U.S. left turn in the UK

tion. Moreover, the adult second language learner is an adult and is therefore not being spoken to patiently and redundantly for ten to fifteen hours per day by attentive parents about a limited range of topics such as food and bodily functions. In contrast, the adult second language learner is talking to other adults and wants to talk about the wide range of topics that interest adults, which certainly go far beyond food and bodily functions. Finally, the child has basically nothing else to do besides learn the language as well as other basic aspects of social interaction, while the adult has many other important and potentially more interesting things to do.

So, to put the difference in the starkest terms, the environment for first language learning, on the one hand, is perfectly well designed to give the child every opportunity to learn her native language. On the other hand, the environment makes it anything but easy for an adult to learn a second language, and the adult's greater maturity and range of interests may actually work against being successful. This being said, the adult does have some potential advantages over the first language learner.

ADVANTAGES

There is no question that compared with a young child, the adult has advantages in learning certain types of knowledge. We have already noted that young children are incapable of learning complex systems of knowledge such as calculus and physics. They are also incapable of learning about grammatical rules, although of course they are capable of acquiring these rules subconsciously.

The adult also has the ability, in principle at least, to consciously structure the learning environment. The adult can focus on particular difficulties, can talk about problems and identify ways to solve them, and can (again in principle at least) make language learning be something that is fun rather than a chore.

Even with motivation, we have seen that adults are handicapped by the fact that they do not have as much **useful** experience with the language that they are learning as the child does. We stress "useful" because it is relatively easy for an adult to be exposed to a second language for hours and hours a day, for example, by listening to the radio or watching television. There is a difference between this type of experience and that of the child's, however. As the child develops and begins to interact with his parents and other adults, her linguistic experience is not only very extensive but also very redundant and overwhelmingly about things that the child cares about and understands. It is this involvement with and understanding of what the language spoken in the environment is about that makes it relatively easy for the child to correlate the words and phrases with the relevant aspects of the physical, social, and emotional environments. Without such understanding, the language that the child hears is noise, and the child can do nothing with it.

The adult learner must therefore enter or create a learning environment where what is being talked about is fully understood by the adult. Moreover, there should be substantial repetition and elaboration, so that the adult, like the child, does not have the opportunity to forget things that are once learned. Some helpful strategies for the adult language learner are introduced in the following chapters.

Activities

1. Think about your own experiences in trying to learn a second language. If you are studying a language now, keep a diary about what aspects of the language you find most challenging, and what aspects you find easiest. For example, are there particular sounds that are very difficult for you? Are there vocabulary items that are hard to remember, no matter how many times you review them? Are there grammatical constructions that you find difficult, while others seem very straightforward? Are there particular environments where language learning seems to be easiest? Keeping track of these things will make it productive for you to reflect on them as you proceed through the various topics covered in this book.

2. Another difference between first and second language learning is that children are typically exposed to many different speakers, while adult learners in the classroom are typically exposed only to the speech of the instructor (and possibly speakers on various media). Do you find it more or less challenging to follow what is being said in another language when you are confronted with a variety of speakers as contrasted with a single speaker? Why do you think that this is the case?

References

Lecanuet, J. P.; C. Granier-Deferre; & M. C. Busnel. 1995. Human fetal auditory perception. *Fetal development: A psychobiological perspective,* ed. J. P. Lecanuet; W. P. Fifer; N. A. Krasnegor; & W. P. Smotherman. 239–62. Mahwah, NJ: Erlbaum.

MacWhinney, Brian. 2000. Tools for analyzing talk, transcription format and programs: The CHILDES project. Mahwah, NJ: Erlbaum.

Tomasello, Michael. 2003. *Constructing a language: A usage-based theory of language acquisition.* Cambridge, MA: Harvard University Press.

2

Brain Training

Understanding Complex Tasks

As we saw in chapter 1, learning a first language is accomplished by the human mind as it is exposed to a vast number of sounds, words, and sentences in meaningful contexts. One of the most remarkable facts about first language learning is that every normal child accomplishes the task without explicit instruction, simply by experiencing the language and subconsciously constructing general rules on the basis of this experience. These rules allow the child to produce new and creative examples that are appropriate to a wide range of situations and contexts.

As we also saw in chapter 1, the task of learning a second language as an adult is similar to the task of learning a first language in some ways and different in others. The most fundamental similarity, which we can take advantage of, is that both the first language and the second language are represented somehow in the mind of the learner. The mind, in turn, is a product of the brain. In learning a first language, a child's brain is "trained" by its everyday experience to be able to understand and produce language right from the start, and development proceeds naturally. In learning a second language, we have to find ways to train our brains so that we can acquire something resembling the ability of the first language learner to deal with language. An important step in this process is to understand what our brains are doing when we speak and understand a language.

Why Understanding What the Brain Is Doing Is Important

- A language is a form of *knowledge.*
- Knowledge is encoded somewhere in the *brain.*
- This knowledge is used for *speaking* and *understanding.*
- Learning a language involves *training* your *brain.*
- You can manage your own brain training if you understand what the *goals* of the training are.

In order to get a feel for what brain training involves, we look first at one complex task that is quite distinct from language, which is juggling, and briefly mention a few others, including playing a musical instrument and learning a first language as a child. Then we return to second language learning.

These complex tasks are all very different in terms of what the objective is. In juggling, we are trying not to let any of the objects fall; in playing a musical instrument, we are trying to get the notes right and play musically; and in learning a first language, a learner is trying to figure out what the relationships are between sounds and meanings and how to physically produce the sounds. But they are similar in that they all involve getting control of and coordinating a large number of simultaneous actions; we look closely at this similarity below. The place where this control resides is the brain. By looking at these, we'll see what the elements are that go into a program for training the brain to perform a particular complex task.

We should note that a good course in a foreign language will incorporate brain training exercises, and lots of them. Our objective at this point is to help you think about what goes on in brain training and what happens if it is not done properly, and to make you aware of what is going on in your own experience of learning a language.

Coordinating Mental Actions

Let's start with juggling, and in particular, bad juggling. When we see what goes wrong in the performance of a complex task, and when we actually get an intuitive feeling for what goes wrong, we can begin to understand what needs to be done right in order for the task to be performed successfully.

"Why juggling?" you might ask. "What does juggling have to do with speaking and understanding language?" In fact, there are a number of similarities. Most importantly, they both require the **active, ongoing, coordinated involvement of the mind.**

Complex Activities like Juggling and Language Require:

The active, ongoing, coordinated involvement of the *mind.*

Juggling is basically a physical activity that is controlled by the mind. Speaking and understanding a language involve physical activity controlled by the mind, as well as many nonphysical (that is, purely mental) activities that go on in the "background." For example, when we hear a word and recognize its meaning, recognition of the meaning is definitely a mental action, but we do not appear to do anything physical when this is happening.

In order to get a better feel for what's going on, we focus on the speaking part of language because we can experience it consciously as it happens. In this way, it is most closely related to juggling.

Here are the major similarities.

Movement

- Juggling involves moving various parts of your body (typically your arms and hands).

Let's begin by juggling one ball or a beanbag. Toss one beanbag up and down in one hand. Don't worry if you're not perfect—that's a good thing: making errors is part of learning.

After a while, try tossing the ball or beanbag from one hand to the other. Notice how you have to coordinate your actions—while one hand is getting ready to toss, the other is getting ready to catch.

In a similar way, being able to speak a language involves simultaneous and coordinated control over the relevant parts of the body to be able to produce the basic sounds.

And in a similar way, being able to play a musical instrument involves control over the relevant parts of the body (depending on the musical instrument). You've got to begin at the beginning, with the basic elements: pressing a key, producing a sound through a reed or a mouthpiece, vibrating a string, and so on.

Coordination

- Juggling involves coordinating various movements; one hand must be doing one particular movement while the other hand is doing another particular movement at the same time.

Coordination becomes a problem when we are dealing with two or more objects. Notice how we have to move both hands at the same time in order to empty the two hands so that they are each ready to catch the new beanbag.

Try it—it's not as easy as it sounds.

In more complicated juggling, the hands are constantly in motion and are coordinating with one another. This is all controlled by the brain. Let's look at an illustration of expert juggling. In figure 2.1 we've put a circle around the right hand and a square around the left hand to track their movements.

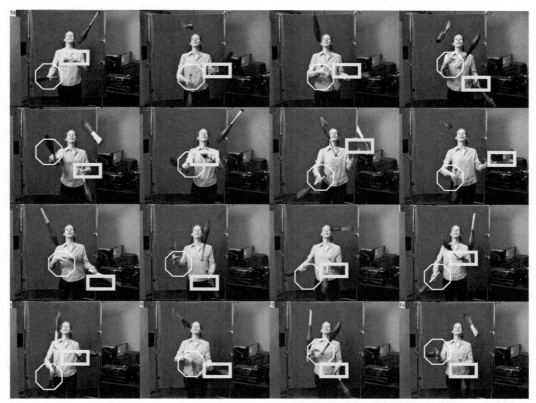

Figure 2.1.

The same kind of physical coordination is true of language, particularly speaking. We must move our lips and tongues in a coordinated way to make particular sounds. To illustrate this for yourself, try pronouncing the words *my tune* together as slowly as you can, and pay attention to the actions that your tips and tongue make when you say the words. It may be helpful to do this in front of a mirror so that you can also see the movements. Notice that for the word *my,* you begin with your lips brought tightly together for the first sound, and then your mouth opens for the sound at the end of the word. Then, before you actually say the word *tune,* you should feel your lips protrude and the front part of your tongue move upward so it is resting against the roof of your mouth behind your teeth. This illustrates that there is sequencing as well as coordination.

Sequencing

- The particular movements in juggling and in language have to be made in a particular sequence; otherwise, disaster occurs immediately.

Notice in figure 2.2 that in juggling, the two hands must not only be coordinated, but the movements must also be carried out in a particular sequence. When we try three objects, this becomes even more important, as we can see. We see in figure 2.2 what happens when the sequence is not followed properly.

Figure 2.2.

The same thing is true of language. In order to speak correctly, we must get the sounds in the right order.

top	versus	**pot**
mat		**tam**
bag		**gab**
gap		**pag**

The order of the sounds determines what word we have, or even whether it is a word. Similarly, the order in which we produce the words determines the meaning of what we say.

Ted loves Alice.   **Alice loves Ted.**

Precision

- Juggling involves making the movements exactly right; otherwise, things start to fall apart.

Precision is essential to good juggling. We have seen what happens when we don't toss the object in exactly the right trajectory—it throws off the sequence and everything comes crashing down. Similarly, getting a language right requires precision. Putting the tongue in the wrong place in the mouth means that the sound that is produced will not be the intended one. There are many other operations where precision counts, like figuring out which word a particular word is (is it *sank* or *thank*?) or understanding its intended meaning. We'll talk a lot more about how to do this later in the book.

Speed

- Juggling involves making the movements in "real time," as they say; that is, you don't have time to think, and choose, and compute, and evaluate, and backtrack. You have to do it right, and you have to do it right now!

The requirement that all of the actions be performed in real time is another common feature of many complex activities, like juggling and speaking. There is no time to think—at least for a novice there's no time to think. The more that is going on, the less time there is to think. The actions must become automatic in order for performance to be successful.

And again, speaking and understanding language involves carrying out a large number of physical and mental operations very, very quickly.

We summarize our comparison of juggling and language in the box.

Basic Physical Components of Performing Juggling and Language

MOVEMENT

- Juggling involves moving various parts of your body (typically your arms and hands).
- Language involves moving various parts of your body (typically your lips and tongue, but other parts that you may not know that you have, back in your mouth and throat!).

COORDINATION

- Juggling involves coordinating various movements: one hand must be doing one particular movement while the other hand is doing another movement.
- Speaking involves coordinating the movements of your lips and tongue (and those other parts that we just mentioned).

PRECISION

- Juggling involves making the movements exactly right; otherwise, things start to fall apart.
- Speaking involves making the movements very precisely; otherwise, the sounds come out wrong (which is what we call a foreign "accent").

SEQUENCING

- The particular movements in juggling have to be made in a particular sequence; otherwise, disaster occurs immediately.
- The particular movements in speaking have to be coordinated in a specific way, either in a sequence or at the same time; otherwise, what comes out is incomprehensible nonsense (that is, a disaster).

SPEED

- Juggling involves making the movements in "real time," as they say; that is, you don't have time to think, and choose, and compute, and evaluate, and backtrack. You have to do it right, and you have to do it right now!
- Speaking involves making the movements in real time, also. The speed is the speed of conversation, and it goes by very fast, as you can attest to if you listen to a language that you don't know spoken at a normal rate of speed.

It is very important to recognize that each of these physical requirements depends on mental control, and of course the mental control of physical action is located somewhere in our brains. That is what we mean by **brain training.** The extent to which we (even with our personal limitations) are able to carry out various complex physical tasks, such as those just described, is determined by how well we've trained our brain to do them.

So, to summarize to this point, juggling and language both require control of movement, coordination, sequencing, precision, and the rapidity that comes with automatic action. How do we acquire these abilities? Do we come into the world able to pick up three beanbags and start juggling? Or to begin speaking right from the start? No, we need to learn.

We won't be studying learning theories here, but we'll talk about some practical aspects of learning that will help you understand what is going on when you learn a language and what kinds of problems you have to deal with and figure out how to solve. Using the discussion of juggling as our starting point, let's think about what needs to be done and some advice to follow.

General Advice

How does one go about training one's brain in order to learn how to perform a complex task with accuracy and in real time? The answer involves an approach to practicing that is well known in the study of music performance and to some extent sports; it is as valid in the learning of a language as it is in these other areas because of the similarity in the physical requirements that we have already noted. For any complex task, it is necessary to break things down into their basic elements and to practice the elements individually so that they become **automatic.** As we master the basics, we can put them together to make units that are more complex. We find that this is true in learning to play a musical instrument and in learning to play a sport (and to become proficient in it). These skills are sometimes called the **fundamentals.** You must identify the fundamentals that need to be learned, and learn them as well as you can by practicing them over and over again. At some point you will know them so well that you will not need to practice them or think about them (and there will always be other things to learn). This approach to complex learning falls under the famous so-called KISS principle.

1. KISS (THE KISS PRINCIPLE—KEEP IT SIMPLE, STUPID)

KEEP
IT
SIMPLE,
STUPID

But here is a problem: If you do not know what you're doing, how do you learn the fundamentals? That's what teachers and coaches are for. Through their experience (and their own training) they know, or should know, what the fundamentals are, how to demonstrate them to you, and how to help you practice them.

There are three basic problems in learning the fundamentals of something, whether it's juggling or German or basketball or the piano or skiing or horseback riding or Chinese or anything else that requires skill. One, it's boring. Two, it's boring. Three, it's boring. So good coaches and teachers embed the fundamentals in exercises and games that are supposed to make them interesting and fun.

Here are three main pieces of advice:

1. First, practice the fundamentals early and often.
2. Second, pay attention to the teacher's attempts to communicate what the fundamentals are and how to practice them, and if that's not clear, make sure you get this clear.
3. In general, it is not efficient to try to learn the complex combinations before the fundamentals that they are composed of have been learned.

Without building the fundamentals, you will have a very hard time going further.

2. START FROM WHERE YOU ARE. DON'T GET AHEAD OF YOURSELF.

Different people have different gifts. Some have the natural gift to be good jugglers and learn very quickly and very well. Some have the natural gift to be good at playing a particular sport or a particular musical instrument. Some are good at a particular language or at languages in general. This is a fact; it cannot be changed. We are who we are, and we can do what we can do. The important thing for those of us who are not naturally gifted in the area where we are trying to achieve something is the following.

Start from where you are. Where this place is doesn't matter because you are what you are, and that's where you have to start. In language learning, the challenge is to see **how far you can get** from your starting point. The one who goes the furthest "wins," in the sense that the further you go, the more you have learned.

3. SLOW PRACTICE

Here's some advice: SLOW PRACTICE! DON'T PRACTICE MISTAKES!

Slow practice is essential to learning activities because it contributes to precision. When we are not that good at something, we make mistakes; we miss the target. If we keep making mistakes, missing the target, then what we are doing is undermining our learning, not contributing to it. We are practicing missing the target, not hitting it! In other words, we are practicing our mistakes.

What does this mean in practical terms? It means not only that you don't just practice slowly, but also that when you make a mistake, you practice more slowly until you are not making any mistakes. In order to do this, you will have to keep things very simple, because when you try to do too many things at once, and don't have control of all of them, it all falls apart. (Recall the juggling disasters above.) Because of the discipline it requires, this is perhaps the hardest thing to do.

Slow practice contributes to the learning of the fundamentals. It is essential in order to be able to achieve precision. It is what we need in order to get the coordination and the sequencing right.

4. GET FEEDBACK AND CORRECTION

In order to avoid mistakes and slow things down when we make mistakes, we have to get feedback and correction. Feedback tells us that something is wrong; correction tells us what is right. Where do you get this feedback? From the instructor, from the language lab, from talking with friendly native speakers. This is exactly what we need in order to learn a musical instrument. It is what is called "coaching" if we are learning to become proficient in a sport, and it is exactly the same when we are trying to learn a language.

Memory

Introduction

W e have said that acquiring a skill like juggling or language involves training the part of your brain where the knowledge is located in order to make the actions **automatic.** Making things automatic is important when we're talking about fundamentals and slow practice. Making just the right things automatic is what we're talking about when we talk about not practicing mistakes and the importance of getting correction and feedback.

In order to get a somewhat deeper understanding of why things work this way, why we have to practice and practice slowly, and why this approach to complex skills works, let's think about one of the most fundamental components of our knowledge, namely, **memory.** When we're learning something, we're building memory, and the techniques that we've been discussing are concerned with building just the right kind of memory with the minimum expenditure of effort.

The problem with memory is that languages have a lot of words. As the actor Steve Martin once said, "Those French have a word for **everything.**" In fact, so does German, Russian, Swahili, and every other language. And that can be a problem when you're learning a new language. You have to remember a lot of words in order to speak a language. It really isn't going to do you much good to know the grammar of a language and be able to pronounce words like a native speaker if you can't remember any of the words.

How many words are there in a language? Here are some numbers for English, based on two dictionaries and an online resource. *Webster's New Pocket Dictionary* lists **19,000** words; the number contained in the online *Carnegie Mellon University Pronouncing*

Dictionary[1] is **125,000**; and *Webster's New Universal Unabridged Dictionary* has over **315,000** words. What about other languages? For Russian, the *Pocket Oxford Russian Dictionary* lists **67,000** words; the *Oxford Russian Dictionary* gives **180,000**; and the *Young & Morgan Dictionary of Navajo,* a Native American language, includes more than **400,000** words.[2]

When you consider the number of words in even the shortest of dictionaries, you might get the impression that it would be impossible to memorize all the words in a language. There is some truth to that—it would be the rare person indeed who knows **all** of the words in *Webster's Dictionary.*

For example, what do you suppose *guttle* means in English? Most people don't know this word. In fact, this example depends on your **not** knowing it. *Guttle* is related to *guzzle* in the same way that eating is related to drinking. So, if someone is guttling and guzzling, it means that he is eating and drinking greedily. Now you know a new word— new to you, but it was already listed in the dictionary.

The point is that even though languages have hundreds of thousands of words, you shouldn't despair. You can operate like a native speaker with a really limited vocabulary. Dewey (1923) found that 1,027 word types comprise 79 percent of all of the word tokens in written English material. In fact, lots of native speakers of all languages do have small vocabularies. (Even if we have learned what *guttle* means, if we don't use it, we are very likely to lose it.) Word learning is a lifelong process that is tied rather closely to formal education. University freshmen know many fewer words than university graduates, and most people continue to learn words throughout life. So there is no need to worry too much about needing to have a 100,000-word vocabulary.

Still, when you're learning a new language, even learning a few thousand words can seem like a lot to have to memorize. In this section we're going to give you some tips and strategies that will help you remember (really remember) lots of words.

Getting Words from Temporary Memory to Permanent Memory

One useful piece of information is that there are two different types of memory: **temporary** memory and **permanent** memory.

Temporary memory is just that: temporary. Have you ever had the experience of remembering something just long enough to take a test on it and then a day later you can't remember the details that you worked so hard to "memorize"? This is what we're talking about when we use the term "temporary memory." It is also called "working memory" or "short-term memory."

---

1. http://www.speech.cs.cmu.edu/cgi-bin/cmudict.
2. Obviously it is impossible to actually list all of these forms in a printed dictionary. Most of them are theoretically possible forms that can be constructed by following a relatively small number of rules for constructing words.

● ● ● ● ● ● ● ● ● ● ● ● ● ● ● ●

One thing that your experience of studying for tests has probably taught you is that rehearsal is important. That is, it is necessary to keep repeating what you want to remember to yourself. If you get distracted, that's it—the word or idea is gone.

Let's try an actual example to see how this works. In Swahili, *kalamu* means 'pen,' like the one illustrated in figure 3.1. If you have a pen handy, hold it in front of you while you say the word *kalamu* over to yourself a few times in order to remember it.

Figure 3.1.

Obviously, the reason why you repeated it to yourself is that rehearsal is necessary for temporary memory. Distraction gets in the way. In fact, if you try to remember the word while someone is talking, she is distracting you from remembering the new word that you just learned and are holding in your temporary memory. You may be trying to rehearse it so that you can impress your instructor with how good your memory is, while the instructor is standing up in front of the class droning on about distraction interfering with working memory!

Psychologists who study memory say that temporary memory is subject to attentional factors. If you can keep your attention focused on the items in working memory—if you can keep rehearsing them in your mind—you can recall them. But if your attention is drawn to something else (like a loud noise), then you may "lose" some of the things in temporary memory.

Now, what was that word we just learned?

Right! *kalamu.* And what does it mean? Right, 'pen.'

When we're learning a new language, we generally have to learn more than one new word at a time. But how much information can we store in temporary memory? Let's try another exercise and find out. In this case, we're going to learn a number of words of Swahili so that we can deal with a set of memories instead of just one new word. Repeat each of the following words to yourself a few times.

o *rafiki* 'friend'
o *kiambo* 'household'
o *sawa* 'equal'
o *zilizala* 'earthquake'
o *ubaya* 'ugliness'
o *taabu* 'suffering'

Now cover the words above to find out many words you're able to hold in temporary memory.

It's been said that the limit is seven plus or minus two (Miller 1956). Let's see if you've hit your temporary memory limit.

What does *ubaya* mean?
What about *kalamu*?

Many of us will have had a harder time remembering *ubaya* than *kalamu*. This isn't surprising. Research suggests that information held in temporary memory fades after 20 seconds.

But then why are some/most/all of us able to remember *kalamu* so much better? There are also several differences in your experience with the two words that help you remember *kalamu* better. First of all, you've had more time to rehearse *kalamu*. The word *kalamu* was also unique when you learned it. It was presented to you as an isolated item, not as a part of a longer word list. In addition, you were given a vivid mental image to go along with the word. You saw a picture of a pen and you picked up a pen and held it in front of you while you repeated the word. Finally, you had a test on *kalamu* which gave you a salient reminder of what it means.

Your experience with *kalamu* highlights four important points that are involved in shifting a memory over from temporary memory to permanent memory.

- The first is **repetition, repetition, repetition.**
- The second is **visualization.** Form a mental image of the word that you're trying to remember.
- The third is **uniqueness.** To the extent possible, focus on one new word at a time.
- The last one is **testing.**

Using these four strategies can help you as a language learner. Since what you want to do is to **really** remember words, this means getting the words to go into permanent memory. If you do this, it means, first, that you don't have to keep rehearsing the words (since you already know them), and second, that you can remember many, many words.

Flash Cards

A common tool that people use to help them learn new words is **flash cards.** Perhaps not surprisingly, not everyone thinks that flash cards are the most effective way of learning words. In fact, some language teachers may say that they hope you won't have to use the old "flash card" method of vocabulary learning in their courses. We'll come back to this point shortly to see why a teacher might aim for an alternative method.

But often when you ask a successful language learner "How did you learn all these words?" you will get an answer like this: "I used flash cards. I find them helpful."

Here are a few tips on using flash cards, in case you decide to try them.

Flash cards will be most effective if you make your own. Get some index cards and write the words on them yourself.[3] Don't buy cards that are already printed, and don't have someone else make the cards for you. You can get a lot out of making up your own cards since this is part of the repetition process. Put the word from Swahili or whatever language you're learning on one side, and then the English translation on the other.

To make your cards even more effective, draw pictures on them. This helps with the visualization strategy. So instead of just writing the English translation of the word you are learning on the back of the card, include a picture. You can draw this by hand or get a picture out of a magazine. So, if you were studying Swahili, you would put *ubaya* on the front of the card and then write "ugliness" on the back. If you have a picture of your really ugly uncle Joe, add it to the card. Of course, some words can be hard to visualize, at least at first, so you may need to be a little creative.

One thing that happens when you have strong visual images to go with words in your new language is that you may not be very good at translating between the two languages, at first, anyway. For example, you might understand the meaning of the concept of *kiambo* ('household') and know how to use it, but you might not be able to come up with the exact English word for it very easily.

When you use flash cards, keep in mind that you're not only trying to remember the meaning of a word and what it looks like when it's written, but you're also trying to remember how it sounds. To help with all three of these aspects, practice by repeating each word **out loud,** not silently. This helps put the word into permanent memory and it gives you practice with your pronunciation. By the way, what were those four tips for getting a word from temporary memory to permanent memory? Right—repetition, visualization, uniqueness, and testing.

We've talked about the first three. What about testing? A large part of using flash cards is about testing your memory. Here's an easy step-by-step strategy for testing yourself with flash cards.

1. Using a stack of flash cards, say the foreign word that appears on the first card out loud. Once you've done this, try to guess the English meaning.
2. If you guess it correctly, place the card at the bottom of the stack and continue with the next word in the stack.
3. What do you do if you don't remember the meaning? Practice! Take a few minutes to study the word and repeat it out loud. When you're finished, place the card seven to ten cards down in the stack.
4. Go to the next word and start with step (1) above.
5. Repeat until you're able to remember the meaning of all of the words in the stack.

Why does this work? The repetition of "missed" words is delayed until after the temporary memory for that word fades—you are being distracted by the intervening words. Yet you are getting repetition at a pretty fast rate in terms of the number of repetitions

3. An alternative to constructing flashcards is to create them using an online resource such as Quizlet (quizlet.com). You can present the flash cards to yourself in a variety of ways, and use them to test yourself as well.

per hour of study. In addition, you are engaging three kinds of sensory input during this kind of practice: (1) visual, as you read the word from the card; (2) pronunciation, or mouth-moving, feedback as you say the word out loud; and (3) auditory, as you hear yourself say the word. These three kinds of sensation help enrich the experience of studying the word. Writing the word out on a piece of paper as you repeat it may also be helpful, as it adds one more sensation to the learning experience.

Flash cards can be helpful when you're trying to get the words into permanent memory—the goal of language learning in the first place! Permanent memory can last for years or decades. In addition, it is structured, with many associations between items that are held in memory. It can also be surprisingly rich with detail.

Here then is what some would argue is the problem with flash cards. They lack richness of detail. Even the pictures that you may put on the flip side of the flash card to help you remember the meaning of a new word in a foreign language are a poor substitute for the "real" meaning. The reason is that memories in permanent memory exist in a web of meaning, a complicated, interconnected structure of meaning, not just isolated translations.

Consider, for example, the meaning of a simple English word like *smell*. What comes to mind when you think of *smell*? Here are a few meanings that you might think of:

- a hot apple pie fresh out of the oven
- a nose
- a garbage can full of rotten food that's been sitting out in the sun for too long
- a dog sniffing a tree
- a locker room

Now try to scan back in your memory. Can you remember hearing the word *smell* as a child? Do you have childhood associations with the word? A particular type of food that you loved, like popcorn or freshly baked bread? What about the place where you used to smell these foods? Or the adults who were with you at the time?

Now look at a flash card for the word for 'smell' in Swahili. Here you have a Swahili word *harufu* that has no childhood connotations for you—no popcorn or baked bread in your past was related to *harufu*. The new word is almost empty of meaning and so very hard to remember. It needs to become rich and powerful and thus memorable. Flash cards can't deliver this kind of richness.

Rich memories are different from poor memories in that they tie together several kinds of information at once. They can be triggered through a variety of routes—a song triggers a memory, a particular sight triggers a sound, the feel of some object triggers an image, an object is associated with a particular place, and so forth. Poor memories, on the other hand, may be limited to a single kind of experience—visual, auditory, tactile, and so on.

In language learning this means that words learned in a rich context (with associated sights, sounds, actions, feelings, places, etc.) are easier to remember and more likely to be retained in permanent memory than words that are learned in a poor context. So, little classroom activities that you might think are hokey are actually better than flash cards or grammar drills at getting words into permanent memory. This doesn't mean that you shouldn't use flash cards at all. What it does mean though is that you shouldn't rely solely on flash cards to get all those new words that you want to learn into long-term memory. Diversify. Learn language in a rich context.

Chunking

We're going to conclude this discussion of memory with one final strategy for remembering words. This involves what's called **chunking** (Miller 1956). If you can store things in temporary memory as "chunks," you will be able to retain more information. Consider phone numbers, for example. Remembering the area code of a phone number will be easier if the area code is meaningful to you. For example, let's say that you remember that 614 is the area code for Columbus, Ohio, and that 416 is the one for Toronto, Canada. If you remember the area code as a meaningful chunk, you don't have to remember each individual digit of the area code 6, 1, 4, or 4, 1, 6. Instead, all you have to do is remember that it is the familiar single code 614 or 416.

In language learning this means that set phrases like *thank you very much* can be treated as a simple familiar chunk rather than a sequence of unrelated words. Spelling is like this too—if you can remember words as chunks rather than as a sequence of letters, then reading goes faster. This means then that you should try to remember the Swahili word for 'smell' as the chunk *harufu* rather than as the sequence of letters 'h,' 'a,' 'r,' and so on. Familiarity is the key to chunking—items that you've seen, repeated, or heard many times will tend to take on chunk status.

Consider another example. In many languages, nouns have gender (masculine and feminine), so words that are translated as English 'the' have to have the same gender as the noun that they are used with. For example, 'the table' in German is *der Tisch* (masculine), while 'the wall' is *die Wand* (feminine). It is much more efficient to memorize the phrase *der Tisch* than it is to memorize that *Tisch* is masculine and then to figure out that the masculine form meaning 'the' is *der*. We will take up this point in more detail in chapter 11.

Procedures can also be remembered as chunks, so that in a sequence of steps that have been chunked as an activity, the first step triggers the memory of the next, and so on. Let's try an example: What are the steps involved in tying your shoes? Think about what you do first, second, third, and so forth. You probably find that it's difficult to explain how to tie your shoes without just doing it or at least visualizing the process in your head. This is because we have stored the memory of the steps involved in tying our shoes as a chunk.

How does chunking relate to language learning? It means that practicing isolated new sounds like the last sound in the German composer's name *Bach* (linguists use the symbols [bax] to represent the sounds in this word) may not be as beneficial as practicing entire words that contain the new sound. In chapter 8, you'll get lots of practice doing just this!

References

Dewey, Godfrey. 1923. *Relative frequency of English speech sounds.* Cambridge, MA: Harvard University Press.

Miller, George A. 1956. Magical number seven, plus or minus two: Some limits on our capacity for processing information. *Psychological Review* 63(2).81–97.

Using a Dictionary

Dictionaries for Language Learners

One of the key tools in building memory is a dictionary. With a good dictionary, you can find out the meanings of words and phrases that you don't know and use this knowledge to expand your capacity to express ideas and understand ideas expressed by others.

It might seem at first that it's not necessary to talk about how to use a dictionary, since surely everyone knows how to do so. While this is probably true in some basic sense, there are particular problems that arise in using a dictionary in order to go back and forth between two languages, particularly when things begin to get complicated. There are a number of tips that can be helpful in avoiding these problems that have been learned through painful experience, and we would like to share them with you.

What's in a Dictionary

A good dictionary is indispensable when you're learning a new language. It can help you do simple things like find the translation of an English word. Or suppose you're given a word in a foreign language but don't know what it means—you check the dictionary.

Of course, you can also use a bilingual dictionary to do the same kinds of things that you would use your English dictionary to do. For example, you might check the correct spelling or pronunciation of a word. A dictionary also provides important information about the parts of speech of words. Here's a sample from English:

leap (lēp) *v.i.* 1. spring through the air; jump; bound. 2. start eagerly.—*n.* a jump or bound. 2. a sudden rise or start.
(*The New Webster Handy College Dictionary,* 4th ed.)

We know that in English, a word like *leap* can be both a verb ('to spring through the air') and a noun ('a jump,' or metaphorically, a 'leap' of faith). In *The New Webster Handy College Dictionary,* for example, this is indicated with the abbreviation *n.* for noun and *v.* for verb. In the example given, the abbreviation for verb is actually written as *v.i.* which stands for intransitive verb, a type of verb that we'll talk more about later in the book.

Not surprisingly, this same type of distinction is found in bilingual dictionaries. In Spanish, for example, the word *como* can be both a verb meaning 'I eat' and a preposition meaning 'as, like.' In this case, the abbreviation *prep.* is commonly used for "preposition" and again *v.* for "verb."

como *v.* eat
prep. like, as

como el pan   = as/like bread
              = I eat bread

In addition to information about the part of speech of a word, you can find other grammatical information that is relevant to the language that you're studying. As mentioned previously, this might include grammatical gender, for example. As we'll discuss more in chapter 11, in some languages, nouns are assigned a particular gender (masculine or feminine). Information about the gender of a word is provided in a good dictionary, just like information about a word's part of speech is. In some cases, gender is the only property of a word that distinguishes its meaning from another word.

This is the case with the French words *page* (feminine) and *page* (masculine), for example. The feminine form of the word, usually indicated by an *f.* in the dictionary entry means a 'page of paper.' When an *m* accompanies the word *page,* it means that we're referring to a person who is a page. Being aware of this information in the dictionary can help you avoid a common mistake of language learners, which is to use the incorrect gender with a particular word.

page *nf* page. **en base de page** at the bottom of the page
page *nm* page, pageboy
(*Collins Dictionary,* collinsdictionary.com)

A bilingual dictionary is also helpful when you're trying to figure out how to actually **use** a word. A good dictionary will show the different meanings of a word in sentence form so that you can get a feel for how the word is used.

As an example, consider the German word *nicht*:

nicht *adv.* not. *er raucht ~.* he isn't smoking; *kommst du?—nein, ich komme ~* are you coming?—no, I'm not (coming); *ich kann das ~ — ich auch ~* I can't do it—neither can I . . .
(*Collins German-English, English-German Dictionary*)

In the *Collins German-English, English-German Dictionary,* the definition is made up almost entirely of sentences illustrating the word's usage. This is very useful to a language learner and is a good sign that you're dealing with a good dictionary. The first sentence *er raucht <u>nicht</u>* means 'he isn't smoking.' (Notice that they use a tilde symbol "~" to indicate where the target word *nicht* is meant to go.)

Now you try.

How do you say: 'No, I'm not coming'? (*Nein, ich komme nicht*).
How about: 'I can't do it'? (*Ich kann das nicht*).

Now you know two new phrases in German!

A good dictionary will also tell you whether a word is slang or whether it forms part of an idiomatic expression. It can also give you information about the level of speech of a word. For example, you might want to find out whether you could use a particular word in polite company—say, with your grandmother or your boss. Or is it a word you would want to say only to a close friend? Or is it a word that you'd want to save for your worst enemy?

To illustrate the many different ways that we can convey the same basic meaning, think about how many different ways you can ask someone to be quiet in English. What would you say to someone if you were trying to be **very** polite? Now, a little less polite. How would you ask a good friend to be quiet? What about your bratty little brother or sister?

Not surprisingly, we find the same kinds of differences in other languages. Here's an example from Greek that covers at least some of these categories.

'Being quiet' in Greek:
Casual:	*kane ligo isihia*	'be quiet'
Very informal:	*vulos to*	'stuff it/shut up'
	skazmos!	'suffocation!'

There are a number of different ways of asking someone to be quiet in Greek, depending on whom you're speaking to. Let's compare casual with **very** informal. The casual way of saying 'be quiet' is *kane ligo isihia.* This is much more polite than *vulos to* which essentially means 'stuff it/shut up' or *skazmos!* which literally means 'suffocation'! This example illustrates why it's important to have a good dictionary when you're learning a new language. It will give you guidelines on how words and expressions are used in everyday speech. This then will help you decide, for example, whether *skazmos,* is really expressing the meaning that you intended!

Choosing a Dictionary

Now that we've considered how a dictionary might be used to help you when you're learning another language, it's time to think about what kind of dictionary you need. Not surprisingly, there are many different kinds of dictionaries; they can differ in size and coverage, by which company publishes it, or, of course, by the year it was published, among other things. With so many choices, how do you decide which one is right for you?

If you're studying a language in a formal language setting, the first thing to do is talk with your language instructor. They will most likely have used many different dictionaries and can tell you which one they prefer. Of course, what's good for them may not be good for you, but at least it's a good starting point.

One important quality to take into account when choosing a dictionary is the age of your reference book. While it might be nice for sentimental reasons to use the dictionary that your grandmother used when she studied French in high school, you'd be best to get yourself an up-to-date dictionary. Why? Language evolves and changes. The meanings of words change, and dictionaries aren't always able to reflect the most current usage of language. Did you know, for example, that *silly* used to mean 'happy, blessed, innocent' and *wench* used to mean 'female child'? The meanings of words clearly change!

Words can also fall out of use. How often to you hear *groovy* nowadays, for example? And unless you're watching old reruns of *Leave It to Beaver,* you probably don't hear too many people saying *neato* or *golly* either!

These examples illustrate an important fact about **all** languages: they change. Because of this, it's very important to equip yourself with a relatively up-to-date dictionary.

Another thing to consider is what you will be using the dictionary for. Will you be using it to do homework assignments for your language class or simply for translating the names of food items on an Italian menu?

Of course when you're traveling, a small dictionary is probably the most practical. But for learning a new language, you'll want to invest in a larger one. Why? Size matters when it comes to dictionaries. Bigger dictionaries give you more information. They have more entries, the entries have more detailed definitions, and, ideally, there is more information on how the different meanings of a word are used in sentences. There will also be more information about how a word is used in everyday speech. More information means that you're less likely to get the wrong meaning of a word.

Here's an example of where too little information can lead you astray. Suppose that during your travels through Québec, Canada, you come across the French word *gibier* [dʒibje] and need to check its English translation in the dictionary. If you were to look up the word in a small pocket dictionary, you might find the first translation 'game.'

gibier, *m.* game.

Compare this with what you get if you were to look in the much larger *Le Robert & Collins Dictionary.* In this dictionary you'd discover that the word *gibier* is referring to one particular kind of English game, the one with feathers. Why the difference between the two dictionary entries? The main reason has to do with the size of the dictionary. The pocket dictionary is small, while *Le Robert & Collins Dictionary* (www.lerobert.com/dictionnaires-bilingues/anglais/le-grand-robert-collins.html) is much larger and more comprehensive.

> **gibier**, *n.m.* game. **gros/menu** ~ big/small game; ~ **d'eau** waterfowl; ~ à poil game animals . . .
> (Le Robert & Collins Dictionary)

Relying on too little information is a common mistake of language learners. So, if you want to know how to play a game of chess in French, for example, make sure you have the right words—otherwise, you might end up playing a "fowl of chess," whatever that means!

Cross-Referencing

But what if all you have is a small dictionary? Is it totally useless? No!—But you have to do a bit of extra work. You need to **cross-reference.** Here are the basic steps involved in cross-referencing.

Begin by looking up the foreign word and get the English translation. Next, go to the English side of the dictionary and look up the English meaning of the foreign word that you found in the first step. For example, if you were looking up the English translation of the French word *gibier,* you might find that it means 'game' (step 1). Now check to see what the French translation of *game* is (step 2). What you would most likely find is that there is more than one French word corresponding to English *game.* You might find words like *jeu, amusement, gibier,* and others. Careful examination of the definition will show you that *gibier* is **definitely** not the word you want when you're trying to translate 'a game of chess.'

Cross-Referencing Basics

1. Look up the translation of the foreign word into English.

    E.g., *gibier* (French) → *game* (English)

2. Cross-reference the translation. That is, reverse the direction of translation and look up the English word *game* and check that the translation that you were given corresponds to the meaning that you want.

    E.g., **game,** jeu, amusement; gibier; *game-bird*, gibier à plumes; *game-preserve*, chasses gardées; *small game*, menu gibier; *to play a game*, faire une partie.

Cross-referencing in the other direction is just as important. This is helpful when you want to find the French translation of an English word, such as *game*, the one referring to an activity like chess. When you look it up in a dictionary, you'll likely be given translations, including *jeu, amusement, gibier*, as well as others, as we just saw. But how do you decide which one to choose? Right, you **cross-reference.**

Go to the French-to-English part of the dictionary and check each of these words until you come across one that has the meaning you want. In this case, there are two possibilities: *jeu* and *amusement*. *Jeu* is translated as 'play, sport, game,' and so on, and for *amusement* we find 'amusement, entertainment, diversion,' and so forth. Based on these translations it looks like *jeu* is the word we want to describe a game like chess. If you want to be extra sure that you've got the right word, you can cross-reference one more time.

In this case, you'll take the translations that have been given for *jeu*, 'play, sport, game,' and so on, and go back to the English side to see if the translation into French gives you *jeu* in each case. Voilà! You have your word. The word 'game' in French as in 'a game of chess' is clearly *jeu*.

Cross-Referencing Basics (continued)

3.   After you've looked up the translation of the English word in French (step 2), cross-reference the translations. That is, for each translation given, for example, *jeu, amusement, gibier*, go back to the other side of the dictionary (here, the French side) and see what meaning is listed for each word. If you were to do this with the three French words just given, you find the translations below.

*   **jeu,** play; sport; game, pastime; fun, frolic . . .
*   **amusement,** amusement; entertainment; diversion . . .
*   **gibier,** game.

4.   If you want to be extra sure, go back to the English side of the dictionary and cross-reference the new translations.

*   **play,** jeu . . .
*   **sport,** jeu, amusement, sport . . .
*   **game,** jeu, amusement; gibier . . .

Using a Dictionary

So let's assume that you've got the dictionary that you want. Now let's talk about how you can get the most out of it. First, and most importantly, you need to familiarize yourself with your dictionary. Part of this involves understanding how the words in it are organized. As we discuss below, another important thing to keep in mind is to read over the entire entry for a given word before deciding on a specific translation. Finally, and most importantly, familiarize yourself with your dictionary (*again*)!

So what can you do to familiarize yourself with your dictionary? First of all, you should read the information provided at the beginning (assuming you're using a book). This is generally a **very** useful resource. There, you can find information on the alphabet of the language, how words are organized in the dictionary, how letters and symbols are pronounced, what form of a given word is listed as the base form, and so on. You'll also get information about the abbreviations and symbols used in the book.

Learning about a language's alphabet is important for a number of reasons. One is the fact that not all languages use the same set of symbols. Another reason is because even if the language you're studying does use the same alphabet as your native language, the letters of the alphabet may not be organized in the same manner in dictionaries of the two languages. Consider the alphabets of Finnish and Turkish, for example.

The Alphabets of Finnish and Turkish

Finnish: a b c d e f g h i j k l m n o p q r s t u v w x y z ä **ö** å
Turkish: a b c ç d e f g ğ h ı i j k l m n o **ö** p r s ş t u ü v y z

The Finnish alphabet is just like the English alphabet except that Finnish has two additional vowels, written as 'ä' and 'å'. Note that words beginning with any one of these vowels are ordered at the **end** of all other words in the language. The Turkish alphabet is similar, but the order of the additional vowels is different. They are ordered next to similar-looking vowels. You can see this by comparing the position of the 'ö' in each language. Notice that in Finnish it comes almost at the end of the alphabet, while in Turkish it comes right after 'o.' Knowing this kind of information before you start searching through a dictionary can be very helpful, and all good dictionaries will have this information.

Now let's consider languages that differ from English not simply in terms of the consonants and vowels that the language has, but in terms of some other property like tone, for example. How do you find out how words with unfamiliar properties are organized? What order are they listed in? Once again, an important starting point is to read the introduction to your dictionary since it will most likely contain this kind of information. Of course, if you're taking a language course, your instructor would also be able to provide guidance in this regard as well.

As an illustration, consider Mandarin, a Chinese language. In Mandarin, words differ not only in the kinds of consonants and vowels that they have, but also in terms of **tones,** a term referring to the use of the different pitch levels of syllables. In Mandarin, as in other tone languages, tones can distinguish the meaning of otherwise identical words. Four different tones are used to do this in Mandarin. The first is called a **level high tone** and occurs in the word [mā] 'mother,' for example. The second is called a **rising tone;** the pitch starts out low and ends up high, as in the word for 'hemp,' [má]. The third tone is called a **falling-rising tone.** It starts out high, dips lower, and then ends high. This is the tone that occurs on the word for 'horse,' [mǎ]. Finally, there's the **falling tone.**

This tone starts out high and ends up low, as in 'to scold,' [mà]. Note that all four words have exactly the same consonant and vowel. Only the tone lets you know which word is which. The order of tones that we have listed here is also the order in which words bearing these tones are listed in a Mandarin dictionary.

Not all tone languages order tones in the same way as Mandarin. Just as languages can differ in how consonants and vowels are ordered, they can also differ in how they order tones. What you need to do is, of course, check your dictionary to find out exactly how words are ordered.

In addition to providing information about how a dictionary is organized, a good dictionary will generally also give you useful information about how a word is pronounced. This typically comes in the form of a symbol guide included with the dictionary, and then following each individual entry there will be a symbolic representation of how the word is pronounced.

Why not simply rely on the spelling of the word, you might ask. For one thing, not all languages use Roman orthography, like we use for English. But even if Roman orthography is used, spelling is not always a reliable guide to pronunciation since a letter in one language is not necessarily pronounced the same way as it is in another language.

As an illustration, let's compare some spellings from French and English. In French, the sequence of vowel letters 'o' and 'u' is pronounced like the 'u' in the English word *Sue*. The letter written as 'u' in French is pronounced differently, however. It's pronounced like the English sound 'i', as in *me*, but made with rounded lips. (You'll get practice making this and other sounds in section II.) Interestingly, there are two words in French that differ solely in the pronunciation of this vowel. The French word for *neck*, which is spelled 'c', 'o', 'u', is pronounced [ku], while the word for 'butt, ass' is spelled 'c', 'u', 'l' and pronounced as [ky] (the 'l' is silent). This distinction is important if you're a native speaker of English learning French since the only difference in the pronunciation of the words for 'butt' and 'neck' is in the vowel! It's either an [u] sound or an [y] sound, and if you get this wrong, you could be talking about a part of the body that you hadn't intended! Our point here is simply to illustrate that you can't assume that a symbol in your native language is pronounced the same way in the language you're learning. Familiarize yourself with how spellings are pronounced by consulting the symbol guide in a good dictionary.

In addition to differences in how letters are pronounced in languages, dictionaries can also differ in terms of what they use as the base form of a given word. By "base form," we're referring to the particular form that is listed at the beginning of an entry in the dictionary. In English, for example, the base form of a verb is the infinitive. This is the form of the verb that begins with *to*, such as *to eat, to listen,* and so forth. In an English dictionary, however, the verb is listed without the *to*. For nouns, the base form is the singular. So the entry for *dog* is *dog* and not *dogs*.

What counts as a base form can differ from language to language. This means that in order to look up a particular form in a dictionary of the language you're learning, you'll first need to become familiar with what the base forms are. In Maltese, for example, the base form of verbs is different from that in English. (Maltese, by the way, is spoken on the island of Malta, located in the Mediterranean Sea off the coast of Sicily.) In this language, the base form of a verb is the form used for the third-person, singular, masculine, past tense. The English equivalent of this would be *he ate, he listened, he wrote.*

Another example concerns verb forms in German. Suppose that you are reading a German text and you run across the sentence *Wann hast du den Film angesehen?* You know what the beginning of this sentence means—'when have you the movie . . .' (*wann* 'when' *hast* 'have' *du* 'you' *den* 'the' *Film* 'movie), but what does *angesehen* mean? You go to the dictionary, but no luck—there is no entry for *angesehen.*

Fortunately, as a student of German, you recognize two things about *angesehen.* First, it is made up from *an-* and *gesehen.* The latter is the past participle form of the verb *sehen* 'to see'—it corresponds with *seen* in English. If you go back to the dictionary, there might be a list of verbs and their past participles, and if there is, you will see *sehen–gesehen.* The syllable *an-* can be attached to certain verbs to form new verbs, and *ansehen* is such a verb. The past participle form follows that of *sehen*—hence we get *an-gesehen* and not *ge-ansehen.*

OK, so we go back to the dictionary and look for *ansehen.* And there it is—it means 'to view; to look at.' That means that *angesehen* means 'viewed; looked at.' The whole sentence is, therefore, 'When have you viewed the film?' or, less literally, 'When did you watch the movie?'

So a little knowledge of how German works, and how the dictionary is organized to take advantage of this knowledge, is very helpful in figuring out the meaning of a word that at first glance simply isn't in the dictionary.

The last dictionary tip that we address in this chapter is this: when you're looking for a word, look over the *entire* entry for the word before choosing the translation that you want. In other words, don't simply choose the first word that's given. It may not be the translation that you want!

Here's an example from Swedish to illustrate. Suppose that you want to find out how to say 'rock' in Swedish. When you look up the English word in a Swedish-English dictionary, you may find that there are several entries given. The word you're looking for could be, for example, *klippa, grasten, karamell,* or even *rockmusik.* Even though there isn't a lot of information contained in this entry, from our discussion above, you know exactly how to go about choosing the right word. Right, you cross-reference!

rock 1. klippa, klippblock; 2. grasten, häleberg; 3. karamell; 4. slända; 5. rock-musik

Using an Online Dictionary

An alternative to using a physical dictionary is to use online resources to find the meanings of words. Most of the advice we gave above also applies to going online and looking up a word. Some excellent online resources are LEO (dict.leo.org) for German and *Larousse* (larousse.fr/dictionnaires) for French and Spanish.

Mögliche Grundformen für das Wort "angesehen"

ansehen

sich ansehen

Adjectives / Adverbs

prestigious *adj.*	angesehen
reputable *adj.*	angesehen
distinguished *adj.*	angesehen
respected *adj.*	angesehen
esteemed *adj.*	angesehen
notable *adj.*	angesehen
respectable *adj.* - *socially approved person*	angesehen
of good standing	angesehen
eminently respectable	hochangesehen *auch:* hoch **angesehen**
well-respected *adj.*	sehr **angesehen**

Verbs

to look at sth.	looked, looked		etw. *Akk.* **ansehen**	sah an, angesehen	
to watch sth. - *on TV*	sich *Dat.* etw. *Akk.* **ansehen**	sah an, angesehen	
to look at so./sth.	looked, looked		jmdn./etw. **ansehen**	sah an, angesehen	
to view sth.	viewed, viewed		etw. *Akk.* **ansehen**	sah an, angesehen	
to see sth.	saw, seen		etw. *Akk.* **ansehen**	sah an, angesehen	
to have a look at so./sth.	had, had		sich *Dat.* jmdn./etw. **ansehen**	sah an, angesehen	
to consider so./sth. as (or: to be) sth.	considered, considered		jmdn./etw. als etw. *Akk.* **ansehen**	sah an, angesehen	
to deem so. sth.	deemed, deemed		jmdn. als etw. *Akk.* **ansehen**	sah an, angesehen	
to inspect sth.	inspected, inspected		sich *Dat.* etw. *Akk.* **ansehen**	sah an, angesehen	
to look upon so./sth. as sth.	looked, looked		jmdn./etw. als etw. *Akk.* **ansehen**	sah an, angesehen	
to put so. down as sth.	put, put		jmdn. als etw. *Akk.* **ansehen**	sah an, angesehen	
to regard so./sth. as sth.	regarded, regarded		jmdn./etw. als etw. *Akk.* **ansehen**	sah an, angesehen	
to treat sth. as sth.	treated, treated		etw. *Akk.* als etw. *Akk.* **ansehen**	sah an, angesehen	
to regard so./sth.	regarded, regarded	- *look at [form.]*	jmdn./etw. **ansehen**	sah an, angesehen	
to account so./sth. sth.	accounted, accounted	*[form.]*	jmdn./etw. als etw. *Akk.* **ansehen**	sah an, angesehen	
to esteem so. sth.	esteemed, esteemed	*[form.] dated*	jmdn. als etw. *Akk.* **ansehen**	sah an, angesehen	
to behold so./sth.	beheld, beheld		jmdn./etw. **ansehen**	sah an, angesehen	
to face so./sth.	faced, faced		jmdn./etw. **ansehen**	sah an, angesehen	
to be considered as so./sth.	was, been		als jmd./etw. **angesehen** werden
to be regarded as so./sth.	was, been		als jmd./etw. **angesehen** werden
to look at so. thunderously	looked, looked		jmdn. grollend **ansehen**
to see over sth.	saw, seen	*(Brit.)*	etw. *Akk.* genau **ansehen**	sah an, angesehen	
to count for lost	counted, counted		als verloren **ansehen**
to get granular on sth.	got, got/gotten		sich *Dat.* etw. *Akk.* genau **ansehen**	sah an, angesehen	
to be challenged by sth.	was, been		etw. *Akk.* als Herausforderung **ansehen**	sah an, angesehen	
to look sth. ⇔ over	looked, looked		sich *Dat.* etw. *Akk.* aufmerksam **ansehen**	sah an, angesehen	
to take sth. for granted	took, taken		etw. *Akk.* als gegeben **ansehen**

Figure 4.1.

The nice thing about an online dictionary is that it can be very comprehensive—you can look up the actual form, like *angesehen,* and you don't have to figure out that it is a form of the verb *ansehen* first. But the online dictionary may provide such a comprehensive answer that it may be more difficult to figure out what the actual meaning is than if you did the work to look it up in a regular dictionary. Figure 4.1, for example, illustrates what LEO tells us about *angesehen* 'viewed.'

LEO is telling us that *angesehen* has many uses. It could be an adjective meaning 'distinguished, prestigious, etc.,' or a past participle meaning 'looked at, watched, beheld, etc.' What is the meaning that we should use? And what do 'etw.^{AKK},' 'sich.^{DAT},' 'jmdn./ etw.' mean?[1]

Such an abundance of information is wonderful, but it might be more than we bargained for if we are at a relatively early stage of learning the language. Perhaps the most important thing to know about a resource like LEO is that it assumes that you already know the language pretty well. With this in mind, we suggest that it is best to use a dictionary that is most suited to your level of expertise in the language—a learner's dictionary at the beginning, and a more advanced or online resource as you progress in the language.

Summary

To summarize, the five most important ways to get the most out of a bilingual dictionary are listed below:

1. Invest in a good dictionary, one that is appropriate to your level of expertise in the language. Recall that this dictionary is one that will give you language usage information, grammatical information, and many other useful things.
2. Use an up-to-date dictionary.
3. Familiarize yourself with your dictionary. Find out about the alphabet, the order of entries, the pronunciation of symbols, what the base forms are, and so on.
4. Look over the entire entry for a given word.
5. Cross-reference!!!

References

Collins German-English, English-German dictionary. 2013. New York: HarperCollins.

Morehead, Philip D. 2006. *The new Webster handy college dictionary,* 4th ed. 2006. New York: Signet Books.

---

1. We won't leave you in suspense: *etw.* is an abbreviation of *etwas,* meaning 'something'; AKK stands for 'accusative case'; and 'DAT' stands for 'dative case.' *jmdn./etw* is an abbreviation of *jemanden/etwas,* meaning 'someone/something.'

Sounding like a
Native Speaker

Foreign Accents

Knowing How to Speak a Language

Being able to speak a language means that you know how to pronounce and understand the words and sentences of your language. If you are a native speaker of English, for example, you know that the letters 's' and 'sh' both represent sounds of the English language since they occur in distinct words like *sin* and *shin*. As a native speaker you have learned how to pronounce these sounds as well as the many other sounds that are used in your language. You also know the way that sounds combine to make English words. For instance, you know that 's' can be followed by 'l' because of words like *slow*. You are also aware, at a certain level of consciousness, that 'l' cannot be followed by 's' at the beginning of a word—there are no words like *lsow* in English.

One of the things that makes languages so interesting for linguists who study them, but so difficult for those trying to learn a new language, is that languages can differ in terms of how sounds are put together to form words. Of course, the way that sounds combine in two languages may be similar in some respects, but you can be almost certain that there will also be differences. A challenging aspect of learning another language then is that languages differ both in terms of the **kinds** of sounds that are used as well as in the **ways** that the sounds combine to form words. To learn another language therefore means that you will at least need to learn new ways of combining sounds to form words, and possibly new sounds as well.

In the next few chapters you will become familiar with some of the ways in which languages differ in terms of how speech sounds are made and used. You should also gain a clearer understanding of how your own language works. With this knowledge, we hope that you will come away with an appreciation for how your native language and

49

the language(s) that you are learning differ. Being aware of how the languages differ is a huge step toward understanding how you can sound more like a native speaker since it will allow you to identify areas to pay special attention to when trying to master your new language(s).

We begin by considering foreign accents and what exactly makes an accent sound foreign. We have all heard someone speak English or some other language that we speak natively and have known right away that they are not a native speaker. What is it about the way the person speaks that makes him or her sound foreign? As you will see, how an individual produces the sounds, words, and sentences of a foreign language is directly influenced by the sounds, sound combinations, and other properties of his or her native language.

Dealing with Unfamiliar Sounds

One of the most basic reasons why an accent seems foreign relates to the sounds that make up the speaker's native language and those of the language he or she is speaking non-natively. We will refer to the collection of speech sounds that are used in a particular language to form words and sentences as a language's **sound inventory.**

A Language's Sound Inventory

A language's sound inventory is the collection of speech sounds that are used in a particular language to form words and sentences.

When the sound inventory of your own language differs from that of a language that you are learning, you may be confronted with unfamiliar sounds. In this case, part of learning the new language obviously means learning how to produce and combine new sounds. In attempting to pronounce these new sounds, you may modify your speech in some way to make it more similar to the sound patterns that you are used to. In this chapter, we focus on the various strategies used by language learners to deal with unfamiliar sounds and sequences of sounds. By using these strategies, you will produce speech that will sound different from that of a native speaker, thus giving you a foreign accent.

One common strategy is to replace an unfamiliar sound with one that is relatively similar to it from the learner's native sound inventory. This can result in an accent quite noticeable to the native speaker's ears.

Strategy 1

Replace an unfamiliar sound with a similar, more familiar one.

We illustrate this first by considering some examples of non-native speakers of English speaking English, and then of English speakers speaking other languages. In each case, a sound that occurs in a word in one language is replaced with some other sound. The reason, of course, is that the particular sound does not occur in the speaker's native language. As a result, the person may not have had experience pronouncing or listening to the sound and therefore may substitute an unfamiliar sound with one that is similar sounding.

AN ASIDE

Remember that it is vowel **sounds** that we are concerned with here, not how these sounds are **spelled** in words. To illustrate the difference, compare the words *beat* and *beet*. They both have the same vowel sound [i], but the sound is spelled as *ea* in *beat* and as *ee* in *beet*.

Let's begin by considering one aspect of Greek-accented English. The sound inventory of Greek, like that of many languages, including Spanish and Korean, differs from American and Canadian English in that it does not include the vowel sound [ɪ], which occurs in English words such as *sit, bit, kit*.[1] That is, there are no words in Greek (or Spanish or Korean) that are formed with the sound [ɪ]. On the other hand, the sound inventories of Greek and English are similar in that they both include the sound that we will symbolize as [i]. This stands for the vowel in English words like *seat, beat, feet*. If an English speaker uses the vowel [i] instead of [ɪ] in a word, it can change the meaning of the word: compare *sit* ([ɪ]) vs. *seat* ([i]); and *bit* ([ɪ]) vs. *beat/beet* ([i]). Notice that it is only the quality of the vowel that distinguishes the meaning of these pairs of words. We therefore say that the vowels [i] and [ɪ] are **distinctive** in English.

Unlike English, the Greek language does not use the distinction between [ɪ] and [i] to change the meaning of words since there are no Greek words with [ɪ]; [i] and [ɪ] are therefore not distinctive in Greek. This means that Greek speakers may not have had practice producing or listening to the sound [ɪ] and may have difficulty hearing the difference between [i] and [ɪ]. They may also replace the unfamiliar [ɪ] sound in English words with the similar yet more familiar [i]. As a result, the words *sit* and *seat*, spoken in Greek-accented English, may both be pronounced similar to *seat*. Speakers of Greek-accented English have used the first strategy for dealing with an unfamiliar sound: replacing an unfamiliar sound with a similar, more familiar one.

Let's look at some common replacements from other languages. Korean, unlike English, does not distinguish between the sounds [p] and [f]. These occur in English words such as the following: [p] *pool, punch, paper, cup*; [f] *fool, photo, caffeine, enough*. The reason for the lack of distinction between [p] and [f] in Korean is that only [p] is part of the language's sound inventory. Therefore, one common trait of Korean-accented English is for the sound [f] to be replaced with a [p] sound in English words.

Why, you might ask, is the [f] sound replaced with [p] as opposed to some other consonant like [t] or [k]? The answer is that to Korean speakers, [p] and [f] sound fairly similar. One of the reasons is that they are both made with the lips. To make the sound

---

1. The symbols used to represent vowel sounds are discussed in chapter 8; see also the symbol reference chart in "The International Phonetic Alphabetic" at the back of the book. To differentiate the symbols used to characterize speech sounds from the letters used to spell words, sound symbols are enclosed in square brackets.

[p], the lips close together tightly and then open, letting the air pass through the lips. The lips are also involved in making the sound [f]. In this case, the bottom lip rests gently against the top row of teeth as the air goes out of the mouth. (We will have more to say about making these kinds of sounds in the next chapter.) It is important to keep in mind that sounds like [p] and [f] may seem very different to a speaker of a language like English who uses them to differentiate words, like *pool* and *fool*. But for speakers of languages where the sounds are not distinctive, the two sounds can be very difficult to tell apart, and the unfamiliar sound can be difficult to pronounce.

As a final example of foreign-accented English, consider one way in which German and English differ. German lacks a distinction between the sounds [w] and [v] as in _wine_ and _vine_; there is no [w] in the German sound inventory. So in German-accented English, in a phrase such as *Victoria's wine shop*, the first sounds in *Victoria* and *wine* may both be pronounced as [v], a sound very similar to [w].

Now let's reverse the process and consider some of the common pronunciations that make English speakers sound foreign in other languages. Continuing with German and English, you may be familiar with how the final sound in the German composer's name _Bach_ is commonly pronounced in English—with a [k] sound and rhyming with _rock_. In German, however, the last sound in this word is actually pronounced with a sound that, though similar to [k], is nonetheless different. The symbol for the German sound is [x], and it is made, like [k], by raising the back of the tongue up to the back of the mouth. In making [k], the tongue briefly touches the roof of the mouth and consequently the flow of air is temporarily interrupted as it goes out of the mouth. (At this point you should convince yourself that [k] is made in this way by slowly saying the word *rock* and paying attention to where your tongue touches the roof of your mouth when you make the sound [k].) For the sound [x], the tongue comes close to the roof of the mouth but does not touch it. In this way the air passes through the narrow opening and creates turbulent noise. Technically speaking, [k] is called a **velar stop** and [x] is a **velar fricative** (see the next chapter for additional discussion). Since the English sound inventory does not include [x], English speakers commonly replace this unfamiliar sound with the more familiar [k], a common trait of English-accented German.

Another characteristic of English-accented German (or French, or Swedish, or Turkish, etc.) has to do with the way that certain vowels are pronounced. German, like many other languages, makes a distinction between the vowels [i], as in English _beat_; [u], as in English _boot_; and [y], as in the German word _Tür_ 'door.' The last sound does not occur in the sound inventory of North American English (it does occur in some English varieties, e.g., New Zealand English). The sound [y] can be thought of as a combination of the sounds [u] (_boot_) and [i] (_beat_): the lips are protruded like in the formation of [u], but the position of the tongue is the same as in [i]. We will work on learning how to make sounds like this in chapter 7. Since some varieties of English lack this sound, speakers of those varieties typically replace foreign words containing the sound [y] with the vowel [u]. The reason that [y] is replaced with [u] (and not [i]) is probably that to English speakers, [y] sounds more like [u] than it does to [i]. It may also be due in part to the fact that in German, at least, the sound [y] is written in words as the letter 'ü,' as we saw with the word *Tür* 'door,' so English speakers unfamiliar with German may equate the letter 'ü' with the English sound [u].

In each of these cases, the English speaker sounds noticeably foreign, and once again, the reason for this is that a sound that belongs to some other language's sound inventory does not occur in English. In order to pronounce words like a native speaker, you will obviously need to learn how to pronounce the unfamiliar sound, should you want to.

A second strategy that non-native speakers use to deal with an unfamiliar sound is to simply omit the foreign sound entirely.

Strategy 2

Omit an unfamiliar sound from a word.

The omission of a sound is a common trait of French-accented English when dealing with the unfamiliar sound [h], as in English *hello, hat, heavy*. There are at least two reasons why the [h] may be omitted from the pronunciation of English words by French speakers. First, there is no [h] sound in French and there is also no sound that is particularly close to [h]. Second, given that the sound [h] is absent from the French sound inventory, French speakers may not be able to hear the sound and thus do not reproduce it. This is because as a child acquires a language, she learns to focus on the parts of the acoustic signal that carry meaning in her language, ignoring others. As such, her perceptual system becomes fine-tuned to the sounds of her own language, which in turn influences what she does and does not hear. What characterizes "foreignness" in this case, then, is the **absence** of a sound.

The example from French allows us to emphasize once again the important distinction between **sounds** and the **letters** that we use to spell words. Note that while the letter 'h' is written in some words in French, such as *haricot* 'bean' and *homme* 'man,' it is never pronounced as [h]. This fact shows that the spelling used in a language does not always reflect what sounds occur in that language. French is not alone in this regard; it is also true of English and many other languages. Consider the letter 'p' at the beginning of some words in English, for example, *psychology*: although the letter 'p' is present in written English, it is not pronounced in this word. Similarly, the 'l' in *salmon* is not pronounced, nor the 'k' in *knife*, nor the second 'b' in *bomb*.

Another aspect of spelling that can be confusing when learning a new language has to do with the fact that languages can differ in the way in which written words are pronounced. Such differences are especially challenging when the same sequence of letters is pronounced differently. For example, the spelling 'ch' in English is pronounced like the initial or final sounds in <u>church</u>, while in Italian, the spelling 'ch' is pronounced with the sound [k]. As a result, the first sound in the Italian word <u>che</u> 'what' approximates the first consonant in the English word <u>Kay</u>.

All of the examples we have considered above underscore an important point when it comes to learning a new language: do not assume that the language that you are learning is identical to your native language in terms of the sounds or the rules for spelling. Be aware of the differences with your native language, learn how to pronounce the new sounds, and, of course, practice!

Dealing with Unfamiliar Sequences of Sounds

As we all know, learning another language involves more than just learning new sounds. We also need to learn how to combine them to form new words. Because of this, it is sometimes the particular combination of sounds, not the sounds themselves, that is unfamiliar to a non-native speaker. Part of knowing how to speak a language involves knowing what **sequences of sounds** are possible, that is, a language's **phonotactics.** An English speaker, for example, has learned that a word can begin with sequences like [bl], [pl], [pr], [sn], [tr], and [gl] because there are words in the language like *blue, please, price, snow, truck,* and *glue.* It is likely than an English speaker would say that *plake* is a possible word of English because it contains combinations of sounds found in English, even though, at the present time, it is not an actual word. On the other hand, there are no English words that begin with the sequences [bn], [pb], [rt], or [gd], and knowing that these are not sequences of English is also part of a native speaker's knowledge of English. As a result, a sequence like *bnark* would sound very strange to an English speaker's ears; in fact, she would probably say that it could not be an English word.

What happens when the language you are learning has unfamiliar combinations of sounds? One strategy often used by native speakers is to omit one of the sounds, as we saw above for French with [h]. A different strategy is to insert a sound in order to bring the sequence more in line with the phonotactics of the native language. In other words, inserting a sound gives the sequence a more familiar structure.

Strategy 3

Insert a sound to make a sequence of sounds more familiar.

Consider the effects of this strategy for an English learner of Polish, a language where words can begin with many different kinds of consonant sequences. For example, in Polish the sound [g] (e.g., English *go, dog*) can be immediately followed by [d] (e.g., English *do, bud*) at the beginning of a word. In fact, the name of one of Poland's major cities, *Gdansk,* begins with just this sequence of sounds. Try saying this word. Most native speakers of English unfamiliar with the sequence [gd] will insert a short vowel between the two consonants so that the word is pronounced like *G^edansk.* If you are a native speaker of another language that does not permit [gd] at the beginning of a word, determine whether you use this same strategy or a different one when pronouncing this word.

Inserting a vowel is also a trait of Spanish-accented English. One difference between English and Spanish is that words beginning with the sound [s] followed by another consonant are common in English, while they do not occur in Spanish. As a result, the consonant sequences at the beginning of the following English words simply are not found in Spanish: *speed, stoop, strike, ski*. For many Spanish speakers learning to speak English, a vowel is generally inserted at the beginning of the word. In this way, a word like *school* is pronounced something like *eschool* with a vowel pronounced before the [s] + consonant sequence.

A similar strategy is used in Korean-accented English. Although English does not have as wide a variety of consonant sequences as Polish, a fair number of different consonant sequences still occur in the language, such as *snow, fifth, strike, fast food*. These kinds of sequences do not occur in Korean. Consequently, Koreans often use the same strategy as English and Spanish speakers: they insert a short vowel, which gives the sequence a more familiar structure. In this way, the word *strike* may be pronounced like $s^et^erik^e$ and *fast food* as fas^et^e *food*. If you are a native speaker of a language that, like Korean, doesn't have these consonant sequences, say the words *snow, fifth, strike*, and *fast food* out loud several times and listen carefully. Are you able to detect a short vowel sound between the consonants in some of the words? Or do you use one of the other strategies that we've discussed?

Your Strategies

If you are learning another language, it is almost certain that you will have a foreign accent when you speak. But what makes your own speech sound non-native? How do you deal with unfamiliar aspects of the language that you are learning? Which of the above strategies are you using?

Introspecting about your own accent can be hard especially if you are trying to do it while speaking. A better approach would be to record yourself saying individual words or small phrases. If you have access to recordings of a native speaker, you could even record yourself repeating what the speaker said. Then listen carefully to each word several times, comparing it to the native speaker's version, if possible. Try to pinpoint parts of the word that differ. What is it that makes them sound different? Are different sounds being used? Are you omitting or inserting sounds in places where the native speaker is not? Having a native speaker of the language help you identify the foreign-sounding aspects of the words will make the task easier.

This is a difficult exercise because how you hear sequences of sounds in words has been strongly influenced by the languages that you learned as a child. Learning to hear in new ways may be possible with lots of practice, however.

Dealing with Unfamiliar Syllable-, Word-, and Sentence-Level Properties

Thus far we have focused on strategies that language learners use when dealing with unfamiliar sound inventories and phonotactics. Yet languages can also differ in terms of other properties relating to syllables, words, and sentences. In this section we will consider three types of properties relating to these elements: **word stress, tone,** and **intonation.** Additional properties will be introduced in the following chapters. Understanding that your native language may differ from the one that you are learning in terms of any of these properties can help you become aware of how you need to modify your speech if you want to sound more like a native speaker of the language you are learning.

STRESS

In most languages, one part of a word may have greater emphasis or prominence than another part. We use the term **stress** to refer to this property and the term **syllable** to refer to the various parts of a word that can have stress. For example, speakers of English would probably agree that the word *baby* has two syllables: *ba-by.* On the other hand, *elephant* has three: e-le-phant. Which syllable of the word *baby* has stress? Do you say *BAby* or *baBY*? Clearly, there is greater prominence on the first syllable. The stress in *elephant* also falls on the first syllable. In the word *computer,* however, stress falls on the middle syllable: *comPUter.* If you are a native speaker of English, you have learned that certain syllables in English are pronounced with more emphasis than others and, as a result, are louder and/or longer and/or have higher pitch. This is part of your knowledge of English. Since languages differ in terms of where stress occurs in words, one common quality of speech that cues us to an accent as foreign involves the misplacement of stress.

In French, for example, stress typically falls on the last syllable of a word. Thus, one characteristic of French-accented English is the misplacement of stress on the final syllable of a word. A French-speaking politician was commonly heard pronouncing the English word *economic* as *econoMIC,* with stress on the last syllable instead of on the third syllable, as a speaker of North American English would say it: *ecoNOmic.* In Czech, by contrast, stress systematically occurs on the first syllable of a word. Therefore it is important to be aware of differences in stress placement between your native language and your new language.

Czech: stress always on first syllable.
French: stress on final syllable

TONE

Another property of syllables that can be challenging to the language learner is **tone.** In many languages, such as the Chinese language Mandarin, the only difference between two words may be the tone, or the pitch, of the syllable. As a result, tones can distinguish the meaning of otherwise identical words. As discussed previously in chapter 4, there are four different tones that are used to do this in Mandarin. The first is called a level high tone and occurs in the word [mā] 'mother,' for example. The second is called a rising tone, where the pitch starts out low and ends up high, as in the word for 'hemp,' [má]. The third tone is called a falling-rising tone. It starts out high, dips lower, and then ends high. This is the tone that occurs on the word for 'horse,' [mǎ]. Finally, there is the falling tone which starts out high and ends up low, as in 'to scold,' [mà]. Note that all four words have exactly the same consonant and vowel. Only the tone lets you know which word is which. For speakers of languages that do not have tone such as English, learning a language like Mandarin Chinese means that you also need to learn a new property of sounds that carries meaning in the language. Not pronouncing the tones correctly is a typical property of English-accented Mandarin Chinese.

INTONATION

A foreign accent can also involve differences relating to the melody, or intonation, of a phrase or an entire sentence. In standard American English, for example, intonation can distinguish a statement from a question. Say the following two sentences, paying close attention to how the pitch levels at the end of the sentences differ.

Statement: Zach eats pizza for breakfast.

Yes-no question: Zach eats pizza for breakfast?

When the pitch falls, as at the end of the first sentence, the utterance is interpreted as a simple statement. When the pitch rises, as in the second sentence, it is a question. Being able to assign the correct interpretation to a sentence according to these different intonation patterns is part of English speakers' knowledge of their language.

But not all languages use different pitch contours to distinguish sentence function. Speakers of Chinese languages, for example, tend to keep the intonation pattern pretty much the same for questions and statements. Instead, they include the marker [ma] in the sentence to indicate that a question interpretation is intended. Finnish is similar in using a marker to indicate the difference between a statement and a question.

It is also interesting to note that even within a single language, the intonation patterns can differ depending on variety. In contrast to the pattern illustrated above for standard American English, African American Vernacular English indicates a yes-no question (e.g., *Did Zach eat pizza for breakfast?*) with a very high flat pitch pattern.

Intonation patterns can appear to differ quite subtly, particularly when you are learning a language. Yet producing an intonation pattern incorrectly, just like mispronouncing a word, can convey a meaning other than what you might have intended. In a study by Hewings (1995), for example, it was observed that Indonesian learners of British English frequently used a falling pitch in inappropriate contexts which in turn led to their being perceived as contentious.

As a native speaker of English, you are biased to perceive and pronounce utterances with the intonation patterns that you have learned for English. (In fact, you are biased toward all aspects of your language!) This is the case whether you are listening to English or to some other language. Learning to undo these patterns is challenging for an adult learner. You can start, however, by trying to pay attention to the melody that accompanies the words in an utterance when you are listening to a speaker of another language. Does the pitch go up at the end of a sentence? Does it go down? Is it a familiar melody, or is it quite different from what you have learned to expect? Some language learning materials focus on intonation patterns and can thus serve as a valuable resource for determining what part of the utterance to pay attention to when learning to produce the melody. If you are learning a language in a formal language setting, you can also turn to your instructor for information about the melodies used in various contexts.

Summary

We hope to have accomplished three goals in this chapter. The first was to help you understand some of the reasons why people speak with a foreign accent. The second was to outline what parts of a language's sound system are affected when speech sounds foreign. The third was to identify some of the strategies that nonnative speakers use to deal with unfamiliar elements.

As we saw, the reason why people speak with a foreign accent is that they are making an unfamiliar structure more familiar. It is important to stress that familiarity in this context is determined by one's native language. For this reason, the accent of an English speaker learning Russian will be different from that of a Swahili speaker or a Korean speaker learning Russian. Virtually any aspect of a language can be modified to make speech sound foreign, including individual sounds, sequences of sounds, stress, tone, and intonation. In making a language structure more familiar, learners will generally do one of three things: (a) replace the unfamiliar element with something familiar, (b) omit the unfamiliar element, or (c) insert another sound. Analyzing the sound system of your language as well as the one that you are learning will help you understand the ways in which the two languages differ, and by being aware of these differences, you will have more control over how you speak.

Reference

Hewings, M. 1995. Tone choice in the English intonation of non-native speakers. *International Review of Applied Linguistics* 3. 251–65.

How to Make a Consonant

Introduction

*I*n this chapter, you will learn how to make a consonant. Of course, you already know how to make many consonants, or you would not be able to speak English or any other language! What we are going to do, though, is focus on what making a consonant involves. This, we hope, will give you tools to learn new speech sounds, as well as to undo aspects of English pronunciation that can give you a foreign accent when speaking another language, should you choose to. Let's start with a short exercise to show you just how skillful you already are.

Learning to speak a language is in some ways like learning to juggle: you have to coordinate many different movements in order to produce an intended effect. To see what we mean by this comparison, say the word *punctuate* out loud very slowly. It may be helpful to watch your mouth in a mirror as you pronounce the word. Pay attention to what you are doing with your lips and tongue as you say the word. You may need to say it over a few times in order to get a feel for what you are doing. Notice that you start out with your lips brought closely together. Feel where your tongue is positioned while your lips are closed. Is it toward the front of your mouth or closer to the back?

Now open your lips and continue saying the word. Notice that by the time you say the 'unc' part of the word, your tongue is bunched up toward the back part of the roof of your mouth. What happens when you continue to pronounce the word? Your tongue is on the move again. This time the front of your tongue should be touching the center of the roof of your mouth. Your lips are probably also protruded.

To complete the word, your lips will likely spread apart a bit, showing your teeth, and your tongue will end up close to the front of the roof of the mouth. And these are only the gestures involving your tongue and lips! Another gesture was needed to allow air to pass through your nose during part of the word, and another gesture was involved to make the air vibrate when you made the vowels and a consonant. How did you get so good at moving the various parts of your mouth around to make these sounds? Much of it has to do with practice, and since you have probably been speaking English for many years, you have had years of practice!

In any activity that requires precise, coordinated gestures, whether it be juggling, playing the violin, driving a car, or playing soccer, the more you practice, the better you get. Learning how to speak a new language is no different. You have to learn how to coordinate gestures in ways that may at first be unfamiliar to you. Beginning to speak another language may seem very complicated at first. However, if you break words and sounds down into smaller parts, the task will hopefully be more manageable. In fact, it may even be easier than you think since you are already familiar with many of the movements required to make speech sounds in other languages. You just may not have had the experience of putting the movements together in the necessary way. But you **can** make new speech sounds based on what you already know.

To illustrate, let's try pronouncing some sounds that may be new to you. We will start by making a vowel that does not occur in the English sound inventory but is found in many other languages, including Chinese, German, French, Turkish, Hungarian, and Swedish. (This vowel was seen in the previous chapter in the German word *Tür* 'door.') The symbol that linguists use to represent this vowel is [y], which is part of the International Phonetic Alphabet (IPA) and displayed at the end of this book. (A common alternative symbol for this sound is 'ü'; in fact this is the symbol used in German to spell words with this sound.) Technically speaking, [y] is referred to as a front rounded vowel. The **rounded** part of the vowel means that the person's lips are protruded when making the vowel, as in the North American English vowel [u] (*boot*, *coupe*). By referring to a vowel as **front,** we are making reference to the position of the tongue in the mouth; that is, the tongue is bunched toward the front of the mouth. You can feel this for yourself by pronouncing the front vowel [i] in words like *beet* and *sea*. We will have more to say about producing vowels in the next chapter.

For the moment, however, let's combine frontness and roundness to make a front rounded vowel sound. Start by making the vowel [i], as noted just above. Pay attention to what you are doing with your lips and your tongue when you make this sound. Your lips are probably spread as if you are about to smile and your tongue is bunched toward the front of your mouth. In order to make the new sound [y], all you need to do is protrude your lips when you say the vowel, as you would if you were going to make an [u]. However, do not change the position of your tongue; just move your lips from a spread to a protruding (or rounded) position. Congratulations, you have just made the front rounded vowel [y], as in the German word *Tür* [tyr] 'door,' seen earlier, or the French word *su* [sy] 'knew'!

Sounds, Not Letters!

Remember that we are talking about **sounds,** not the letters of the alphabet. Languages can use many different letters and symbols to characterize what is essentially the same sound. Even in a single language there can be more than one way to write a single sound. For example, in English, the letters and letter combinations 'f,' 'ph,' and 'gh' are all used to represent the same sound, as in _food_, _photo_, and _enough_. To simplify matters, we will use only one symbol to refer to a specific sound, regardless of what language it occurs in; for example, [f] refers to the sound at the beginning of the English words _food_ and _photo_ and at the end of _enough_. The IPA chart of these symbols is available for your reference at the back of the book.

Let's try another one. You may have heard of sounds called "clicks" that occur in some African languages like Zulu. The term _click_ is used to describe a group of sounds that are made with a noise that sounds like clicking (hence the name). You should be able to make some click sounds quite easily since you already know how to make the various gestures involved. Although there are many types of click sounds (just as there are many kinds of vowels, for example), we will experiment with what is called an "alveolar click," characterized by the IPA symbol [!]. Begin by making the English sound [k] as in the word _back_. As you say _back,_ hold your tongue in place when you make the [k] sound. Feel how your tongue is bunched up toward the upper back of your mouth. In fact, the top back portion of your tongue will be touching the roof of your mouth.

Now make the English sound [t], like in the words _table, two._ Feel where the front part of your tongue is. It will probably be touching the hard ridge located a short distance behind your teeth. To make the alveolar click, you need to put your tongue in both of these locations at the same time; that is, place the back of your tongue at the upper back part of your mouth (as in [k]), and put the front of your tongue up against the front top of your mouth (as in [t]). There should be a small space left between the back and front of your mouth above your tongue. Now create suction in this space, for example, by breathing inward, and release your tongue abruptly from the roof of your mouth. If you hear a clicking sound, congratulations: you have just made an alveolar click found in the Zulu language!

The goal of these brief demonstrations is to show that learning to pronounce new sounds is doable if you start with some investigative work regarding the sounds. You can begin by getting information about what the various movements, or **gestures,** of the new sounds are. You should be able to get this from, for example, a language instructor, a language textbook, and websites, or even by having a native speaker describe how he or she makes the sounds.

The next step is to compare the new sound with similar sounds in English. What components of the new sound are different from sounds that you are already familiar with? Use the knowledge that you already have and apply it to sounds of the language that you are trying to learn. The gestures that combine to make sounds are independent from one another to a great extent and so can be combined in different ways to produce different sounds.

By understanding how you make the sounds in your own language, we believe that you will have tools to produce all kinds of new, exotic speech sounds. We include some exercises below to help you analyze the sounds of the language(s) that you are learning. Yet before proceeding, we need to point out that not all information about making speech sounds is presented in the following pages. Instead, we have chosen to focus on those aspects that we feel are most relevant to the language learner. Many universities offer courses in phonetics and phonology, the fields concerned with this subject matter, and should you be interested in expanding your knowledge about these topics, we would encourage you to consider taking courses.

Creating Speech Sounds

Most speech sounds are created when air is pushed out of the lungs and up through the vocal tract. The term "vocal tract" refers to the passage that air follows from the vocal folds (or cords) to the front of the mouth, as shown in figure 6.1. It also includes the nasal cavity since air can also flow out of the nose to make sounds. If you think of the vocal tract as a long tube, it is easy to see how different qualities of sound can be created. When there is nothing to obstruct the air as it moves up through the mouth, you will make the sound [h] as in _hi, ha, aha,_ or something similar to it. However, if you narrow the tube

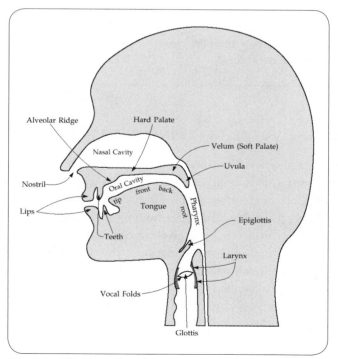

Figure 6.1. The Human Vocal Tract

at various locations along the tube, these modifications will result in differing acoustic effects and, as a result, different sounds.

You can get a feel for how this works by shaping your hand into a tube. To do this, put your hand in a loose fist so that you are making an "O" with all fingers touching the tip of your thumb. Bring the "O" up against your mouth with the end of the tube by touching your thumb to your face. Blow air through the hole (you may need to blow pretty hard). Listen to the kind of noise that is produced. Now close your fist just a bit and blow again. Did you hear a difference in the quality of noise? Try it again, closing your fist even more. You should have noticed that by narrowing the diameter of the tube created by your fist, you were able to create different sounds.

In a similar fashion, we make speech sounds by varying the width of the air passage from the vocal folds to the lips. Narrowing the passage in one part of the mouth will filter the air to create a particular sound, while narrowing it in a different location will produce a different sound. In the case of clicks, as we saw above, the passage is narrowed in two locations, giving rise to a clicking sound.

In order to make a consonant, you will need to keep several general points in mind, as shown in the box. Each of these questions will be addressed below.

Making a Consonant Sound

- What parts of the vocal tract are involved in making the sound?
- Where in the vocal tract is the air passage narrowed?
- How narrow is the air passage?
- Does air flow through the nose and/or the mouth?
- What is the position of the vocal folds?
- How long is the consonant?

PARTS OF THE VOCAL TRACT INVOLVED IN MAKING SOUNDS

Let's begin by familiarizing ourselves with the parts of the mouth that are important for making speech sounds, beginning with the **vocal tract** where sounds are produced. Starting at the front of the mouth shown in figure 6.1, sounds can be made using the **lips** and the **teeth.** Just behind the upper teeth you can see a change in the angle of the roof of the mouth; this is called the **alveolar ridge** and is also an important location for consonants in English and other languages. The roof of the mouth is divided into the **hard palate** and the **soft palate,** or **velum.** You should be able to feel the difference between these two parts of the palate with your tongue—as you run your tongue from front to back along the roof of your mouth, you should feel that the surface is harder in the front than it is in the back. At the back of the throat is the **uvula,** the soft dangling tissue that hangs down at the back of the soft palate. As noted above, above the roof of the mouth is the **nasal cavity.**

Shifting our focus to the **tongue,** as you may know, the tongue is one of the most flexible complex of muscles of the human body. Different sounds are made by using the tongue to filter the air as it moves through the vocal tract. Some of the tongue positions that are particularly important for making speech sounds are listed below. Can you figure out which consonants are made at each of these locations?

(1) **Tongue positions**
raised toward the top of the mouth
pulled back toward the back of the throat
tongue tip curled back so that it touches the top of the roof of the mouth
tongue front pushed up against the upper set of teeth
tongue tip pushed between the upper and lower sets of teeth

For our purposes, it is helpful to divide the tongue into four parts; moving from front to back, we have the **tip,** the **front,** the **back,** and the **root.** As we show below, each of these parts plays a key role in making consonants. Below the root of the tongue, you will see the **epiglottis,** a fold of tissue that helps cover the larynx during swallowing, to help make sure that food goes into the stomach and not the lungs. The **larynx** houses the **vocal folds** (or vocal cords), and the space between the folds is known as the **glottis.**

PLACES WHERE THE AIR PASSAGE IS NARROWED FOR CONSONANTS

In this section, we discuss where in the vocal tract the air passage is narrowed and identify some of the consonants that correspond to these locations. In the IPA charts of consonants at the back of this book, this aspect of a consonant is referred to as its **place of articulation.**

We begin with the lips. Sounds that make crucial use of the lips in their production are called **labial** sounds. If both lips are used, the sounds are called **bilabials.** English has the bilabials [p, b, m, w], which occur in words such as [p] p̱eet, [b] ḇeat, [m] m̱eat, [w] w̱heat.

(2) **English bilabials**
[p]   p̱eet, cap̱
[b]   ḇeat, caḇ
[m]   m̱eat, cam̱era
[w]   w̱heat, tow̱er

The sounds [f] (f̱an) and [v] (ṿan) are also made with the lips: in this case, the bottom lip rests on the upper teeth. These sounds are called **labiodentals.** In addition to raising the lip to the teeth as in making labiodentals, you can also put your tongue between your teeth. Sounds made with this gesture are called **interdentals** and correspond to the sounds [θ, ð] in the English words ba̱th and ba̱the, respectively.

(3) **English labiodentals and interdentals**
   [f]   <u>f</u>an, lea<u>f</u>
   [v]   <u>v</u>an, lea<u>v</u>e
   [q]   <u>th</u>in, ba<u>th</u>
   [ð]   <u>th</u>e, ba<u>the</u>

You can also push the tip of your tongue against the back of your teeth to make a con-sonant. Sounds made in this manner are called **dentals** and occur in many languages, including French, Spanish, and Italian. The Italian word for 'table,' for example, begins with the dental consonant [t̪] *tavola.*

The Italian sound differs from the 't' in English in part because the English 't' is made further back in the mouth, against the alveolar ridge. Sounds made in this area are called **alveolars.** English has the alveolar consonants listed in (4). Note that [l] is only pronounced as alveolar in some parts of the word; see (6) for the pronunciation of the velarized version of this sound.

(4) **English alveolars**
   [t]   <u>t</u>wo, boa<u>t</u>, re<u>t</u>ire
   [d]   <u>d</u>o, ri<u>d</u>e, re<u>d</u>uce
   [ɾ]   le<u>tt</u>er, ma<u>dd</u>er
   [s]   <u>s</u>ue, fa<u>c</u>e, bat<u>s</u>
   [z]   <u>z</u>oo, ri<u>s</u>e, dog<u>s</u>
   [n]   <u>n</u>ew, bo<u>n</u>e, ba<u>nn</u>er
   [l]   <u>l</u>ike, si<u>ll</u>y

A common pronunciation error made by English speakers is to pronounce dental con-sonants as alveolars. Although the consonants sound quite similar to English ears, they are a certain mark of a foreign accent to native speakers of the language with dentals. In chapter 9 we discuss some strategies for overcoming this pronunciation error.

Moving further back in the mouth, the tongue can be raised so that it touches or comes near to the **hard palate,** the hard part of the roof of the mouth. Sounds made in this area are called **palatals.** They are sometimes also referred to as **palato-alveolars** or **alveopalatals,** but to keep things simple, we will just use the term **palatal.** English has the following palatal consonants.

(5) **English palatals**
   [ʧ]   <u>ch</u>eck, ba<u>tch</u>
   [ʤ]   <u>j</u>ack, ba<u>dge</u>
   [ʃ]   <u>sh</u>ack, ba<u>sh</u>
   [ʒ]   <u>J</u>acques, gara<u>g</u>e
   [j]   <u>y</u>ak, v<u>i</u>ew

Another type of sound made with the tongue close to or in contact with the hard palate is a **retroflex** consonant. A retroflex sound is made by curling the tip of the tongue back toward the hard palate. For some speakers, the English "r" sound is made in this way.

The tongue can also approach or make contact with the velum (soft palate) to produce what is referred to as a **velar,** or velarized in the case of [ɫ], consonant. You should be able to feel this for yourself when you say the first consonant in the English word c̲old. The velar consonants that occur in English are given in (6).

    (6) **English velars**
        [k] c̲old, joc̲k̲
        [g] gold, jog
        [ŋ] son̲g̲, min̲g̲le
        [ɫ] pail̲, sal̲t

Let's continue to move back in the mouth toward the uvula. While the English language does not use the uvula for any of its consonants, knowing how to make sounds using it will be helpful for people learning, for example, French, Hebrew, or Arabic languages.

Try this small exercise to get a feel for where the uvula is located. Begin by making the sound [k] as in c̲at. Notice that the back of your tongue is bunched up toward the upper back part of the roof of your mouth (the velum). What you need to do now is move your tongue back just a bit further. It should now be making contact with the uvula, the soft dangling tissue that hangs down at the back of your throat. In some languages, the back of the tongue is moved up toward the uvula to make sounds. These sounds are called, not surprisingly, **uvulars,** and the sound that you were just attempting to make, [q], is a common sound in Hebrew and many Arabic languages, for example, Hebrew *qeber* 'grave.'

The leftmost image in figure 6.2 shows a drawing of an Arabic speaker producing the uvular consonant [q]. Notice how the tongue back is located right up against the uvula.

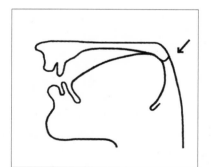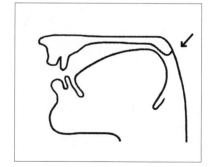

Figure 6.2. The Uvular Stop [q] (Left) and Uvular Fricative [ʁ] (Right); Consonants, as Pronounced by a Speaker of Arabic (based on Zeroual 2000)

You can compare this with how you would say the velar consonant at the beginning of *cat,* where your tongue would be touching the soft palate, and therefore slightly further to the front of your mouth.

Another uvular consonant, shown on the right in figure 6.2, occurs in some Arabic languages, as well as in many varieties of French, including Parisian French, where it is spelled with the letter 'r,' for example, *rouge* 'red.' This sound, characterized by the IPA symbol [ʁ], has the same place of articulation as the [q] sound, but it is made by letting a bit of air pass between the tongue and the uvula. This creates the turbulent noise that you can often hear associated with the sound. We will return to this topic in the next section.

We will go back one more step in the mouth, to the pharynx. If you move the root of the tongue back toward the pharyngeal wall, that is, the back of your throat, you can make what is called a **pharyngeal** consonant. While English does not have consonants made at this location, many Arabic languages include pharyngeals in their inventory of sounds. The Maltese language, spoken on the island of Malta just south of Italy, has the pharyngeal sound [ħ], for example, *ħeles* 'he set free.' The consonant sounds a bit like the English [h] in *hat,* but the tongue is pulled further back which then affects the acoustics of the sound. Figure 6.3 shows the tongue position for [ħ], as pronounced by a speaker of Arabic.

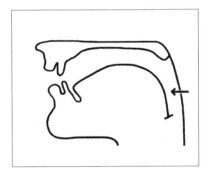

Figure 6.3. The Pharyngeal Consonant [ħ], as Pronounced by a Speaker of Arabic (based on Zeroual 2000)

Two additional places in the vocal tract are used to make consonants: the epiglottis and the glottis. Since epiglottal sounds are extremely rare, we will focus only on consonants made at the glottis. You will recall that the vocal folds are located at the glottis. By manipulating the position of the vocal folds with respect to one another, different **glottal** sounds can be produced. One such sound is English [h] (*hi*), which we discussed above. In the case of [h] the vocal folds remain open and the air passes freely through the vocal tract. The other most common glottal sound is made by closing and then quickly opening the vocal folds. This produces a sound called the **glottal stop** [ʔ], which occurs in the English expression *uh_oh,* for example. While it is not used to differentiate words in English like, for example, the consonants [b] and [p] do (e.g., *bat* vs. *pat*), it is distinctive in other languages, including Hebrew, Arabic, and Maltese. Notice that the only difference between the Maltese words for 'to taste' and 'this' is the quality of the last consonant, that is, whether it is [ʔ] or [n].

(7) **Maltese glottal stop: differentiating words**
daʔ   vs.   da<u>n</u>
'to taste'   'this'

Thus far, we have been focusing largely on consonants made where the air passage is narrowed in one location in the vocal tract. Interestingly, in some languages the air passage is narrowed in two places creating what are called **doubly articulated consonants** (recall that the click consonant described above has two articulations). With the possible exception of 'r' or velarized 'l', the closest English comes to this type of consonant is the sound [w], for example, <u>w</u>ill and to<u>w</u>er. Most English speakers pronounce [w] with the lips protruded (first location) as well as the back of the tongue raised toward the velum (second location). Hold your mouth in the position to make the [w] sound and see if you are making a sound with two places of articulation.

While not common in English, other languages can have many doubly articulated sounds, and these can pose a challenge to the language learner. Russian's sound inventory, for example, is rich in doubly articulated consonants. The language combines a palatal sound similar to [j] in <u>y</u>ellow with what would otherwise be a basic labial, dental, or velar articulation to create what are called **palatalized** consonants. Recall that a palatal is made with the tongue raised up toward the hard palate. A palatalized consonant is similar to sequences of consonant + [j] at the beginning of English words like *view, cue, hue, pew.*

English Consonant + Palatal

Say the pairs of English words below out loud, focusing on the beginning of the word. Notice the [j]-like sound after the beginning consonant, that is, [vj] in *view,* [kj] in *cue,* [hj] in *hue,* and [pj] in *pew.* (Try not to be distracted by the spelling of the words; spelling does not consistently represent the palatal.) Compare the pronunciation of each word on the left with the similar word to its right. The words in the column on the right do not have a [j] sound after the first consonant while those on the left do.

1st consonant sound + [j]	1st consonant sound, no [j]
pew	Pooh
hue	who
cue	coupe
view	voodoo

● ● ● ● ● ● ● ● ● ● ● ● ● ●

An important difference between English and Russian is that, psychologically, a native English speaker will generally consider the consonant and palatal [j] to be a sequence of two consonants, while a Russian will hear the consonant and palatal as a single sound.

Russian Palatalization

Practice saying the following Russian words first with a plain consonant and then with a slight [j]-like pronunciation added. Notice that by adding the palatal articulation, you change the meaning of the word.

Russian plain and palatalized consonants

Plain		Palatalized	
mal	'little'	m^{j}al	'crumple'
nos	'nose'	n^{j}os	'he carried'
sok	'juice'	s^{j}ok	'he lashed'
zof	'call'	z^{j}of	'yawn'

A [w]-like sound can also be added to a basic consonant sound to create what are called **labialized** consonants, for example, [p^w], [t^w], [k^w]. Labialized consonants occur distinctively in Ancient Greek, in Siberian Eskimo, in some languages of Africa (e.g., Hausa, Berber, Igbo), and in some Native American languages (e.g., Navajo, Chipewyan, Bella Coola), among others. These sounds are similar to the consonant + labial glide that occurs at the beginning of English words like *twist* and *quick*. In English, however, the sounds are generally considered to be sequences of two consonants, while in the languages noted above, a labialized consonant is perceived as a single consonant. In addition, the presence vs. absence of the labialized part of the sound is used to distinguish words. In English, on the other hand, lip protrusion is pronounced with some consonants, including [ʃ], for example, *shock,* and [ɹ] *run,* but the labial property in such words does not serve to differentiate one word from another. That is, pronouncing the word *run* without your lips protruded does not change the meaning of the word.

NARROWNESS OF THE AIR PASSAGE

In addition to thinking about where in the mouth a particular consonant is made, it is also important to take into account how narrow the passage is for the air to move through. This property is typically referred to as a consonant's **manner of articulation.** For example, if you jam your tongue up against the roof of your mouth, you will produce a different sound than if you leave a small space between the tongue and the roof. Try this by saying the following pairs of sounds:

(8)   [t] vs. [s], for example, two vs. sue
       [d] vs. [z], for example, do vs. zoo

The consonants in each pair are alveolars because the tongue front is at or near the alveolar ridge. The place of articulation is then the same. What distinguishes [t] from [s] and [d] from [z] is the narrowness of the passage between the tongue and the alveolar ridge. When you pronounce [t] or [d], you will notice that your tongue actually touches the ridge, which has the effect of blocking the passage of air momentarily. Sounds made in this way are called **stops** (or plosives). Now pronounce [s] or [z]. Unlike [t] and [d], notice that the air is not blocked at all. Instead, your tongue rests very close to the alveolar ridge without touching it. This is what gives [s] and [z] their noisy quality. Consonants that have this turbulent noise quality are called **fricatives.**

There are basically three degrees of narrowness that we need to take into account when describing how narrow the air passage is at a consonant's place of articulation. Below each category, we list the corresponding consonants from English.

Degree 1: complete closure. There is no space for air to pass through. Sounds produced in this way are called **stops** (or **plosives**).

(9)   [p, b]   pat, bat   bilabial stops
       [t, d]   toll, doll   alveolar stops
       [k, g]   cage, gauge   velar stops
       [ʔ]   uh_oh   glottal stop

English has another stoplike sound [ɾ] that occurs in words such as *letter, matter,* and *madder.* Like a stop, the airflow is briefly interrupted passing through the mouth. The term **flap** is used to describe sounds made in this way. It may be difficult for you to hear the difference between [t], [d], and [ɾ] if you are a native speaker of English because the presence of [ɾ] in a word is completely predictable and so we tend not to pay attention to it. Since the flap is used in languages like Spanish to distinguish the meaning of words, it will come up again in chapter 9 when we discuss common pronunciation errors.

(10) [ɾ]   ladder, letter   alveolar flap

Degree 2: near closure. There is just enough space so that noise is produced when the air passes through. These sounds are called **fricatives.**

(11) [f, v]   fat, vat   labiodental fricatives
       [θ, ð]   bath, bathe   interdental fricatives
       [s, z]   sip, zip   alveolar fricatives
       [ʃ, ʒ]   shack, Jacques   palatal fricatives
       [h]   hello   glottal fricative

You can actually combine degrees 1 and 2 and make another type of sound. We call this **degree 2½.** These sounds have a complete closure, like a stop, followed by a near closure, like a fricative. These sounds are called **affricates.**

(12) [ʧ, ʤ]   C̲h̲o, J̲oe   palatal affricates

Degree 3: relatively open. The air passage is narrowed, but the air can still pass through without making a lot of noise. These sounds are called **approximants** and include all **vowels, glides,** and **liquids** (some examples below).

(13) [w]   w̲hack, w̲in   bilabial glide
     [l, ɹ]   l̲ack, r̲ack   alveolar liquids
     [j]   y̲ak   palatal glide

Bilabial Fricatives

Unlike some languages, English does not have bilabial fricatives. This exercise is designed to help you practice making a bilabial fricative, using the degrees of narrowness discussed above.

Start with degree 1. Close your lips and open them. You have made a **labial stop** like in English p̲at and b̲at. Now open your lips only slightly for degree 2. This will allow you to make **labial fricatives,** like you find in the African language Ewe (you can ignore the vowel symbols).

Ewe labial fricatives
eva   'he polished'   vs.   English 'epa'
ɛβɛ   'Ewe (the language)'   vs.   English 'ebe'

Now open your lips even further for degree 3. By doing this, you make a **labial glide** as in English [w] w̲in. The position of your lips for bilabial fricatives is just between what you would be doing to make a bilabial stop and a bilabial glide. Congratulations! You've made a bilabial fricative!

AIRFLOW THROUGH THE NOSE AND MOUTH

Whether the air passage is open or closed is important for distinguishing between sounds that are made with the air flowing through the mouth and those where it also passes through the nose. Say the following pairs of words out loud, and see if you can determine whether the air is coming out of the mouth or the nose. It may help to put your hand in front of your face to try to feel the air.

(14) [b] ba   vs.   [m] ma
     [d] da   vs.   [n] na
     [g] ag   vs.   [ŋ] ang

If you determined that the air is exiting the mouth for [b, d, g] and is going through the nose (and perhaps also the mouth) for [m, n, ŋ], you are absolutely right. In distinguishing these pairs of sounds, what matters is whether the air passage going into the nasal cavity is open or closed. When it is open, the air is able to go through the nasal cavity, and a nasal sound such as [m, n, ŋ] is made; when the air passage is closed, the air can only go through the mouth, and the sound is oral, for example, [b, d, g]. The **velum** (soft palate) is responsible for controlling the flow of air through the nasal or oral cavities. If the velum is lowered as is the case in figure 6.1, there is an opening that allows air to flow out through the nose. If the velum is raised, the opening is blocked, and no air can flow through the nose.[1] As stated above, sounds made with air coming out of the nose are called **nasals.** The English sound inventory includes the following three nasal consonants.

(15) **English nasal consonants**
    [n]   nose, can
    [m]   mouse, same
    [ŋ]   sing, mingle

Most if not all languages have at least one nasal consonant. The Dravidian language Malayalam is particularly impressive in this regard because it has five nasals: labial, dental, alveolar, retroflex, and velar, as shown below (the symbol [ʌ] characterizes the vowel sound in the English word *butter*).

(16) **Malayalam nasals**
    Labial: kʌmmi 'shortage'
    Dental: pʌn̪n̪i 'pig'
    Alveolar: kʌnni 'virgin'
    Retroflex: kʌɳɳi 'link in chain'
    Velar: kuŋŋi 'crushed'

Nasals

Practice trying to move your velum to contrast nasal and oral sounds. Start by saying the vowel [ɑ], as in *father*, several times; the velum is raised in this case. Now say [ɑŋ] as in *song*, several times. In this case, the velum is lowered to let the air pass through the nose. Now alternate: [ɑ], [ɑŋ], [ɑ], [ɑŋ], [ɑ], [ɑŋ], [ɑ], [ɑŋ]. Focus on your velum and try to sense it moving up and down. With enough practice you should be able to feel the movement of the velum as it lowers and rises to create nasal and oral sounds. If you are able to do this, you should be able to pronounce unfamiliar nasals by turning a familiar oral sound into its corresponding nasal sound.

---

1. Have you ever experienced milk getting up your nose when you are talking and laughing and drinking milk at the same time? That's the lowered velum opening up the passage between the oral and nasal cavities.

POSITION OF THE VOCAL FOLDS

The narrowness of the air passage through the vocal folds can also affect the quality of sound that is being produced. The vocal folds are tissue that stretch across the airway to the lungs and can vibrate against each other, providing much of the sound that we hear when someone is talking. Just like the tongue, the vocal folds are used to filter the air as it comes out of the lungs. Depending on their position, the quality of the air differs, and, as a result, so does the sound produced. Let's consider a number of different vocal fold positions that are used in languages to make consonants.

The vocal folds can be closed tightly and then released. This produces a sound called the **glottal stop** [ʔ] which, you will recall, is used marginally as in the English expression *uh_oh*. The vocal folds can also be held very close together though not closed, which allows them to vibrate. Sounds made in this way are called **voiced** sounds. Vowels are voiced, as are some consonants, including [z] (vs. [s]), *zoo* vs. *sue*, and [d] (vs. [t]), *do* vs. *two*. Nasal consonants, for example, [m, n, ŋ], are also voiced. Sounds that are made without the vocal folds vibrating are called **voiceless** sounds.

(17) **English voiceless sounds**
[p]	ca*p*	voiceless bilabial stop
[f]	cal*f*	voiceless labiodental fricative
[θ]	pa*th*	voiceless interdental fricative
[t]	ca*t*	voiceless alveolar stop
[s]	Ca*ss*	voiceless alveolar fricative
[ʃ]	ca*sh*	voiceless palatal fricative
[ʧ]	ca*tch*	voiceless palatal affricate
[k]	pa*ck*	voiceless velar stop
[h]	*hi*	voiceless glottal fricative
[ʔ]	*uh_oh*	voiceless glottal stop

(18) **English voiced sounds**
all vowels, nasals, liquids, and glides
[b]	sla*b*	voiced bilabial stop
[v]	slee*ve*	voiced labiodental fricative
[ð]	see*the*	voiced interdental fricative
[d]	see*d*	voiced alveolar stop
[z]	sei*ze*	voiced alveolar fricative
[ʒ]	sei*z*ure	voiced palatal fricative
[ʤ]	sie*ge*	voiced palatal affricate
[g]	slu*g*	voiced velar stop

Many languages differentiate words just on the basis of the voiced and voiceless distinction in consonants. This means that the only difference in the pronunciation of two words will be that the vocal folds are vibrating for some sound in one of the words, while they are not vibrating in the other. This is the case with English words like *cab* (voiced) and *cap* (voiceless), ignoring possible differences in the length of the vowel.

Voiced and Voiceless Consonants

Try to get a feel for what the difference is between a voiced and a voiceless consonant. To do this, touch your palm to your throat by your larynx (Adam's apple). Now say the following pairs of words, paying special attention to the underlined sounds:

zoo	sue
vat	fat
do	to

Can you feel your vocal folds vibrating when you say the first consonant of the words on the left? For the words on the right, there will be vibration associated with the vowel, but you should still be able to notice that there is no vocal fold vibration associated with the first consonant.

The vocal folds can also be kept wide apart. When there is a considerable amount of air passing through them in this state, a small puff of air will be released at the end of a consonant made in this way. Say the pairs of words below with your hand in front of your mouth. Notice the difference between the underlined sounds of each pair.

(19) pot   spot
     top   stop
     core   score

You should be able to feel a small puff of air after [p, t, k] at the beginning of the words in the left column. These sounds are called **aspirated** sounds. The corresponding stops in the right-hand column are **unaspirated,** since no puff of air accompanies the consonant.

While English has both aspirated and unaspirated consonants, the presence or absence of aspiration is never the only property distinguishing two words. As a result, there are no two words that both begin with a voiceless stop that are identical in all respects but where one is aspirated while the other is unaspirated; English only has voiceless *aspirated* stops in this position, for example, *Pam.* Nor are there two words beginning with [s] followed by two identical voiceless stops except that one is aspirated and the other is unaspirated: only unaspirated voiceless stops occur in this position, for example, *spam.*

In Hindi, on the other hand, pronouncing an aspirated consonant without aspiration, or an unaspirated consonant with aspiration, can change the meaning of a word. Compare the pairs of words. The only difference between the members of each pair is aspiration: the word on the left is aspirated while the one on the right is unaspirated.[2]

---

2. We thank Ila Nagar for supplying us with these Hindi examples.

Hindi aspirated and unaspirated voiceless stops

[pʰal] 'knife-edge'   [pal] 'take care of"

[tʰan] 'roll of cloth'   [ʈan] 'mode of singing'

[kʰal] 'skin'   [kal] 'era'

[ʈʰal] 'place for buying'   [ʈal] 'postpone'

Because aspiration is not distinctive in English, native speakers will generally not be aware of the difference in pronunciation of the two types of sounds. As a result, it is easy for an English speaker to mispronounce aspirated and unaspirated words in languages that have rules that are different from English rules. In chapter 9, we review some of these errors and ways to avoid them.

LENGTH OF THE CONSONANT

An interesting property used to distinguish words in some languages concerns consonant length, that is, how long the articulation of the consonant is held. To say a sound in an English word longer or shorter does not change the meaning of the word. Take the word *sun,* for example. If you hold the 's' twice as long as you normally would, the word may sound rather strange, but it does not make it a new word. Yet this is exactly what happens in many languages. In Italian, for instance, the words for 'fate' and 'made' are distinguished solely by the length of the consonant 't.' In 'made' the consonant is about twice as long as its counterpart in 'fate,' a quality indicated in the Italian spelling system by doubling the letter.

(20) **Italian consonant length**
     fato 'fate'   vs.   fatto 'made'

While English words can also be spelled with double letters, for example, *matte, assure, babble,* this doubling is not telling the reader that the consonant is to be made twice as long as a word with only a single letter, for example, *matte* vs. *mate.* As noted above, consonant length is not used to distinguish word meaning in English. Double letters in English can nonetheless give us clues about how words are pronounced. In *matte* (vs. *mate*), for instance, the double letters provide information about the quality of the preceding vowel.

Summary

To summarize what we have covered in this chapter, we have identified a number of points concerning the production of consonants. They are as follows:

1. The parts of the vocal tract that are involved

   - lips, teeth, alveolar ridge, hard palate, velum, uvula, pharynx, vocal folds
   - tongue tip, tongue front, tongue back, tongue root

2. Places where the air passage is narrowed for consonants

   - lips, teeth, alveolar ridge, hard palate, velum, uvula, pharynx, vocal folds

3. The narrowness of the air passage

   - Degree 1: closure (no sound; airflow is interrupted)
   - Degree 2: near closure (turbulent noise produced)
   - Degree 2½: a combination of 1 and 2, closure followed by near closure
   - Degree 3: relatively open (no turbulent noise)

4. Does air flow through the nose and/or the mouth?

   - through the mouth: oral consonants (and vowels)
   - through the nose (and mouth): nasal consonants (and vowels)

5. What is the position of the vocal folds?

   - tightly closed and released: glottal stop
   - close together to produce vibration: vowels, voiced consonants
   - opened without vibration: unaspirated
   - opened with increased volume of air: aspirated

6. How long is the consonant?

   - longer
   - shorter

Keeping these points in mind, you should be able to tackle the pronunciation of new sounds. To do so, start by understanding how a new sound is made. This may involve asking your language teacher to say it for you slowly so that you can repeat it. Some language books actually describe the particular sounds using labels similar to the ones used above. Once you understand the components of the new sound, go slowly, putting the components together. Finally, **practice, practice, practice!** And practice slowly. Remember: you have had years to practice making the sounds of your native language!

Additional Exercise: Comparing Consonants

Here is an exercise to help you better understand how the consonants in a language that you are learning differ from those in English.

At the end of this book you will find consonant charts from the International Phonetic Association giving the symbols needed to describe the speech sounds in all the languages of the world (many more than you will ever need!). On the preceding page you will see a simplified chart containing the consonants of English.

- Make a copy of the IPA consonant chart (or draw your own).
- Circle all the consonants from English.
- Then, taking information that you have gathered from your language book, your instructor, the web, or other sources, draw a triangle around the consonants of the language you are learning. You could also sit down with a native speaker of the language and have them say each sound individually. You can either ask them to describe how he/she is making the sound or, you can imitate the sound, asking him/her to let you know how native-like you sound. You can then determine for yourself how the consonant is made and put a triangle around the appropriate symbol in the chart.

The next step is to compare the sounds in circles and triangles. Are there triangles without corresponding circles? If so, look for English consonants that share some of the same properties, for example, place of articulation and voicing quality, and use your knowledge of producing these familiar sounds to create new ones, as we did at the beginning of this chapter with clicks and front rounded vowels.

Reference

Zeroual, Chakir. 2000. *Propos controverses sur la phonétique et la phonologie de l'arabe marocain.* PhD dissertation. Université Paris 8.

How to Make a Vowel

Introduction

W hen you are learning how to pronounce vowels of a new language, it is useful to keep a number of points in mind. As with consonants, you will obviously want to be aware of the parts of the vocal tract that are involved in making the vowel. The narrowness of the passage for the air to exit the mouth is also important. For consonants, we saw that by varying the degree of narrowness of the air passage between, for example, the tongue and the hard palate, different consonants are created. The same is true for vowels, and we will look at the types of narrowing relevant for vowels below. It is also important to consider where in the mouth the narrowing occurs, just as we found for consonants, as well as whether the air exits just out of the mouth or out of the nose as well. Also, just as consonants can be long or short, we will also want to be aware of how long a vowel is and whether the quality of the vowel changes during its production. Finally, the shape of the lips is also relevant, perhaps more so than for consonants; that is, whether they are protruded to form a small 'o' or are spread apart.

Making a Vowel Sound

- What parts of the vocal tract are involved in making the vowel?
- Where in the vocal tract is the air passage narrowed?
- How narrow is the air passage?
- What is the shape of the lips?
- Does the quality of the vowel change from start to finish?

(continued)

- Does air flow through the nose as well as through the mouth?
- How long is the vowel?

Parts of the Vocal Tract Involved in Making Vowels

Since all speech sounds are made by filtering the air as it passes through the mouth or nasal cavity, you should not be surprised to learn that similar parts of the vocal tract are used to create consonants and vowels. Yet vowels differ from consonants in a number of ways. For example, we do not generally use the tip of the tongue to make a vowel. For vowels, movements involving the middle and back of the tongue are especially important; together these two areas are often referred to as the **tongue body**. In addition, the airflow is never completely obstructed in the vocal tract as it is for some consonants (stops). Despite this, vowels are differentiated by more degrees of narrowness than consonants are. Because of these differences, it is worthwhile having a closer look at the production of vowels in English and other languages.

Places Where the Air Passage Is Narrowed for Vowels

In this section we discuss an important function of the tongue: its back-and-forth movement in the mouth. While we illustrate using the vowels from the variety of English spoken in parts of North America, it should be noted that all languages use this movement to distinguish vowels even though the specific vowels may differ from those given below.

Horizontal Tongue Movement

To get a feel for your tongue moving back and forth, first say the vowel in [æ] as in c<u>a</u>t and then say the vowel [ɑ] as in c<u>o</u>t. Repeat a number of times, concentrating on where in your mouth the tongue body is. It may help to look in a mirror while you are doing this.

You can also use your index finger to sense the movement: touch the tip of your index finger to the front of your tongue when you say the vowel in c<u>a</u>t; now, make the vowel in c<u>o</u>t without moving your finger. Your tongue should be moving away from your finger, toward the back of your mouth, when you say the vowel in *cot*.

There are three basic positions used by speakers of most languages to make vowels. The first involves bunching the tongue toward the front of your mouth, as in [eɪ] (*b<u>ai</u>t*). This may be more noticeable when you contrast it with the pronunciation of [oʊ] (*b<u>oa</u>t*), though you should ignore any differences in the shape of your lips. Vowels that are made with the tongue bunched forward are called **front** vowels.

(1) **Front vowels in North American English**

    [i]   b<u>ee</u>t
    [ɪ]   b<u>i</u>t
    [eɪ]   b<u>ai</u>t
    [ɛ]   b<u>e</u>t
    [æ]   b<u>a</u>t

In the second position, the tongue is pulled toward the back of the mouth; vowels made in this way are called **back** vowels. Comparing again the front vowel [eɪ] (*b<u>ai</u>t*) with the back vowel [oʊ] (*b<u>oa</u>t*), notice that when you say [oʊ], the back of your tongue is pulled back so that it almost touches the back of your throat. The front-back distinction is very important and used in virtually all languages.

(2) **Back vowels in North American English**

    [u]   c<u>oo</u>l
    [ʊ]   c<u>oul</u>d
    [oʊ]   c<u>oa</u>t
    [ɔ]   c<u>au</u>ght[1]
    [ɑ]   c<u>o</u>t

In the third position, the tongue is neither bunched up at the front of the mouth nor pulled all the way back, but rather it is positioned in between the two. This is the case in English for the sound that occurs in the word *b<u>u</u>t*; vowels with this third tongue position are called **central** vowels.

Compare the pronunciation of **front, central,** and **back** vowels in North American English. To do this, say just the vowels in the following words slowly one after the other: *b<u>ai</u>t* [eɪ], *b<u>u</u>t* [ʌ], *b<u>oa</u>t* [oʊ]. Try to feel where your tongue is for the front vowel [eɪ], the central vowel [ʌ], and the back vowel [oʊ]. Practice this until you are able to feel your tongue moving back as you pronounce the three vowels. (Note that the vowel in *but* is sometimes written as [ə], a vowel referred to by linguists as 'schwa.')

(3) **Central vowels in North American English**

    [ʌ] or [ə]   c<u>u</u>t

Taking what you know about tongue placement in English, consider the front-central-back distinction among some vowels in the Korean language, as shown by the three forms below. North American English has [i] (*b<u>ee</u>t*) and [u] (*b<u>oo</u>t*), but not the central vowel [ɨ].

---

1. Not all speakers of North American English make a distinction between the vowels in *caught* and *cot*. For those who do not, the vowel [ɑ] is generally used. See relevant discussion in the next section.

(4) **Korean**

front	*central*	*back*
[i] [kil] 'road'	[ɨ] [kɨl] 'letters'	[u] [kul] 'oyster'

In both languages, the vowel [u] is pronounced with the lips protruded. Similarly, in both English and Korean the vowel [i] is made with the lips spread, not protruded. Korean obviously differs from English in that it also has a central vowel [ɨ] where the tongue body is positioned between where it would be for [u] and [i]. You can come fairly close to making a Korean [ɨ] by drawing on your knowledge of English vowels. Start by making [i] (*beet*). Now, without protruding your lips, draw your tongue back toward its position for [u] (*boot*), though not completely. By doing this, you are approximating the pronunciation of the central vowel [ɨ], which occurs not only in Korean but in Chinese languages, Turkish, and many others.

Narrowness of the Air Passage

We turn now to the narrowness of the air passage. The different degrees of narrowness that are used to distinguish vowels are generally referred to as **vowel height** distinctions. To be more precise, it is the height of the **highest part of the tongue** with respect to the roof of the mouth that is relevant. The higher the tongue, the narrower the air passage.

To get a feel for what we mean by the height of the tongue, say the vowel in the word *beet* and then the vowel in *bat*. Repeat several times, focusing on the position of the middle of your tongue in relation to the roof of your mouth. Notice that for the vowel in *beet*, your tongue is very high in your mouth, almost touching the hard palate. If it were any higher, you would be making a fricative or stop consonant. For the vowel in *bat*, on the other hand, the space between your palate and tongue is much greater. Your jaw will be much lower in this case as well. This is why doctors ask us to say "aaah" and not "eeeh"!

The image in figure 7.1 shows X-ray tracings of the tongue position of a North American English speaker saying the vowels [i] (*beet*), [u] (*boot*), [æ] (*bat*), and [ɑ] (*bottle*, *bought*). Look for the narrowest passage between the tongue and the roof of the mouth in each case; it is closer to the middle of the mouth for [i] and closer to the back of the mouth for the other three vowels. Compare the very different tongue heights for the vowels you were just saying: [i] (*beet*) and [æ] (*bat*). Of all of the vowels illustrated, [i] and [u] have the highest tongue positions and so are referred to as **high** vowels. The vowels [æ] and [ɑ] are called **low** vowels because the tongue is low in the mouth.

There are five different degrees of narrowness or vowel height used in most varieties of North American English, illustrated by the front vowel sounds in (5). They can be described on a scale from high to mid to low, with the height of the two intermediate vowels labeled "higher mid" and "lower mid."

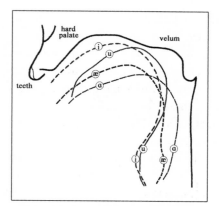

Figure 7.1. Side View of Tongue Positions in the Production of Four English Vowels: [i], [u], [æ], [ɑ] (based on Joseph Perkell 1969, with permission from the publisher)

(5)   **Vowel height in North American English front vowels**

High	[i]	b<u>ee</u>t
Higher mid	[ɪ]	b<u>i</u>t
Mid	[eɪ]	b<u>ai</u>t
Lower mid	[ɛ]	b<u>e</u>t
Low	[æ]	b<u>a</u>t

Practice feeling the height differences among the vowels in (5). Begin by pronouncing the vowel in *b<u>ee</u>t* by itself, without the two consonants. Notice that the tongue is very high in your mouth, close to the hard palate. Add a small bit of space between the tongue and the palate while keeping everything else in the same position. By doing this, you will be making the vowel in *b<u>i</u>t*. Lower the tongue a bit more and you will have the vowel in *b<u>ai</u>t*. Lower it one more step and you will be making the vowel in *b<u>e</u>t*. Now lower the tongue even further and drop the jaw, and you will have the vowel in *b<u>a</u>t*. Try this a few times to familiarize yourself with the feeling of your tongue moving closer to and further away from the roof of your mouth.

North American English also uses different vowel heights to distinguish back vowels as shown below.

(6)   **Vowel height in North American English back vowels**

High	[u]	c<u>oo</u>l
Higher mid	[ʊ]	c<u>ou</u>ld
Mid	[oʊ]	c<u>oa</u>t
Lower mid	[ɔ]	c<u>au</u>ght
Low	[ɑ]	c<u>o</u>t

As noted earlier, not all speakers of North American English use five height distinctions for back vowels. For many speakers, the vowels [ɔ] and [ɑ] are not differentiated. Instead, words like *cot* and *caught* are both pronounced as [kɑt]. Determine for yourself whether you distinguish between these two vowels or not.

English is rather uncommon in having five vowel heights, given that most languages have three or four. This is good news for people who already know English and are learning another language. The odds are that you will already be familiar with the heights of the vowels in the new language. This means that producing the vowels and hearing differences among them will probably not be as difficult as it would be if you were going from, for example, a three-height to a five-height system.

Many languages have three vowel heights, including languages such as Arabic, Bulgarian, Greek, Hawaiian, Hebrew, Hungarian, Japanese, Korean, Latin, Persian, Serbo-Croatian, Spanish, Swahili, Turkish, and Yiddish. In Spanish, Hawaiian, and Swahili, for example, the three back vowels are [u], [o], and [ɔ].

A number of other languages have four vowel heights. These include Dutch, French, German, Italian, Polish, Russian, and Swedish. Dutch, for example, has the back vowels [u], [o], [ɔ], and [ɑ].

The Shape of the Lips

We saw in the last chapter that some consonants are made with the lips protruded, as in [w] <u>win</u>. Lip protrusion is often referred to as *lip rounding* because the lips form a small circle when protruded. Rounded vowels are quite common in languages. English, for example, has a number of rounded vowels, including [u] <u>boot</u>, [oʊ] *boat,* and in some dialects [ɔ] <u>bought</u>. While in North American English all the rounded vowels are also back vowels, in other languages front vowels can be rounded as well, for example, French, German, Hungarian, Korean, Swedish, and Turkish, to name a few.

French, for example, has an especially rich inventory of front rounded vowels, as in (7).

(7)   **French front rounded vowels**

high front rounded [y]	*pu* [py] 'could'	*lu* [ly] 'read'
mid front rounded [ø]	*peu* [pø] 'little'	*le* [lø] 'the'
lower mid front rounded [œ]	*peur* [pœr] 'fear'	*leur* [lœr] 'their'

Making front rounded vowels is not difficult if you start with vowels that you are familiar with. Picking up from our discussion above, begin by making the vowel [i] as in <u>beet</u>. Now protrude your lips as you would if you were producing [u] (<u>boot</u>), remembering to keep your tongue near the front of your mouth. You have just made the high front rounded vowel [y]! Now practice it a number of times to give your muscles a chance to remember how they are positioned when you make this vowel.

Let's try another. To make the front mid rounded vowel [ø], start by making the English vowel [eɪ], as in b*ai*t. Now protrude your lips, again without moving your tongue. This is the vowel in French words like [pø] *peu* 'little' and [lø] *le* 'the.'

To produce the remaining French front rounded vowel, that is, the lower mid front rounded vowel [œ], begin with the lower mid front vowel [ɛ], as in North American English b*e*t. Once more, protrude your lips. You have now made the vowel that occurs in words like [pœr] *peur* 'fear' and [lœr] *leur* 'their.' Congratulations!

Now practice pronouncing all three vowels one after another: [y], [ø], [œ].

Once again we have illustrated how you can make unfamiliar sounds from another language by drawing on the knowledge that you already have from your own language.

Changing Vowel Quality from Start to Finish: Diphthongs

Most of the vowels that we have discussed so far are similar in that the quality of the vowel stays the same from beginning to end. For instance, the vowel [i] in b*ee* is consistently pronounced as [i] from when it starts after the consonant [b] to when it ends. Vowels of this type are called **monophthongs.** Not all vowels have this property, however. The vowel [ɔɪ] in the word b*oy*, for example, begins as a mid back rounded vowel [o] but ends up as a higher mid front unrounded vowel [ɪ]. A vowel of this type is called a **diphthong**: a vowel that starts out with one quality and ends up with another quality.

The full set of diphthongs in American English is shown below, including two that we have already seen: [eɪ] (bait) and [oʊ] (boat). Note that the change in quality is most detectable when the diphthong occurs at the end of a word since in this position it is fairly long, allowing the end of the vowel to be more fully produced: compare b*ai*t vs. b*ay*. Other varieties of English may have different sets of diphthongs. If you are a speaker of one of these varieties, consider how you pronounce the vowels in the words in (8). If they are different, in what way do they differ from the diphthongs transcribed?

(8) **English diphthongs**

    [aʊ]   c*ow*, tr*ou*nce
    [oʊ]   g*o*, s*ew*, t*oa*d
    [aɪ]   b*uy*, b*i*de
    [ɔɪ]   s*oy*, b*oy*
    [eɪ]   r*ay*, s*ay*

Many languages do not have diphthongs and only have monophthongs; these include Arabic, Bulgarian, Ewe, French, Greek, German, Hawaiian, Hebrew, Hungarian, Italian, Japanese, Navajo, Spanish, Swahili, Zulu, and many others. In fact, all languages have monophthongs, while only some, like English, have diphthongs.

Pronunciation Errors with Diphthongs and Monophthongs

Substituting a diphthong for a monophthong is a common pronunciation error made by English speakers when learning a language without diphthongs. This error is especially easy to make when the monophthong of the foreign language is similar to a diphthong of English. For example, the English diphthongs [eɪ] and [oʊ] are very similar to the vowels [e] and [o], which occur in most of the languages noted just above. If you are a native speaker of English and you want to sound more like a speaker of the foreign language with [e] and [o], see chapter 10 for some suggestions on how to accomplish this. And, again, remember to beware of spelling! While languages may use the same letter to spell a sound, this does not mean that the letters correspond to the same sounds.

Airflow through the Mouth and Nose

In addition to the topics above, another point to keep in mind when producing vowels is whether the vowel is nasal or oral. Just as we saw for consonants, whether the air exits out of the nose or the mouth can be meaningful. If the air only exits the mouth, we have what is called an *oral* vowel. If it also exits the nose, the vowel is called *nasal.*

The vowels of English are all basically oral. That is, we do not use the distinction between nasality and orality in vowels to change the meaning of words like we do with vowel height, for example, ([i] b*ee*t vs. [ɪ] b*i*t). This means that there are no two words in English that differ solely on the basis of whether the vowel is nasal or oral. Yet many languages do use this distinction, including French, Polish, and Portuguese.

Recall that to make a nasal consonant, the velum is lowered so that air can exit out of the nose. This is the case with consonants like [m] *so*m*e*, [n] *su*n, and [ŋ] *su*ng. Not surprisingly, nasal vowels are also made by lowering the velum.

Try to make a nasalized [ɑ] (the oral [ɑ] occurs in words like *father*). Start by pronouncing the sound [ɑ], followed by [ŋ], as in *so*ng. Notice that the back of your tongue is touching the roof of your mouth in order to make the consonant. To remove the consonantal articulation but keep the nasality, lower the back of your tongue slightly so that it is no longer touching the top of your mouth. You should still be making a nasal sound, and if you are, this means that your velum is in a lowered position. You might even be able to feel air coming out of your nose. Now try to make just the vowel [ɑ] with the velum lowered; that is, the nasal vowel [ɑ̃] (A tilde over a vowel indicates that the vowel is nasal.) Practice this several times to get a sense of what a nasal vowel feels and sounds like.

As we mentioned above, in some languages the only difference between two words can be whether the vowel is nasal or oral, and so the meaning of a word depends on this quality of the vowel. In Polish, for example, there are two mid nasal vowels, spelled 'ę' [ɛ̃] and 'ą' [ɔ̃]. The nasal quality of a vowel can differentiate the words 'I, me' (contains an oral vowel) and 'she, her' (contains a nasal vowel), as in (9). Notice that in these two words, the consonant [j], the height of the vowel, and the position of the tongue body and lips are all the same; the only property that distinguishes the two words is whether or not the vowel is nasal.

(9) **Polish oral and nasal lower mid back rounded vowels**
   [jɔ]   'I, me'
   [jɔ̃]   'she, her'

In Polish, nasality on a vowel is "spelled" with a diacritic under the vowel, that is, 'ę' and 'ą.' Another common way to denote nasality in spelling is to write a nasal consonant after the vowel, as is done in French and Portuguese. In French, for example, the word for *good* is spelled *bon* yet pronounced as [bɔ̃]; the 'n' in the spelling is not pronounced as a consonant but instead indicates that the preceding vowel is nasal. A common mistake made by English speakers is to pronounce the 'n' as the consonant [n], rather than as nasalization on the vowel. Understanding the spelling conventions of the language that you are learning will help you to avoid this kind of error.

Length of the Vowel

An additional property of vowels that may be important is vowel length. In some languages, the amount of time that you hold the pronunciation of a vowel can be used to distinguish the meaning of words. Examples from the Turkish language shown in (10) illustrate that in some words it is only the length of the vowel that differentiates words (a colon after the vowel indicates that the vowel is longer than the same vowel without the colon). For example, the words for 'beware' and 'quiet' are identical, except that the first word ([sakin]) has a short [a] while the second word ([sa:kin]) has a long vowel [a:].

(10) **Turkish short and long vowels**

shorter duration	*longer duration*
sakin 'beware'	sa:kin 'quiet'
meme 'breast'	me:mur 'official'
iman 'faith'	i:man 'imam'
surat 'face'	su:ret 'manner'

English vowels can also differ in duration, but these differences do not change the meaning of a word like they do in Turkish. Rather, the duration of the vowel is completely predictable from its context. A vowel is pronounced with a shorter duration if it comes before a **voiceless** consonant, like [t, p, k, s, . . .], as in the word *beat*. A vowel is longer when it comes before a **voiced** consonant, such as [d, b, g, z, . . .], as in *bead*. Compare the vowel [i] in *beat* to the one in *bead*. Can you tell that the second one is longer? Now compare these two to the vowel [i] in *bee*. It should sound even longer. This is because in English the duration of a vowel is longest when it comes at the end of a word. A vowel in English is then short before a voiceless consonant, longer before a voiced consonant, and longest at the end of the word. Since we can predict the relative length of a vowel by knowing what, if anything, follows it in a word, vowel length in English is not distinctive. It is, on the other hand, in Turkish, as we saw in (10).

Summary

In this section we discussed six areas involved in the production of vowels that may be important to you as you learn new vowels.

(11)   **Dimensions of difference for vowels**
    a. the height of the vowel: high, higher mid, mid, lower mid, low
    b. the horizontal position of the tongue body: front, central, back
    c. the position of the lips: rounded, unrounded
    d. whether the vowel is a monophthong or a diphthong
    e. whether the vowel is oral or nasal
    f. whether the vowel is long or short

These are the most common properties associated with vowels, and if you learn these, they will take you a long way in learning how to produce the sounds of another language.

Being familiar with these aspects of vowels, as well as the additional components that we discussed in the previous chapter for consonants, should enable you to produce, with practice, almost any speech sound, even those very unusual sounds that may occur in only a few languages. Remember that when you are learning to make a new sound, it can be helpful to start from a sound that you already know. Recall that this was our strategy for producing the front rounded vowel [y]: we started from the English vowel [i], *beet,* and added lip rounding, similar to English [u], *boot.* If you are unsure about how the new sound is produced and you are studying in a formal language learning setting, ask your instructor to describe where in the mouth and how the sound is made. Alternatively, you could ask a native speaker. Watch as the person pronounces the sound and listen carefully. Then imitate as best you can, asking them for feedback on your pronunciation. Once you have it, there is only one thing left to do: practice, practice, practice! There is no substitute in language learning for practice.

Additional Exercise: Comparing Vowels

This exercise is similar to the one for consonants at the end of the previous chapter. The goal is to help you better understand how the vowels in a language that you are learning differ from those in English.

At the end of this book you will find charts with symbols for vowels in English and other languages.

- Make a copy of the English vowel charts (or draw your own). Note that there is one for monophthongs and one for diphthongs.
- Taking information that you have gathered from your language book, your instructor, the web, or other sources, draw a triangle around any English vowel that also occurs in the language you are learning. Take care to determine whether the vowels of your new language are monophthongal or diphthongal. Add any vowels from your new language that do not occur in English.

Now compare the vowels in the two languages. What differences in the two systems do you notice? If there are vowels in your new language that do not occur in English, in what ways are they similar/ to or different from English vowels? What aspect of pronouncing the new vowels do you find particularly challenging? How can you draw on your knowledge of English vowels to help overcome the challenges?

Reference

Perkell, Joseph. 1969. *Physiology of speech production* (Research Monograph No. 53). Cambridge, MA: MIT Press.

8

Putting Sounds Together

Introduction

Our focus in the preceding two chapters has been on learning how to pronounce consonants and vowels. Obviously, learning to do this is crucial if you want to sound like a native speaker of some other language. But sounds rarely occur by themselves. Instead, sounds combine to form words, and learning to speak another language also involves learning to pronounce new words. In many cases this requires learning how to combine sounds in unfamiliar ways.

As with any new activity that involves the coordination and sequencing of complex movements, learning to pronounce new words requires lots of practice. In this chapter we look at how the sequences of sounds in English differ from those in other languages. Perhaps not surprisingly, we will see that some languages have systems that are more complex than those of English while others have simpler ones. Of course, knowing which sequences of sounds can and cannot occur in English is not going to make you a master of some other language. We believe that it will, however, help you to think analytically about the sound system of English, a system that you already have lots of experience with. Equipped with this knowledge, you can then use it as a basis for comparison with any new language that you choose to learn. Being familiar with the sound sequences of English will also give you a glimpse into potential areas of difficulty that you might expect to encounter when learning a new language.

So how can you learn to combine unfamiliar sounds in unfamiliar ways to create new words? It may be helpful to break a difficult word down into smaller, more manageable sequences and practice pronouncing these shorter sequences **very slowly.** Practice the sequence over and over to give your vocal organs a chance to learn the new combination. Slowly combine the smaller chunks, practicing larger and larger chunks. The important point through all of this is to practice, practice, practice.

But what constitutes an unfamiliar sequence of sounds? To answer this question, we will start by going over which strings of sounds occur in English. Notice again that we say **sounds,** not spelling! Depending on the dialect of English, there are approximately twenty-four distinctive consonants in English. By this we are referring to the sounds that are used to distinguish the meanings of words, for example, [n, m], *ru<u>n</u>* vs. *ru<u>m</u>*. A list of the consonants that occur in most dialects of English is given in (1). Stops, fricatives, and affricates are grouped together under the cover term **obstruent,** while nasals, liquids, and glides form the group of **sonorant** consonants.

(1) **Obstruents**:

				Sonorants:		
Stops:	[p]	<u>p</u>ill		**Nasals:**	[m]	ru<u>m</u>
	[b]	<u>b</u>ill			[n]	ru<u>n</u>
	[t]	<u>t</u>ill			[ŋ]	ru<u>ng</u>
	[d]	<u>d</u>ill		**Liquids:**	[l]	<u>l</u>ock
	[k]	<u>k</u>ill			[ɹ]	<u>r</u>ock
	[g]	gill		**Glides:**	[w]	<u>w</u>ar
Fricatives:	[f]	<u>f</u>ace			[j]	<u>y</u>our
	[v]	<u>v</u>ase				
	[θ]	<u>th</u>in				
	[ð]	<u>th</u>is				
	[s]	<u>s</u>ue				
	[z]	<u>z</u>oo				
	[ʃ]	<u>sh</u>ack				
	[ʒ]	<u>J</u>acques				
	[h]	<u>h</u>i				
Affricates:	[ʧ]	<u>ch</u>uck				
	[ʤ]	<u>j</u>ug				

What combinations of consonant sounds can begin a word in English? We know that [bɹ], [st], and [pl] are possible combinations because of words like <u>br</u>own, <u>st</u>op, <u>pl</u>ease. But are all combinations of two consonants possible at the beginning of a word? If they were, with about twenty-four consonants in the language we'd expect 24!/(24 – 2)! possible combinations, that is, 552. In reality, there are fewer than fifty in the language. As a native speaker of English, you already know this, even though you may not be consciously aware of the fact that you do. Yet for a non-native speaker of English, these combinations have to be memorized. In the next section, we will look in more detail at what the possible sequences of English are. With this as a basis, we will then consider sequences in other languages and the challenges that an English speaker might encounter when learning them.

Sound Sequences in English and Other Languages

Knowing the sequences that occur at the beginning of a word and at the end of the word will generally tell us the kinds of sequences that can occur within a word. Word-internal sequences are typically a combination of possible word-final sequences and word-initial sequences. For example, we know that [ɹt] is a possible word-final sequence in some varieties of English because it is pronounced after a vowel in words like *cart, Burt, sort*. We also know that [m] is a possible word-initial consonant in English because it occurs before a vowel in words like *men, map, melon*. Given this, it is not surprising to find the sequence [-ɹtm-] occurring between vowels in an English word like *apartment*. So although we do not talk specifically about word-internal sequences in what follows, conclusions can be drawn from the other information provided.

ENGLISH SOUND SEQUENCES: WORD-INITIAL

Before looking at what occurs in other languages, let's begin by thinking about possible sequences of sounds in English. The term **phonotactics** is used to refer to which sequences occur and do not occur in a language. We start by considering English phonotactics at the beginning of the word.

In English, words can begin with either a consonant or a vowel sound, for example, *big, supper, in, airplane*. The number of consonants that can come before a vowel at the beginning of a word ranges from one to three. Any consonant can start a word, with two exceptions. First, there are no words in English that begin with the sound [ŋ] (the sound that occurs at the end of words like *song* [sɔŋ]). Second, the sound [ʒ] is very uncommon at the beginning of an English word, and those that do occur generally have a foreign flavor to them, for example, *Jacques, Zsa Zsa (Gabor)*.

As we increase the number of consonants at the beginning of a word, the number of restrictions also increases. In most English words that begin with **two consonants,** the first consonant is a stop or a fricative, and the second is a liquid ([ɹ, l]), or glide ([j, w]). The only exception to this rule is that there are sequences of two consonants in which the first is the fricative [s] and the second is either a nasal consonant, for example, *snore, smoke*, or an oral plosive, for example, *spot, stop, sky*. Some examples of two-consonant sequences are given in (2). (An asterisk before a sequence indicates that the sequence does not occur.)

(2) p + consonant: [pl]   please
                     [pɹ]   price
                     [pj]   pure
                     *[pw] (except in foreign words like *pueblo*)
     b + consonant: [bl]   black
                     [bɹ]   brother
                     [bj]   beautiful
                     *[bw]

t + consonant: [tɹ]   trim

                     [tw]   twin

                     *[tl], *[tj] (though [tj] is possible in some dialects as in
                 tune)

d + consonant: [dɹ]   drug

                     [dw]   dwell

                     *[dl], *[dj] (though [dj] is possible in some dialects as in
                 dude)

k + consonant: [kɹ]   crutch

                     [kl]   clean

                     [kw]   quick

                     [kj]   cute

g + consonant: [gɹ]   grow

                     [gl]   glad

                     [gw]   Gwen

                     *[gj]

θ + consonant   [θɹ]   three

                     [θw]   thwart

                     *[θl], *[θj]

f + consonant: [fɹ]   fresh

                     [fl]   flat

                     [fj]   few, funeral

                     *[fw]

v + consonant   [vj]   view

                     *v + cons. (except in foreign words, e.g. *Vladimir*)

s + consonant: [sp]   spot

                     [st]   stop

                     [sk]   score

                     [sm]   smile

                     [sn]   snore

                     [sl]   slimy

                     [sj]   Sierra (for some speakers)

                     [sw]   swim

                     *[sɹ]

ʃ + consonant   [ʃɹ]   shriek

                     *[ʃl], *[ʃj], *[ʃw] (except in foreign words, e.g. *schlep*,
                 schtick)

    *z + consonant, *ʒ + consonant, *ð + consonant

You may have noticed that voiced fricatives generally do not occur before a consonant at the beginning of a word, so you do not get words like *znew* or *vlop*. An exception is found with the Russian name *Vladimir,* which when used in English provides a nice illustration of how the introduction of words from other languages can expand the inventory of sound sequences in one's own language. Also missing are sequences made up of the consonants [t, d, θ] + [l], [θ] + [j], and [p, b, f] + [w]. None of these sequences occur at the beginning of words in English.

Word-initial sequences of **three consonants** are even more restricted. In fact, in English the first consonant in this kind of sequence has to be [s], the second consonant has to be a voiceless stop ([p, t, k]), and the third consonant has to be an approximant ([ɹ, l, w, j]), for example, *sprain* [spɹejn], *spleen* [splin], *spew* [spju], *strew* [stɹu], *scream* [skɹim], *sclerosis* [sklǝɹosis], *squall* [skwɑl], *skew* [skju].[1] You will see in (3) that even within this restricted set, not all possible combinations are found (√ means that the sequence occurs, × means that it does not).

(3) **Possible word-initial three-consonant sequences in English**

	j	w	l	ɹ
sp	√	×	√	√
st	×	×	×	√
sk	√	√	√	√

WORD-INITIAL SEQUENCES IN OTHER LANGUAGES

Consider word-initial sound sequences: languages can differ from English in a number of ways. A language may allow fewer consonants to occur at the beginning of the word, or it may allow more consonants. Or a language may permit a similar number of consonants as English but have different restrictions on which consonants can combine with each other. A language can also differ in the types of sounds that words can begin with.

Arabic is an example of this last point: it is more restrictive than English concerning the types of sounds a word can start with. Recall that in English, words can begin with either a consonant or a vowel. In Arabic, however, all words must begin with a consonant sound. This means that, unlike in English, there are no words like *apple, inside, eat* that begin with a vowel.[2] Interestingly, there are no languages where all words must begin with a vowel.

Other languages are more restrictive than English in terms of the number of consonants that can occur at the beginning of a word. Fijian (Boumaa), for example, allows only a single consonant to occur at the beginning of a word, though any consonant in the language can occur in this position (Dixon 1988). In Zulu, Swahili, Mandarin Chinese, and Korean, to name a few, no more than two consonants can begin a word, and the second consonant can only be a glide (e.g., [w, j]).[3] Some examples of Korean words

---

1. Note that in some dialects of English, [ʃ] can occur in these three consonant sequences, particularly before [tɹ], for example, *street* [ʃtɹit].

2. Although some words in Arabic may appear to have a vowel at the beginning of a word, these are preceded by a glottal stop or another type of consonant when they are pronounced.

3. Some scholars have claimed that the glide actually forms a diphthong with the following vowel. If this is the case, Korean is even more restrictive since we would need to say that words can begin with no more than one consonant.

beginning with two consonants are [kwicok] 'nobleman,' [tjulip] 'tulip,' [pʰjemul] 'jewelry.' One consequence of this restriction was noted in chapter 5 where it was pointed out that when Korean speakers pronounce English words that begin with a sequence of consonants, they may insert a vowel between the consonants; for example, the word *strike* may be pronounced with a short vowel between each of the three initial consonants.

Languages that allow fewer consonants at the beginning of the word, such as those just mentioned, often pose less of a challenge to an English speaker learning the language than those that allow more consonants or a greater variety of consonant sequences. Polish, for example, exemplifies a language that allows more consonants in sequence at the beginning of the word, as discussed below, and thus may pose particular problems to the language learner. At the same time, problems may be encountered when the specific consonant sequences that are allowed in a given language are *different* from those of the native language, even if they are not more numerous. Greek provides a good example of a language with a similar number of permitted consonants as English but different phonotactics.

Greek is similar to English in that up to three consonants can occur at the beginning of a word (Joseph & Philippaki-Warburton 1987). A number of the clusters with three consonants will be familiar to English speakers, for example, [spl] [splína] 'spleen'; [spr] [spróxno] 'push'; [str] [stratós] 'army'; and [skr] [skrápas] 'idiot.' Three other possible Greek sequences are not found in English: [skl] [sklirós] 'hard'; [skn] [sknípa] 'kind of mosquito'; [sfr] [sfrajíða] 'stamp.' Sequences of two consonants also present some patterns not encountered in English. These include sequences of fricative + fricative ([sθ, sx]), fricative + stop ([ft, xt]), and stop + fricative ([ps, ts, ks]). Notice how a word of Greek origin like *psychology* with the non-English [ps] is pronounced in English with a single [s] (see chapter 5 for discussion).

In Polish, between one and four consonants can begin a word. Words beginning with two consonants are most frequent, making up approximately 88 percent of words beginning with consonant clusters; those with three consonants make up about 9 percent; and those with four consonants count approximately 2 percent. It is impressive to note that there are over 230 different types of two-consonant sequences and close to 200 different three-consonant clusters (Bethin 1992).

Despite the large number of different consonant clusters, there are several generalizations about how strings of sounds combine that the language learner can use to learn the sequences, rather than memorizing each string of sounds individually. For example, not unlike English, most consonant clusters that come before a vowel are made up of an obstruent (stop, fricative, affricate) followed by a sonorant (nasal, liquid, glide), for example, [sn, sm, ʂr], or a fricative followed by a stop, for example, [sk, zb, st]. Unlike English, however, a sonorant consonant can also precede an obstruent at the beginning of the word, giving sequences such as [rv, rt, rd]. Another difference is that for some consonants, both orders are possible, for example, [bz] *bzu*, [zb] *zbir*.

ENGLISH SOUND SEQUENCES: WORD-FINAL

Now let's consider possible sequences at the ends of words. Words in English can end with up to four consonants, for example, *sick* [sɪk] (1), *six* [sɪks] (2), *sixth* [sɪksθ] (3), *sixths* [sɪksθs] (4). Of course, words can also end in only a vowel, for example, *see* [si]. The only consonant that is systematically excluded from occurring at the end of an English word is [h]. As we noted above, [h] only occurs before a vowel. (Remember, we are talking about sounds—the *letter* 'h' can come at the end of a word in English, for example, *wash*, but the *sound* [h] cannot. Which sound occurs at the end of *wash*?)

In some dialects of English, [ɹ] has a distribution similar to that of [h] in that it does not occur after a vowel, only before one. This is the case, for example, in the variety of English spoken by the Queen of England (referred to as Received Pronunciation or RP English), in New Zealand[4] and Australian English, as well as in the American variety of English spoken in the Boston area. Speakers of these dialects share similar pronunciations of words like *car* [kɑ] and *park* [pɑk] (though the quality of the vowels can differ).

When a vowel is followed by two consonants in English, the first may be a fricative, a stop, or a sonorant (nasal or liquid). If the first is a fricative or a stop, the second will also be a fricative or a stop as in *act* [ækt], *desk* [dɛsk], *rest* [ɹɛst], *wisp* [wɪsp], *fifth* [fɪfθ]. If the first consonant is a sonorant, then the second needs to be a stop, a fricative, or an affricate, as in the words *send* [sɛnd], *camp* [kæmp], *sink* [sɪŋk], *cinch* [sɪntʃ], *art* [ɑɹt], *help* [hɛlp], *twelve* [twɛlv], *Welsh* [wɛlʃ], *welch* [wɛltʃ].

There are, however, some further restrictions on word-final sequences in English. For one, when a nasal is followed by an oral stop [p, b, t, d, k, g], both consonants must have the same place of articulation, for example, *rant* [rænt] (alveolar), *sink* [sɪŋk] (velar), *pump* [pʌmp] (labial). There are no words like *ranp* or *pimt* where the consonants differ in terms of place of articulation. This restriction is relaxed if the final consonant is the past tense marker [t, d]; these consonants can follow any verb ending in a consonant whether they have the same place of articulation or not, for example, *banged* [bæŋd], *rammed* [ɹæmd].

An additional restriction holds between a vowel and the consonants that follow. If a nasal + stop consonant sequence follows a diphthong, the nasal can only be [n] and the stop can only be [t, d]. Note that for this restriction, [i] and [u] behave like diphthongs and are written [ij] and [uw]. Examples can be seen in (4). Interestingly, there are no words in English with these diphthongs followed by a velar or labial nasal and stop.

(4) **North American English diphthongs plus [nt] or [nd]**

[ɑɪ]	pint, find, mind
[ɑʊ]	count, mount, mound, ground
[oɪ]	point, anoint
[ij]	fiend
[eɪ]	paint, faint
[uw]	wound ·
[oʊ]	won't

---

4. The Southland variety of New Zealand English differs in that [ɹ] is pronounced after a vowel.

But when the vowel is a monophthong, there is no such restriction: you can get a velar or a labial nasal consonant followed by a stop, as illustrated by the examples in (5).

(5) **North American English monophthongs plus nasal and stop sequences**
    [æ] land, lamp, bank
    [ɪ] lint, limp, ink
    [ɛ] tent, hemp
    [ʌ] hunt, hump, hunk

In sequences of three consonants at the end of a word, the first two consonants can be any of the permissible two-consonant sequences noted above. However, the consonant coming after these consonants can only be alveolar ([t, d, s, z]), for example, *acts* [ækts], *wounds* [wuwndz], *lamps* [læmps], *inked* [ɪŋkt], *calmed* [kɑmd].

WORD-FINAL SEQUENCES IN OTHER LANGUAGES

As with word-initial sequences, languages can differ from English in a number of ways when it comes to possible sequences at the end of words. Some languages, like Maori (spoken in New Zealand), have no words at all that end in a consonant. Others permit only a limited number of consonants, like Japanese. Although there are approximately twenty consonants in the language, only one, [ɴ], can occur at the end of a Japanese word.

Greek is also interesting from the perspective of the consonants that occur at the end of a word. There are only two consonants that can appear at the end of a word of Greek origin: [s] and less frequently [n] (Joseph & Philippaki-Warburton 1987). Words of foreign origin can end in other types of consonants, for example, [kláb] 'club,' [rúz] 'rouge.' Final consonant clusters are also uncommon except in words of foreign origin, for example, [fjórd] 'fjord.'

Polish would appear to be at the other end of the spectrum since words can contain up to five consonants at the end of a word. It should be noted, though, that four- and five-consonant sequences are not very common. The vast majority of final consonant sequences contain two consonants. Like English, in many clusters the first consonant is a sonorant, for example, [rm, ln, mp, rʧ, rf, lk]. Polish also has words with final obstruent-obstruent sequences such as [ʒb, ʃʧ, kʃ, ps, pʧ]. However, the language differs most from English in allowing some words to end in an obstruent followed by a sonorant, for example, [ʒm, kl, zn, dr, tr]. In English, recall that a sonorant can only precede an obstruent at the end of a word, for example, *ramp, fault, art.*

Summary

As we have seen, English seems to be situated in the middle of the continuum when it comes to phonotactics. There are many languages that have fewer possible sound sequences, but there are also many others that allow for more possibilities. As noted above, those with a subset of the combinations that English allows should pose less of a problem for the learner, assuming that the sounds are the same as well. For those with unfamiliar sounds or sequences, a useful strategy in learning them is to begin by breaking the word or sequence of sounds down into smaller parts. If possible, begin with what you know and build on that, as we did with individual sounds. Practice pronouncing the smaller parts slowly, and then slowly combine the sounds, getting feedback on your pronunciation from a native speaker, if possible.

Additional Exercises

1. **Investigating Word-Initial Consonant Sequences**

   Do some investigative work into the consonant sequences that occur at the beginning of words in a language that you are learning. Here is one method of doing this:

   • Start with a list of all the consonant **sounds** that occur in the language.

   (a) **Sequences of two consonants**:
   • Make a chart with a **row** for each consonant in the language. Put the IPA symbol for each consonant in the leftmost column of a single row. Each row should then be assigned to a particular consonant. It can be useful for seeing patterns later to list the consonants in order of manner and place of articulation, for example, [p, b, t, d, k, g, s, z, m, n, l, r, j, w].
   • Add a **column** for each consonant in the language, and label the top of the column with the IPA symbol for the sound in the same order as above.
   • Beginning with the consonant in the first row, go across each column, checking each cell where the consonant can occur at the beginning of a word. Proceed with the consonants in each of the other rows until your chart is complete.

   What **generalizations** can you make about the place and/or manner of articulation of consonants that can begin a word? What generalizations can you make about consonants that can come second? How do these patterns compare to the sequences that can occur in English? Given the differences between English and your new language, where do you anticipate having difficulty? How might you deal with these challenges?

   (b)   **Sequences of three consonants**:
   - If your language allows three consonants at the beginning of the word, create a chart similar to the one above with the modifications below.
   - Since three-consonant sequences will be composed of possible two-consonant sequences, label each row with one of the two-consonant sequences that you have identified above.
   - Columns are identical to the ones in (a).
   - Follow the same procedure as in (a), putting a check in each cell that corresponds to a possible three-consonant sequence.

   (c)   **Sequences of more than three consonants**:
   - Follow the same procedure as above, delimiting the rows of the new chart to only those sequences that were possible in the preceding chart.

2.   **Investigating Word-Final Consonant Sequences**

To discover what consonant sequences can occur at the end of a word, follow the same procedure as in exercise 1 above for word-initial sequences, with the following modifications:

   - The consonant that appears in each **row** will correspond to the consonant that comes immediately after a vowel.
   - The consonant at the top of a **column** will be the consonant that potentially follows the consonant occurring in a row.
   - Follow the same procedures as for word-initial sequences, putting a check in each cell that corresponds to a possible consonant sequence.

Repeat with additional charts if more than two consonants can occur at the end of a word. Each sequence identified in the previous chart will appear in its own row in the new chart.

References

Bethin, C. Y. 1992. *Polish syllables: The role of prosody in phonology and morphology.* Columbus, OH: Slavica Publishers.

Dixon, Robert M. W. 1988. *A grammar of Boumaa Fijian.* Chicago: University of Chicago Press.

Joseph, Brian D., & I. Philippaki-Warburton. 1987. *Modern Greek.* London: Croom Helm.

Common Pronunciation Errors

*I*n the previous chapters we have seen a number of ways in which English differs from other languages in terms of how words and sentences are pronounced. Because of these differences, an English speaker is bound to make mistakes when learning to speak another language, and that, of course, is what makes his or her accent sound foreign. Hopefully the preceding discussion will make it easier for you to pinpoint the areas where you are most likely to have trouble and give you some tools to help deal with them.

In this chapter we bring together some of the typical pronunciation errors made by English speakers when learning another language. Perhaps these are some of the same errors that you make. If so, we hope that the following discussion will remind you of the differences between English and other languages and offer some guidance about how to avoid common errors.

Interpreting Unfamiliar Symbols

As we saw in earlier chapters, each language has its own conventions for representing in writing how a sound is pronounced. These conventions are arbitrary rules decided upon at some stage in the language's development. Because they are arbitrary, the same sound could potentially be represented by as many different letters combinations as there are languages! It is not quite as bad as that, but conventions do differ, as we have seen.

Nasalized vowels are a good example of a type of sound that is represented in different ways. Recall from chapter 7 that in Polish, the language's two nasal vowels are represented with a cedilla under the vowel: 'ę' and 'ą.' In French and Portuguese, on the other hand, nasalized vowels are written with the letter for the vowel followed by the letter for a nasal consonant, as shown below for French.

(1) **French nasal vowels**

pronunciation	spelling and example
[õ] on	bon 'good'
[ã] an	banc 'bench'
[ɛ̃] ain, aim, in	bain 'bath,' faim 'hungry,' fin 'end'

As you know, when 'n' or 'm' follows a vowel in English, we typically pronounce the consonant, like in the words 'sun' and 'some.' As a result, a native English speaker may be inclined to pronounce French and Portuguese words that have similar letter sequences the same way as in English and, thus, pronounce them incorrectly. That is, the speaker may tend to pronounce the vowel followed by a nasal consonant rather than just a nasalized vowel. Native speakers of French and Portuguese will be quick to identify this speech as foreign. You can avoid this pitfall. If you, the learner, are familiar with the spelling conventions for nasal vowels in these languages, you will know that the same sequence of letters in English and in French or Portuguese are pronounced differently.

Where can you find this kind of information? The front matter of a bilingual dictionary is a very good place to start. A good dictionary, whether it be in electronic or written format, will contain a key to how the spelling symbols of the language are pronounced. Alternatively, you could check with your language instructor or consult an introductory language textbook; it should also contain important information about pronunciation.

Aspiration

Another common error made by native speakers of English involves the property of aspiration. You will recall from chapter 6 that an aspirated consonant is made with a small puff of air expelled (typically) after the consonant. We find this with the English stops [p, t, k] when they occur before a stressed vowel and are not preceded by [s]. If you place your hand a couple of inches in front of your mouth when you say the pairs of words in (2), you should feel a puff of air after the consonants at the beginning of the words on the left, but not after the corresponding unaspirated consonant on the right. As a native speaker of English, you learned at a very early age that in some contexts stop consonants are pronounced with aspiration and in other contexts they are not.

(2) **English aspirated and unaspirated stops**

aspirated stops	unaspirated stops
p̲ot [pʰat]	sp̲ot [spat]
t̲o [tʰu]	st̲ew [stu]
k̲ey [kʰi]	sk̲i [ski]

The unaspirated stops that occur after [s] actually sound very much like [b, d, g]. To discover this for yourself, try saying *spot, stew,* and *ski* first as you would normally and then as follows: replace the [p] in *spot* with [b], the [t] in *stew* with [d], and the [k] in *ski* with [g]. Can you tell the difference between, for example, *spot* and *sbot*? If not, you are like most English speakers in not being able to distinguish a voiceless stop from a voiced stop when it comes after [s]. This is because voicing differences between stop consonants in this position are not used to distinguish the meaning of words in English. That is, there are no words in English like *ski* and *sgi* which differ only in whether the stop after [s] is produced with vocal cord vibration or not. If, on the other hand, there were pairs of words such as this in the language you learned as a child, part of acquiring your language would have involved learning to listen for the subtle acoustic details when these or comparable words were spoken that would have then enabled you to tell them apart.

Turning to errors that English speakers make, two of the most common mistakes involve aspiration: in the first case, English speakers produce aspirated stops where they do not occur in the language being learned, and in the second, English speakers fail to produce aspiration where it does occur in the new language. In the first case, English speakers transfer the aspiration rules of English to the pronunciation of words in languages that do not have aspirated stops, such as French, Italian, Spanish, and Greek. As a result, English speakers pronounce voiceless stops before a stressed syllable with aspiration. The problem is that aspiration is simply not a feature of these languages. In Italian, as with the other languages mentioned, voiceless stops like [p, t, k] are *unaspirated* regardless of where they occur.

Pronouncing stops with aspiration is a common characteristic of English accented speech and one that can be avoided with lots of practice. But first, it is important to be able to hear and feel the difference between an aspirated and an unaspirated stop. Recall that you should feel a small puff of air come out of your mouth when pronouncing an aspirated consonant, as in 'to,' but not with an unaspirated consonant, as in 'stew.' The unaspirated 't' in this latter context is similar to how 't' is pronounced in Spanish, French, and Italian (and many other languages with unaspirated stops). The tricky part for an English speaker is to be able to produce the unaspirated stop in contexts where, in English, one would normally find an aspirated stop, for example, at the beginning of a word as in 'to.' In other words, you will need to learn to **undo** the rule of aspiration that you acquired as a child. (See exercise 1.)

In English, there is no difference in spelling between the aspirated and unaspirated consonants, probably because they are not distinctive and so do not serve to distinguish the meaning of words like place of articulation does, for example, [t] 'tea' vs. [k] 'key.'

As we saw in chapter 6, aspiration can be distinctive in languages. In Hindi, for example, pronouncing an aspirated consonant without aspiration, or an unaspirated consonant with aspiration, can change the meaning of a word. Because aspiration is not distinctive in English, it is easy for an English speaker to mispronounce Hindi words. The speaker may incorrectly pronounce a voiceless unaspirated stop at the beginning of a word with aspiration or pronounce a voiced aspirated stop without aspiration. Each pronunciation will give the speaker English-accented Hindi and perhaps even change the meaning of the Hindi word.

Before leaving Hindi, note that, interestingly, aspiration does not only appear on voiceless consonants like in English. As the examples in (3) show, voiced consonants also contrast for aspiration.

(3) **Hindi aspirated and unaspirated voiced stops**
   [bʱal] 'forehead'   [bal] 'hair'
   [dʱan] 'paddy'   [ḍan] 'charity'
   [ḍʱal] 'shield'   [ḍal] 'branch'
   [gʱal] 'confusion'   [gal] 'cheek'

This fact makes Hindi particularly fascinating since it results in a four-way distinction for consonants in terms of voicing and aspiration.

(4)   [kʰal] 'skin'   [kal] 'era'
   [gʱal] 'confusion'   [gal] 'cheek'

Being aware of the difference between English and languages with distinctive aspiration like Hindi is a good start in learning how to pronounce the words more native-like. With this knowledge you can focus on hearing and producing aspirated and unaspirated consonants in unfamiliar contexts.

Exercise 1: Aspirated and Unaspirated Consonants

Try this simple exercise to get practice pronouncing unaspirated stops in unfamiliar contexts (i.e., contexts that you are not accustomed to when you speak English).

- Begin by pronouncing a word with an unaspirated stop, such as *Stan* from column A. Notice that there is no puff of air after the 't' like there is in the word *tan*, for example.
- Now try pronouncing the same word from column A again, but this time, suppress the 's' at the beginning (e.g., by saying the 's' silently before saying the rest of the word out loud). If you are doing it correctly, you will be pronouncing the stop consonant as unaspirated. In fact, pronouncing the word *tan* with an unaspirated stop will, to an English speaker's ears, make the word sound very much like 'dan,' which begins with an unaspirated (voiced) stop.
- Try this a few times for each of the words in column A or at least until you can comfortably produce an unaspirated voiceless stop at the beginning of an "English" word.

Column A	Column B	Column C
Stan	Stan	dan
span	span	ban
scan	scan	gan

Alveolar vs. Dental Consonants

Not only are sounds similar to English 't' and 'd' common in the world's languages, they are also the most frequent consonants in English. This means that we have had lots and lots of practice pronouncing and listening to them.

The challenge for learners of other languages is that these sounds are not always pronounced exactly like the sounds of English even though they may be spelled with the same letters *t* and *d*. We have already seen that they can be aspirated, unaspirated, or both in a given language. They can also be made at a different place of articulation than the sounds of English.

Recall from chapter 6 that the consonants [t] and [d] in English are **alveolar** stops: they are made by raising the front part of the tongue against the alveolar ridge as approximated in figure 9.1.

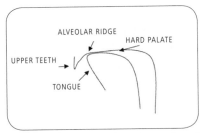

Figure 9.1. Alveolar Place of Articulation of English [t, d]

In some languages, such as Italian, Spanish, and French, the sounds spelled by the letters 't' and 'd' are classified as **dental** as opposed to alveolar. This means that the front of the tongue (including the tip) is positioned behind the upper teeth, as illustrated in figure 9.2.

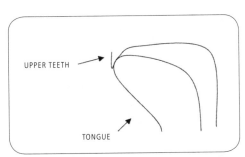

Figure 9.2. Dental Place of Articulation of [t̪, d̪]

While positioning the tongue against the teeth as opposed to the alveolar ridge may seem like a small difference, it is enough to alter the acoustics of the sound. For example, if an English speaker pronounced the first sound in the Italian word *tavola* 'table' with an alveolar stop instead of a dental stop, an Italian speaker would be able to identify the accent as foreign. Similarly, if an Italian speaker said the English word *table* with an initial dental stop, we would likely consider the pronunciation non-native.

Making a dental sound is not difficult; it just takes practice remembering to shift the position of your tongue slightly forward when you are speaking a language that has them. Try exercise 2 in the box below to familiarize yourself with the difference between dental and alveolar consonants. This exercise focuses on dental and alveolar voiced stops ([d̪, d]), though it is important to note that the distinction between dentals and alveolars is not limited to voiced stops. The voiceless counterpart of 'd' can also be dental ([t̪]) or alveolar ([t]), as can nasal consonants ([n̪], [n]). Similarly, there are both dental ([s̪], [z̪]) and alveolar ([s], [z]) fricatives.

As a rule of thumb, in a given language, all sounds in these categories will typically be either dental or alveolar. In English, for example, the voiced and voiceless stops [t, d], the fricatives [s, z], and the nasal stop [n] are all alveolar. In French, on the other hand, the stops ([t̪, d̪]), fricatives ([s̪], [z̪]), and nasal ([n̪]) are all dental. This does not mean that a language cannot have both dental and alveolar consonants, though it is uncommon. Malayalam, seen in chapter 6, is a language with both: [pʌɳɳi] 'pig,' [kʌnni] 'virgin.'

Exercise 2: Dentals and Alveolars

This exercise is most effective if you do it in front of a mirror.

Practicing an alveolar:

- Begin by slowly repeating the English syllables [da, da, da]. While you are saying these sequences, look at your mouth closely in the mirror and focus on the position of your tongue while making the alveolar consonant.

- Continue to repeat the syllables [da, da, da, . . .] slowly focusing now on feeling where your tongue is touching the top of your mouth. The front part of your tongue behind the tip will be positioned slightly behind your teeth, touching the alveolar ridge.

Practicing a dental:

- Now move the front and tip of your tongue forward so that it rests behind your top teeth. When you look in the mirror, you will likely be able to see your tongue protruding slightly below your top teeth. It shouldn't protrude as much as when you make a 'th' sound, as in *the*.

- With your tongue in the dental position, slowly repeat the sequences [d̪a, d̪a, d̪a] (to make the IPA symbol for a dental sound, add [̪] below the symbol used for the alveolar). Feel and see the position of your tongue when you make the dental consonant. When you feel confident that you can make a dental sound, try the following exercise.

(continued)

Exercise 2, continued

Practicing both together:
- Compare the pronunciation of the two types of sounds by slowly repeating the following sequences:

    - [da, da, d̪a, d̪a, da, da, d̪a, d̪a, . . .]
    - [da, d̪a, da, d̪a, da, d̪a, . . .]

Feel the difference between the pairs of sounds. Look in the mirror and pay attention to where your tongue is. Listen closely and see if you can hear the difference between the alveolar and dental consonants.

To further hone your skills at producing alveolar and dental consonants, you may want to do exercises 3 and 4 involving voiceless stops, nasals, and fricatives.

Exercise 3: Voiceless Alveolar and Dental Stops [t, t̪]

Repeat exercise 2, but replace the voiced stop with the voiceless alveolar stop [t] and the voiceless dental stop [t̪].

Note: It is typical for dental stops to be **unaspirated,** as is the case in French, Italian, and Spanish.

Exercise 4: Dental and Alveolar Nasals and Fricatives

Nasals:
Repeat exercise 2, but replace the voiced stop with the alveolar nasal [n] and the dental nasal [n̪].

Fricatives:
Similarly, repeat exercise 2, but replace the voiced stop first with the voiced alveolar fricative [z] and the dental fricative [z̪], and second with the voiceless alveolar fricative [s] and the voiceless dental fricative [s̪]. When you make the fricatives, your tongue will be close to but not touching the alveolar ridge and top teeth.

Flapping

Say the English words *atomic* and *atom,* paying attention to how you pronounce the *t* in each word. If you are a native speaker of North American English, you probably pronounce the *t* in *atomic* as a voiceless aspirated alveolar stop. In *atom,* on the other hand, the letter *t* is most likely voiced and unaspirated, sounding similar to a quick *d* sound. This latter sound is called a **flap,** characterized by the phonetic symbol [ɾ], and is the typical pronunciation of English *t* and *d* when, simplifying somewhat, they occur between vowel sounds and if the first vowel is stressed. The flap pronunciation is a characteristic of North American speech but is also used by some speakers of other varieties, such as in New Zealand English, though to a lesser extent. Compare *atomic* and *atom,* once again paying attention this time not only to how the *t* is pronounced but to which syllable is stressed in each word. In *aTOmic,* the second syllable is the most prominent syllable in the word, while in *Atom,* the first syllable has the most stress. The *t* in *atom* therefore occurs between vowels of which the first is stressed, the context where flapping occurs. Other examples of words with a *t* or *d* pronounced as a flap include *writing, rudder, fatter, out of here.*

Here are some facts about the flap in North American English. First, it is an alternate pronunciation of *t* and *d.* This means that pronouncing the *t* in the word *writer* as the flap [ɾ] as opposed to [t] does not change the meaning of the word; that is, [t] and flap are not distinctive in English, nor are [d] and flap. Second, the flap occurs in only one context in English: between vowel sounds if the first is stressed. Thus, where the flap is pronounced is completely predictable. The predictable, nondistinctive nature of English flap tends to make speakers less conscious of its presence; in fact, if we had not specifically drawn your attention to the fact that the *t* in *writer* is pronounced differently than say, the *t* in *top, stop,* or *pot,* you may not have been aware of any differences. But now that you are aware, you are in a better position to correct any mispronunciations you may have involving this sound when speaking another language!

In other languages, the flap may not be a predictable pronunciation of another sound. Rather, it may be a distinctive sound in and of itself. This is the case with the flap in Spanish, written as a single letter *r* in, for example, *pero* 'but,' *para* 'for,' *tocar* 'to play.' We know that the flap is distinctive in Spanish because replacing it with a similar sound can affect word meaning. Compare the two words *pero* [peɾo] 'but' and *perro* [pero] 'dog' (rr is pronounced as a trill). The fact that the flap in Spanish is written with *r* instead of *t* or *d* as in English may lead a learner of Spanish to conclude that the letters represent different sounds. This is incorrect. Regardless of spelling, American English speakers already know how to produce the flap sound. This should then make it relatively easy to pronounce words such as Spanish *pero* where the flap occurs in the same context as in English.

Pronouncing a flap at the end of a word as in *tocar* [tokaɾ] 'to play' may be more challenging since it is not a context where flaps are produced in English. An exercise to practice doing this is given in (5), using the Spanish words *cara* 'face' and *tocar* 'to play.' Begin by repeating the word *cara* several times (5a), taking notice of how you are making the flap; *cara* [kɑɾa] will sound similar to English *gotta* [gɑɾə], though beginning with an unaspirated [k] instead of a [g]. Now try the sequences in (5b). In this case, the final vowel in the second word of each pair is suppressed. While you should not hear a full vowel after the flap in *cara*, releasing the front of your tongue from the roof of your mouth when making the flap may create a very small vowel sound. Now try row (5c) in which *tocar*, with a word-final flap, has been added. Notice that the final syllable in *tocar* will essentially be pronounced the same way as *cara*. Finally, repeat *tocar* several times alone, paying attention to your pronunciation of the flap at the end of the word.

(5) a. cara, cara, cara
     b. cara cara, cara cara, cara cara
     c. cara cara tocar, cara cara tocar, cara cara tocar
     d. tocar, tocar, tocar

Spanish provides a good example of a language that has a flap like English, though it uses the flap distinctively and in different contexts. Not surprisingly, many other languages do not use the flap sound at all. In these languages, native speakers of varieties of English that have flaps commonly mispronounce *t* and *d* as a flap if they occur in the English flapping context. As subtle as it may seem to American English ears, pronouncing a word like *data* as [daɾa] instead of [data] can sound foreign to a native speaker of a flapless language. Obviously, the way to avoid this type of error is to try to suppress the flap pronunciation. This is much more challenging than it sounds because pronouncing a flap for a *t* or *d* is automatic for an American English speaker. However, awareness of the English flapping rule and the tendency to pronounce *t* and *d* as [ɾ] is half the battle. Practicing to say [t] between vowels in words like [data] is the other half!

Released and Unreleased Stop Consonants

Another characteristic of English pronunciation involves the pronunciation of the stops *p, b, t, d, k, g,* particularly at the ends of words. To illustrate, say each of the sentences in (6) out loud several times at a normal speaking rate. Listen to how you say the consonant at the end of each of the underlined words.

(6) The <u>cat</u> stood on the <u>sack</u>.
     I called a <u>cab</u>.
     The <u>rug</u> she <u>bought</u> was <u>neat</u>.

Was there a small burst of aspiration at the end of any of the final consonants (called a consonant *release*)? Or did you hold the closed part of the consonant a bit longer so that the air was not released after the consonant? Experiment a bit pronouncing each of the consonants at the end of the underlined words. Practice producing the consonants with a release and then without a release.

This short exercise is intended to illustrate that whether a stop consonant is released at the end of a word in English or not is optional. Both are acceptable pronunciations of the same word. This is not the case in all languages. As potentially subtle as this property may seem, the presence or absence of a consonantal release can contribute to creating a foreign accent.

In some languages, such as Korean, stop consonants are never released at the end of a word. In other languages, stops are always released in this position. German is an example of this latter type. Note that adding a release to a Korean consonant or pronouncing a stop in German without a release will not change the meaning of the word. It will, however, characterize the pronunciation as non-native.

Avoiding a foreign accent in this case does not require learning how to make a new sound or gesture because English speakers already know how to pronounce a consonant with a release as well as without. Rather, it begins by having an awareness that whether a consonant is released in English or not is optional and that there may be differences between English and the language being learned.

Full and Reduced Vowels

Let's look at another property of the English language that can give away your identity as a non-native speaker in no time at all. It involves pronouncing full vowels as reduced vowels. It is probably easiest to explain the difference between full and reduced vowels with an illustration.

In the section on flapping above, it was pointed out that the words *atom* and *atomic* differ in terms of which syllable in each word is stressed, that is, which is the most prominent. In *atom* the first syllable is stressed, while in *atomic* it is the second. Recall that the pronunciation of 't' as a flap [ɾ] or an aspirated stop [tʰ] depends in part on the stress of adjacent syllables, as indicated in the phonetic transcriptions of the two words: [ǽɾəm], [ətʰámɪk]. Notice that there is also a change in the quality of the vowels across the two words. Compare, as shown in the diagram below, the first vowel of each word. In *atom* the 'a' is pronounced as [æ] while in *atomic* it is a schwa [ə]. Schwa also occurs as the second vowel of *atom*, even though the second vowel in *atomic* is [ɑ]. Can you predict when schwa occurs?

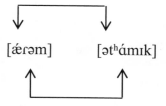

[ǽɾəm]   [ətʰámɪk]

If you said that it is when the syllable is not stressed, you are absolutely right. As a native speaker of English, you will typically pronounce any vowel in a nonprominent syllable as [ə] or [ɪ], sometimes called *reduced vowels*. This means that all the vowels in the following words that do not have an accent mark indicating stress are pronounced as a reduced vowel: *message* [mɛ́sɪdʒ], campus [kǽmpəs] (or [kǽmpɪs]), computer [kəmpjútəʁ], porcupine [póʁkjəpàjn].[1] Vowels that occur in a stressed syllable in English are referred to as *full vowels*. This observation about English may seem confusing because the spelling does not generally distinguish between full and reduced vowels. However, by paying careful attention to how a word is pronounced, you should be able to identify the syllable(s) in a word with the most prominence, those with the least prominence, and hence those with full and reduced vowels.

The challenge for speakers of English is that not all languages distinguish between full and reduced vowels. In Czech, Greek, Spanish, and many other languages, vowels are always pronounced in their full form regardless of whether the syllable they appear in is stressed or unstressed. So the Greek word for 'bicycle' is [poθílato] with no reduced vowels at all. An English speaker not aware of the fact that he learned to pronounce vowels differently in stressed and unstressed positions (regardless of the spelling) will then probably turn the vowels in Greek [poθílato] into the incorrect form *[pəθílətò] and be immediately recognized as a non-native speaker!

To avoid this, determine whether unstressed vowels are reduced in the language you are learning. Listen to and ask your instructor; listen to and ask native speakers. Are some syllables more prominent than others? Is an 'o' in the spelling pronounced the same in all positions in a word and in all types of syllables, stressed or unstressed? What about 'u' or 'a' or 'i,' or whatever the vowels in the language are? If so, you will need to pay special attention to how you pronounce vowels, especially in syllables without stress. In short, you will need to unlearn the pattern that you so successfully learned and have practiced for so many years.

Monophthongs vs. Diphthongs

As we saw in chapter 7, the English vowel system is quite complex since it contains monophthongs like [i] *beat*, [ɪ] *bit*, [ɛ] *bet*, [æ] *bat*, and [ʌ] *but*, as well the diphthongs in (7).

(7) **English diphthongs**
   [aʊ] c<u>ow</u>, tr<u>ou</u>nce
   [oʊ] g<u>o</u>, s<u>ew</u>, t<u>oa</u>d
   [aɪ] b<u>uy</u>, b<u>i</u>de
   [ɔɪ] s<u>oy</u>, b<u>oy</u>
   [eɪ] r<u>ay</u>, s<u>ay</u>

1. The two different accents (ˊacute, ˋgrave) on the word *porcupine* represent the two types of stressed syllables in English: primary stress and secondary stress. As the terms suggest, primary stress is the strongest. Secondary stress is not as prominent as primary stress, but it is more prominent than a syllable with no stress at all.

A great many languages have only monophthongs and no diphthongs. In chapter 7 we identified the following list of languages, though many more could be added: Arabic, Bulgarian, Ewe, French, Greek, German, Hawaiian, Hebrew, Hungarian, Italian, Japanese, Navajo, Spanish, Swahili, and Zulu. It should be clear what the challenge is for a speaker of English when pronouncing vowels in these languages: to try to avoid saying a monophthong as a diphthong.

Substituting a diphthong for a monophthong is a common mistake made by English speakers when learning a language without diphthongs. This mistake is especially easy when the monophthong of the foreign language is similar to a diphthong of English. The English diphthongs [eɪ] and [oʊ], for example, are very similar to the vowels [e] and [o], which occur in most of the languages noted just above. If you are a native speaker of English and you want to sound more like a native speaker of a foreign language with [e] and [o], you will need to practice saying the vowels [e] and [o] without adding an [ɪ] or [ʊ] pronunciation to the end. Below is a small exercise designed to help you accomplish this.

Exercise 5: Diphthongs to Monophthongs

- Say the vowel in <u>say</u> slowly. Concentrate on not moving your tongue or jaw upwards toward the end. This will have the effect of making the vowel seem much shorter and end more abruptly. Note that the tongue and jaw movement may be very subtle.
- Repeat with the vowel in <u>so</u>.
- Once you feel that you are able to pronounce the vowels as monophthongs, try saying a short word in the language that you are learning that contains these vowels. If you are learning French, for example, you might choose the words *fée* [fe] 'fairy' and *faux* [fo] 'false.' You could compare your pronunciation of the French words with the monophthongs to the English words *Faye* and *foe*; the English words end in a diphthong while the French ones do not.
- Repeat with other monophthongal vowels from your new language.

Unrounded High Central or Back Vowels

The final common pronunciation error discussed in this chapter involves high central or back unrounded vowels, particularly the central vowel [ɨ] in languages such as Korean and Turkish, and the similar back vowel in Japanese [ɯ]. Remember from chapter 7 that [ɨ] is made a bit like the [u] in *suit* but without rounded lips. Try saying *suit* as you would normally. Now say it with your lips somewhat spread as if you were smiling. Your pronunciation should be similar to [sɨt]. This vowel really is not that hard to make for a native English speaker. In fact, some people already use the vowel in English words such as roses [rozɨz] (others may say [rozɪz] or [rozəz]).

Yet it is not uncommon for English speakers to pronounce a high unrounded vowel as rounded; for example, to pronounce [ɨ] as [u]. One of the reasons for this is that in some languages the vowel [ɨ] is spelled or transcribed with the letter 'u.' This spelling can be confusing unless you are aware that it does not match up with how you would pronounce 'u' in English.

Another reason for the mispronunciation can be that an English speaker may actually perceive the foreign vowels [ɨ] or [ɯ] as [u] since the sounds share some similar acoustic properties. From this perspective, when a person says the misperceived [ɨ] or [ɯ] as [u], she is then simply repeating what he/she heard.

While there are certainly other reasons why an English speaker may mispronounce a back unrounded vowel, we note one more to conclude this chapter: the person has simply not had sufficient practice making a back vowel without rounding the lips since all non-low back vowels in English are rounded.

Knowing that vowels and indeed all sounds are composed of independent gestures that can be combined in different ways, you should be in a better position to understand how to control your lips independently of where the back of your tongue is positioned. In short, you can learn to undo some of what you have spent so many years practicing in order to sound more like a native speaker of the language that you are studying.

Summary

In this chapter we have focused on a few of the more common errors of pronunciation that North American English speakers make when learning a new language. Naturally the types of errors you might make will depend on how the languages that you speak well and the language that you are learning differ. We hope that the information covered in this chapter and the preceding ones will provide you with tools to analyze these differences and, should you choose, modify your speech.

SECTION III

Thinking like a
Native Speaker

●●●●●●●●●●●●●●●●●●●●●●●●●●●●●●●●●●●●●●

The Role of Form in Language

*I*n this chapter we look at the factors that determine how a sentence of a language is understood. The basic idea is that the **form** of a sentence, that is, how the words are ordered with respect to one another in time (or on the printed page) and the precise shape of the words, that is, how the words are pronounced, determine the kind of sentence that is being uttered. This form determines the basic **function** of the sentence (e.g., whether it is a statement, a question, or a command). The form of the sentence, together with the context in which the sentence is uttered, defines the **meaning** of the sentence, the idea that the speaker is intending to convey.

Accent: A Feeling for Form

Part of a native speaker's knowledge of language involves the proper form of words, that is, how they are to be pronounced. In chapter 6 we discussed the fact that non-native speakers of a language typically have a **foreign accent** because they are unable to precisely match the form of the words that they are trying to pronounce. To a considerable extent, the foreign accent arises from the fact that the sounds of their native language are produced in ways different from the sounds of the non-native language.

In the same way, non-native speakers may typically show a "foreign accent" in the way that they construct the form of sentences. They may put things in the wrong order, use the wrong form of a word, leave things out, or put things in that don't belong.

Now let's look at some examples that will help us distinguish form, function, and meaning. Here are some typical things that non-native speakers of Standard English say.

(1) a. Sun is hot.
   b. He lives in the Peru.
   c. The Professor Smith is very dynamic.
   d. She avoids to go.
   e. I want that you stay.
   f. We will a pizza eat.
   g. Is raining.
   h. Four new lamp . . .
   i. I have helpfuls friends.

What we want to focus on at this point is that these sentences don't sound like "correct" English, regardless of how they are pronounced. Native speakers of English understand them, but recognize that they deviate in certain ways from what is understood to be "correct."

Let's look at these examples. (1a), *Sun is hot*, is less than perfect English because in English we have to say *The sun is hot*. Other languages, such as Japanese, do not have a word for *the*. Speakers of such a language might leave out *the* either because they don't know how English works or because they are unable to always remember to put in *the* where it belongs.

On the other hand, we do not use *the* for the names of places (*Peru* in (1b)) or people (*Professor Smith* in (1c)), while some other languages, such as French, do. Examples (1d, e) illustrate that verbs like *avoid* and *want* determine the form of the verb that combines with them—we say *avoid going*, not *avoid to go*, and *want you to stay*, not *want that you stay*. But the forms in (1d, e) are literal translations of how to express these ideas in French.

Example (1f) contains an error in the order of words—in English, *a pizza* should follow *eat*, but in other languages, like German and Japanese, the order in (1f) would be the correct order. In (1g) the word *it* is missing; in some languages, such as Spanish and Italian, there is no form used with verbs referring to the weather, like *rain*.

Finally, (1h) illustrates the fact that in English, a plural noun—one that refers to more than one item—must be marked as plural, typically with *-s*. But there are languages, like Chinese, that do not use such a marking. And (1i) is a case where the adjective *helpful* is incorrectly marked as plural along with the noun. This type of marking, called "agreement," is found in many languages, such as Italian, French, Spanish, and Russian, but not in English.

As we work through our survey of what speakers of English know about their language, and what speakers of other languages know about theirs, we use errors of this type to highlight precisely what it means to speak "without an accent." In an important way, recognizing what causes the accent helps us to recognize what it means to speak without an accent.

Grammar: Knowing the Rules

Knowledge of a language consists in part of knowledge about the proper form of sentences and phrases in that language, that is, what is grammatical. Exactly what do we mean by *form*? Consider the English sentence (2).

(2)   She gives me a cup of coffee.

This sentence has **declarative** form and functions as a statement. Notice that the "giver" of the coffee is explicitly mentioned. Now compare the English sentence (3).

(3)   Give me a cup of coffee.

This is an **imperative** sentence, used to make a direct request or order. Notice that the sentence lacks a phrase that refers to the hearer. There is no word *you* in this sentence. In this respect it has a special form that distinguishes it from the declarative, such as example (2). The function of the imperative in (3) is thus defined by this aspect of its form. In another language, the same function might be signaled in other ways.

For example, in Italian the imperative sentence may have a special form of the verb. The imperative form of the verb meaning 'give' in Italian is *da*, while the declarative form is *dà*, as illustrated in (4) and (5). Notice also that the word for 'me', marked in boldface, goes in a different position in the imperative and in the declarative—it follows the verb in the imperative and precedes it in the declarative!

(4)   Dam**mi**   una   tazza di caffè.
      give-me   a   cup   of coffee
      'Give me a cup of coffee.'

(5)   **mi** dà   una   tazza di caffè
      me (s)he-gives   a   cup   of coffee
      '(S)he gives me a cup of coffee.'

These properties of sentences—where the words go with respect to one another and how the words are constructed—are what we mean by "form."

The form of a sentence plays a critical role in determining its meaning. In English, where a phrase goes in a sentence determines whether it is the actor in an event or the object that is undergoing the action. For example:

(6)   a.   The dog bit Sandy.
      b.   Sandy bit the dog.

The same individuals are involved in an event of biting in these two sentences, but the relationship between them is not the same. In (6a), the dog is the biter and Sandy is the one who gets bitten, but in (6b), Sandy is the biter and the dog is bitten. Big difference!

A fundamental part of knowing how a language works is knowing how to distinguish the actor from what is acted on.

The relationship between form and meaning, particularly the form part, is familiar to many readers as "grammar." And for many of those readers, "grammar" is something that they were made to learn about in high school, might have disliked intensely, and may well have largely forgotten.

The reason that the study of grammar is hard or boring for many people is that it does not appear to have any immediately useful purpose. When we know our native language, we know the grammar intuitively—why do we have to study it? What does knowledge about grammar give us that we don't already have?

There are two reasons that some understanding of grammar is useful. The first reason is that there are important differences between spoken language and written language, and these differences can be most effectively described in terms of grammatical concepts and categories. To get a feel for this point, consider the following actual spoken sentence of English.

(7) "Who knows? He may be that type of dominant guy who it really doesn't make a difference" (Lloyd McClendon, the manager of the Seattle Mariners baseball team, quoted in the *New York Times*, 6/13/14).

While this sentence is perfectly understandable and acceptable in an informal style, it would probably not work in a written term paper. We would most likely write *to whom it really doesn't make a difference* or *who it really doesn't make a difference to* instead of *who it really doesn't make a difference*. This is a difference in form and can be described and understood in terms of grammar.[1]

Knowing about grammar helps us write better because we are more aware and in control of what is required in the two styles of language. Moreover, in thinking about the written language, we can talk explicitly about the differences in form between two or more ways of expressing the same content and evaluate which works better to convey our ideas, and why.

The second reason, which is most central to the focus of this book, is that the grammar of a language is a summation of the knowledge that a speaker has about how that language works. We have already seen that an understanding of how form works is essential to understanding how languages express meaning, that is, how they allow us to communicate. We already know intuitively how our own language works; the challenge is to acquire knowledge about how another language works. And we want that knowledge to be usable.

To put it another way, the grammar of a language is the set of "rules" (or "instructions," if you like) that specify how to arrange units to form phrases and sentences and how the parts of a sentence correspond to its meaning. For anyone who wants to learn

---

1. There are also differences in the words that we would be likely to choose in a more formal written style. We would probably write *the type of dominant person* instead of *that type of dominant guy.*

how to communicate thoughts in another language, some insight into the grammar of that language can be very useful, and in some cases it may even be essential.

For these reasons, we introduce in this section of the book the most important grammatical terms and concepts. Wherever possible, we illustrate them first using English and then look at examples from other languages to provide a broader perspective. Because the rules involve both form and meaning, we compare languages in two basic respects.

First, we look at how languages differ in their form. In learning a second language, it is very important to be aware of the grammatical differences. Knowing how a language arranges its units allows us to focus on the areas where we have to devote special attention to expressing things in the right way.

Second, we look at the various aspects of meaning that languages can express. Different languages use different grammatical devices to express the same meaning components. Some languages explicitly express certain components of meaning that are implicit in another language; as speakers, we have to know what has to be said explicitly and what needs to be implied. Such differences pose particular difficulties for the language learner and warrant special attention and practice.

What Is Structure?

A little while back we introduced the term **structure** of a sentence or a phrase and said it was another way of referring to the form. The word **structure** refers specifically to how the sentence or phrase is organized into parts, how the parts are grouped together, and how they are ordered with respect to one another. Consider again sentence (3).

(3) Give me a cup of coffee.

There are several things that our intuitions as speakers of English tell us about the structure of this sentence. First, we recognize that the words are of different categories or types: *give* is a verb, *me* is a pronoun, and so on. Second, we recognize that the order of words is special; scrambling them up would not produce a sentence of English.

Exercise

How many ways can you scramble up the words of *Give me a cup of coffee*? Are any of them possible sentences of English? Exactly what are the properties of *Give me a cup of coffee* that make it a sentence of English, in contrast to the other arrangements of words?

Third, we recognize that *a cup of coffee* is a phrase that is used to refer to a particular thing. *Me a* is not a possible phrase in English, nor is *Give me a.*

We explore aspects of structure in the remaining chapters of this section of the book. We introduce some minimal terminology that will allow us to refer clearly to the parts of sentences and phrases.

To illustrate the structure of sentences, we use the simple device of bracketing words together to show how the parts of a sentence are arranged and what they consist of. For example, the structure of *Give me a cup of coffee* can be shown as follows:

(8)   [Give me [a cup of coffee]]

Putting brackets around *a cup of coffee* represents the fact that it is a phrase. And grouping *give* and *me* with [*a cup of coffee*] represents the fact that *give me a cup of coffee* is also a phrase (a **verb phrase,** to be precise).

The arrangement of the words into phrases and the sequencing of these phrases in time (or on the page) are what constitute the structure of a sentence. Those familiar with "sentence diagramming" know how to sketch out the structure of a simple sentence and how to assign a function to each part of the structure. This type of exercise may not be especially challenging for simple examples like *Give me a cup of coffee*. However, it becomes quite challenging when sentences get complicated, even in one's own language. Having the ability to see clearly the structure of one's own language, and to understand in what ways it corresponds to the structure of another language, can substantially facilitate the task of learning that other language.

Categories

Let us consider in more detail how languages have rules about structure that are known to the speakers of those languages and how these rules can vary from language to language. Think of the words *the, dog,* and *barked*. How many different ways can we arrange these three words? The following list shows that there are in fact six ways to arrange three words.

(9)   1. the dog barked   4. dog the barked
      2. the barked dog   5. dog barked the
      3. barked the dog   6. barked dog the

Are all of these sentences of English? No, only number 1 is. Someone who knows English has to know not only what *the, dog,* and *barked* mean, and that they can be combined to express the thought 'the dog barked,' but also that they have to be placed in a particular order.

When we have more than one participant in an action, each of whom plays a particular role in the action, the English sentence uses the order of words to indicate who is doing what to whom. We already saw this with the sentences in (6).

(6)   a.   The dog bit Sandy.
      b.   Sandy bit the dog.

The words used in the two sentences are exactly the same, but the meanings are vastly different.

This example illustrates a very important point about the meaning of a sentence that we will get into in more detail later in this book: the structure of a sentence specifies the roles played by the participants in a relationship expressed by a sentence; the rules of the language say how the parts of the structure match up with these roles.

If you are aware of such facts about English, will that help you when you try to learn another language? Not directly, it turns out, because some other languages work differently than English does. Of course, it does help to know that another language could use a different order of words, but we have to know precisely what that order is. In other words, we know what questions we should ask about how another language forms questions, but we do not necessarily know what the answers are going to be.

How would we say *John read that letter* and *Did John read that letter?* in Japanese, for example? We could say these sentences in this way.

(10) John ga   sono   tegami o   yon-da.
     John   that   letter   read-PAST
     'John read that letter.'

     John ga   sono   tegami o   yon-da-**ka.**
     John   that   letter   read-PAST-QUESTION
     'Did John read that letter?'

Notice that the verb comes at the end in these Japanese examples. In fact it **must** come at the end of the sentence that it belongs to; this is a rule of Japanese. And in the second sentence, the particle *ka*, shown in boldface, is added to the verb at the end of the question sentence to indicate that it is a question. Japanese also has the particles *ga* and *o* that have the function of indicating which phrase is the subject and which is the object.

What about Bulgarian? Here we have other possibilities.

(11) Kuche-to   lae-she.
     dog-the   barked
     'The dog barked.'

     Lae-she   kuche-to.
     barked   dog-the
     'The dog barked.'

Both orders of subject and verb are possible, appropriate to different contexts. Notice also that the Bulgarian word for *the* follows the word for *dog*, in contrast to what happens in English.

What about Spanish? In Spanish we could say

(12) El   perro   raspó.
      the   dog   barked
      'The dog barked.'

or, depending again on the context,

(13) Raspó   el   perro.
      barked   the dog
      'The dog barked.'

El perro raspó answers the question 'What did the dog do?' while *Raspó el perro* answers the questions 'What happened?' or 'Who barked?'

Spanish is like English in that it has a word for *the* that appears before the word for *dog*, but there seem to be other differences in terms of what order the words appear in.

We can see that observations about what the order of words is in English are not special things about the particular words *the, dog,* and *barked,* and similarly for other languages. If we think about similar English examples with *a, this, that,* and *cat, pig, rooster,* and *hissed, grunted, crowed,* and so on, we find that the pattern holds true for the entire language. *A, this, that* have similar functions, and *cat, pig, rooster* have similar functions. Let's look at table 10.1.

● **TABLE 10.1**
Menu for Simple English Sentences

A	B	C
the	dog	barked
a	cat	hissed
this	pig	grunted
that	rooster	crowed

Using the "menu approach," suppose that we take one word from column A, one from column B, and one from column C. Doing so will give us reasonable sentences, if we go straight across a row.

(14) The dog barked.
A cat hissed.
This pig grunted.
That rooster crowed.

But we can also skip around, still going from left to right, column by column, but moving up and down between the rows, and combine these words in funny ways, for example, *This cat crowed* or *That rooster hissed.* These may not be natural sounds for a cat or a rooster to make, but these are definitely sentences of English and we understand what they mean.

This last point is important enough to restate: A string of words that has all the words in the right place and is completely interpretable, but has a strange meaning, is a grammatical sentence of the language. But if a string of words has the words in the wrong order, it is ungrammatical, even if we can figure out some kind of intended or approximate meaning. So *This dog hissed* may be strange, but it is grammatical; while *Pig the grunted* is **not** a grammatical sentence, even if you and every other native speaker can reliably decipher the meaning.

The reason why this works is that all of the words in column A are members of the same **category** (or 'part of speech'), all of the words in column B are members of the same category, and all of the words in column C are members of the same category. We'll look more closely at categories in the next section.

Notice that we must take just **one** word from column A, **one** from column B, and **one** from column C. And we must order the words according to this order of the columns. If we do not, then in general we get a string of words that is not a sentence of English—for example, **The barked, *Cat hissed, *Grunted crowed, *Dog a cat, *This that pig,* and so on. (We use the symbol * to indicate that a string of words is not a possible expression of the language under discussion, in this case, English.) And we cannot take more than one word from each column in some haphazard way; doing so also produces ungrammaticality: **the a dog barked, *the dog cat rooster crowed barked; *the dog barked a.*

Not surprisingly, it is possible to construct a menu for simple sentences of any language. Consider the following sentences of Mandarin Chinese.

(15) a. Zhè shì shū.
this is book
'This is a book.'
b. Wǒ shì xuésheng.
I am student
'I am a student.'
c. Lǎoshī shì zhōngguó rén.
teacher is Chinese person
'The teacher is Chinese.'

Table 10.2 will produce these sentences if we take one word from each column in left-to-right order. Notice that there is only one item in column B, so we have to take that one for any sequence of words from this menu.

> ● **TABLE 10.2**
> **Menu for simple Mandarin Chinese sentences**
>
> | A | B | C |
> |---|---|---|
> | zhè | shì | shū |
> | this | is | book |
> | wǒ | | xuéshēng |
> | I | | student |
> | lǎoshī | | zhōngguó rén |
> | teacher | | Chinese person |

The words of a language group together into *categories*. (These are sometimes called "parts of speech.")

Because of the sorts of patterns that we have just seen, we say that the words in a language are members of **categories.** A category consists of all those words that can go in the same column. The words in the columns in tables 10.1 and 10.2 are just a small sampling of the total set of words in each of the categories. And sometimes a word can be a member of more than one category, like the word *can* in English, as in "She **can** run fast" and "She bought a **can** of beans."

For convenience, we give the categories names like **noun, verb, determiner,** and so on. The nouns of a language form one category, the verbs another, and the determiners yet another. We look more closely at what determines the membership of the most important categories in the next three chapters.

Sentences of a language are formed by arranging words of particular categories in specific orders. Statements about the particular categories and the particular orders in which they can be arranged are often called **grammatical rules.** Words in the same category participate in the formation of phrases in the same way. The rules of grammar that native speakers know are not about individual words but about categories of words.

A grammatical rule of a language says how to form a sentence: by taking a word from one category, followed by a word from another category, and so on. For example, table 10.2 illustrates a rule of Chinese that we can state as follows: "Make a sentence by taking a noun (that is, a word from column A), followed by *shì* 'is,' followed by another noun (that is, a word from column C)."

Word Order

Every language has rules that specify how to properly arrange words and phrases in order to construct a sentence with an intended meaning. These are "word order" rules, and they vary from language to language. For example, consider just the ordering of the subject (S), the object (O), and the verb (V) in a typical sentence that conveys a simple relationship between a person and a thing, such as *Chris(S) ate(V) the pizza(O)*. We find that of the six imaginable arrangements, three are very common in the world's languages, and the other six are relatively rare. Here are some examples (from *The World Atlas of Language Structures,* online at wals.info).

COMMON WORD ORDERS

SVO: Bulgarian, Cantonese, English, Estonian, Finnish, French, Icelandic, Hausa, Indonesian, Latvian, Russian, Spanish, Swahili.
SOV: Amharic, Burmese, Georgian, Hindi, Hopi, Japanese, Korean, Navajo, Nepali, Persian, Tibetan, Turkish.
VSO: Arabic, Berber, Cebuano, Gaelic (Scots), Hawaiian, Ilocano, Irish, Māori, Tagalog, Squamish, Welsh.

RARE WORD ORDERS

OVS: Cubeo, Hixkaryana
VOS: Malagasay, Tzotzil
OSV: Kxoe, Tobati

Keep in mind that these are basic orders—every language allows for word-order variation that is sensitive to the discourse context. Furthermore, some languages, like German, Hungarian, and Samoan, are claimed to have no dominant order.

Summary

So what do we have to know in order to speak and understand the sentences of a language?

- We have to know the words, what they mean, and how they are pronounced.
- We have to know what category (or categories) each word is a member of.
- We have to know the grammatical rules that say how to arrange the words.

(continued)

And we also have to know how the meaning of a sentence is determined by the meanings of the words, their precise shapes, and the structure of the sentence. In the next few chapters we look more closely at the ways in which languages use form to express meaning.

What we have summarized in this chapter is the fact that the speaker of a language has to know how to arrange the words to form a sentence in that language, and the hearer has to know how to interpret this arrangement of words. **Every speaker of every language** knows precisely how to do this for his language. **Every language** has a complex set of rules for how to do this; there are no "primitive languages" that lack rules.

As we discuss later in this book, there are often very closely related languages or varieties of the same language that share many rules but also differ slightly in a few rules. In such cases, speakers of each language variety may feel that the speakers of the other language do not obey the rules of the language. But this is not true—they are all obeying rules: it's just that there are different rules for different language varieties. Speakers of a language are extremely sensitive to language differences and can always tell when someone does not speak exactly like they do. Speakers follow the rules of their own language variety. It is important to understand this phenomenon because there are often social and cultural factors associated with the different languages, as we discuss in chapters 17–19.

When languages are more distantly related, applying the rules of one to the other often produces very noticeable errors. For example, many languages do not have different forms of the verb to express relationships between the time of speaking and the time of an event, while English does. Speakers of such languages may simply fail to produce the correct English forms, giving rise to errors such as *He have a good time yesterday* and *The singer have big band.* Or they may misuse certain forms: *I am wanting to leave now* and *She enjoys to play tennis.* Understanding the differences in rules between languages allows the learner to anticipate and deal with likely errors.[2]

Additional Exercises

1. Look again at the sentences in (1). If you are a competent speaker of English you should be able to correct each error fairly easily. It is more challenging to say what the error is and why the correction works. In the text we suggested what you might say about sentence (1a). Do the same for the remaining sentences in (1).

2. It is possible to ask for a cup of coffee in a restaurant by saying, "A cup of coffee, please." Think about what the conditions are for such a request to be successful.

---

2. A good sample of these "transfer errors" can be found in Raimes and Miller-Cochrane (2013).

Does it matter whom this phrase is addressed to? Why? What would happen if the same thing was said in a different environment, say, the post office or the ticket counter at an arena? Why? How do things work at the post office and the ticket office? What sorts of phrases would produce the desired result in a restaurant and what wouldn't (e.g., "a chair, please"; "a dog, please"; "ten dollars, please")? Why? Does it matter if you don't say "please"?

3. An English noun phrase typically contains a noun, like *dog*, and may contain a number of descriptive words that specify a property of the thing that the noun refers to. Some of these words are called **adjectives**: for example, *furry, happy, smart, pink*. Construct a menu that shows how these adjectives can combine with the nouns *dog, cat, pig,* and *rooster* and the words *the, this, a*. Are all combinations predicted by the menu grammatical noun phrases in English? Are there any combinations that are fully grammatical but strange because of their meaning? What does this tell you about the relationship between grammatical form and meaning?

4. Construct four English verb phrases that have structures that are different from the one in (8) and different from each other. Each of these will be a verb phrase that lacks something that the one in (8) has, or has something that (8) lacks, or both. To do this, start by observing that *give me [a cup of coffee]* contains a verb and two noun phrases.

5. Construct two verb phrases in a language other than English that you know is different in structure from the sentence in (8). Describe the difference between these verb phrases and the one in (8) in terms of the phrases that they contain and the order in which they appear.

6. For a language other than English that you know, state as clearly as you can how that language forms imperatives. Compare with how English forms imperatives, focusing on where English is the same and where it is different.

References

Dryer, Matthew S. 2013. Order of subject, object and verb. *The World Atlas of Language Structures,* ed. Matthew S. Dryer & Martin Haspelmath. Leipzig: Max Planck Institute for Evolutionary Anthropology. Online: wals.info.

Peking University. 1971. *Modern Chinese: A basic course.* Mineola, NY: Dover Publications.

Raimes, Ann, & Susan Miller-Cochrane. 2013. *Keys for writers.* Boston: Houghton-Mifflin.

Talking about Things

Introduction

*O*ne of the basic functions of language is to talk about things. We need to refer to things in the world and describe them. This chapter is about how languages perform these functions.

The basic words that refer to things are typically called "nouns." We explore these questions about nouns:

- What kind of meaning does a noun have?
- Where do nouns go in the ordering of words in a phrase and in a sentence?
- How do nouns contribute to the meaning of a sentence?
- What special form does a noun have (in particular languages)?

In the simplest cases, a single word can be used to refer to something, for example, *Susan* or *computers*. But in more complex cases, where we want to express some properties of what we are referring to, it is necessary to construct a phrase, for example, *this computer*, or *every red chair*, or *the person whom you said you were talking to*. Although all languages can perform the function of expressing such properties, they vary dramatically in terms of how they do this, in terms of the linguistic form.

For example, in some languages, the words for 'my' and 'red' would follow the noun, not precede it as in English. Here is an example from Tukang Besi, a language of Indonesia. (The case marker *te* indicates the function of the phrase in the sentence.)

(1) te   wunua   molengo = su
     CASE   house   old   = my
     'my old house'

Other languages lack words meaning 'the' and express the meaning conveyed by 'the' by locating the phrase containing the noun in a particular position in the sentence. For example, in the Chinese examples in (2), the phrase *shu* 'book' is interpreted as 'the books' when it appears in the initial position in the sentence, as in (2a), but as 'books' when it follows the verb, as in (2b) (Huang et al. 2009:200).

(2) a. shu,   wo   hui   kan.
          book, I   will   read
          'The book(s), I will read.'
     b. wo   hui   kan   shu.
          I   will   read   book
          'I will read books.'

Nouns

To get some perspective, we begin with some errors that non-native speakers make in English.

(3) a. Sun is hot.
          Store on corner is closed.
     b. He lives in the Peru.
          The Professor Goldmund is very dynamic.
     c. Student in this class very friendly.
     d. I bought a book. He was very expensive.

Let's compare these sentences with their correct counterparts. In (4), an underlined word is one that we have added to correct the sentence, and a word marked with strikeout has to be removed to correct the sentence.

(4) a. <u>The</u> sun is hot.
          <u>The</u> store on <u>the</u> corner is closed.
     b. He lives in ~~the~~ Peru.
          ~~The~~ Professor Goldmund is very dynamic.
     c. <u>The</u> student<u>s</u> in this class <u>are</u> very friendly.
     d. I bought a book. ~~He~~ <u>It</u> was very expensive.

The examples in (4a) were discussed in chapter 10; in English, words like *sun* (when referring to our sun) must be preceded by *the* (which is called the **definite article**). The examples in (4b) show that phrases in English that refer to particular people or places typically do not have an article. Example (4c) shows that English makes a distinction in the form of the noun between singular and plural. And example (4d) shows that English uses the neuter pronoun *it* to refer to inanimate objects, rather than the pronouns *he* and *she,* which distinguish masculine and feminine gender.

We will see later on that some other languages in fact omit the definite article and use other ways to express the notion of definiteness. Other languages distinguish categories of words as "masculine" and "feminine," a distinction that may get translated literally (but incorrectly) into English as *he* and *she* instead of *it.* And some languages do not distinguish singular and plural by marking the word, as English does. Speakers of such languages are likely to make errors of the sort seen in (3c), and speakers of English are likely to have comparable difficulties in learning such languages.

A word that refers to a thing, like *dog,* is a type of **noun.** Words of this type can appear in English after *the, a,* and so on. Let us look more closely at the English examples that went into the construction of table 11.1, which we also used in chapter 10.

● **TABLE 11.1**
Menu for Simple English Sentences

A	B	C
the	dog	barked
a	cat	hissed
this	pig	grunted
that	rooster	crowed

The words in column B are similar to one another in two ways. First, their meanings have something in common (they all refer to physical objects and, in particular, to animals). Second, they appear in similar sequences of words to form sentences—they can follow *the, a, this,* and *that,* and they precede words like *barked, hissed,* and so on.

The fact that these similarities go together is not accidental. In general, words that share some essential part of their meaning in a particular language tend to behave the same in terms of their distribution in phrases and sentences. For this reason, we group them together into the same **category.** But the converse does not hold—not all the words in a category share some part of their meaning. Within the category containing *dog, cat,* and so forth, for example, there are words that refer to substances, such as *water;* to abstract entities, such as *unicorn;* to emotions, such as *anger;* and so on. But it is correct to say that the category noun contains groups of words that do have many properties in common.

Recognizing that category and meaning generally tend to go together makes language learning much easier than if we had to learn the specific properties of every word. For example, if we know that *dog* refers to a type of animal, and if we know that it is possible to say *The dog is sleeping* (i.e., we know that this is a good sentence of English), then if we learn that *cat* refers to another kind of animal, we can pretty well guess that *The cat is sleeping* will be a good sentence of English, too, with a very similar meaning. Even if we make up a new word for an animal that doesn't exist, say *benoxicobe*, we can say *The benoxicobe is sleeping*. The only thing that is odd about this sentence is the fact that it contains a word that doesn't exist. But that word is in the "right" place as far as English grammar is concerned.

Exercise 1: Grammatical and Ungrammatical Sentences

Make up some nonsense word referring to a type of animal. Make up a half-dozen sentences with the word *dog* used in different ways, and then replace the word *dog* with this new word. Are all of these new sentences grammatical?

A rough but fairly accurate test of whether something is a noun is that it can appear with *the,* as in *the dog* and the other words in table 11.1. Using this test, we find that a noun may be a word that refers to:

- a physical thing, like *dog, cat, apple, foot, moon, President*
- physical substance, like *milk, air, dirt, wind*
- a nonphysical thing, like *idea, sentence, number*
- organizations and other social entities, like *government, presidency, family*
- nonphysical qualities that we are able to perceive in ourselves or in others, like *imagination, sincerity, anger, aggressiveness, friendship*
- times, like *day, hour, month*
- places, like *inside, city, backyard*

This list is not exhaustive.

There are several basic types of nouns in English:

- Times and locations, like *Christmas, tomorrow, Paris*. These do not appear with *the*.
- Countable things, either physical or nonphysical. These can appear with *the* and with words like *every* and *the,* as in *every dog, every cat, the apple, the foot*. These are **count** nouns.

(continued)

- A count noun can be used with a **singular** or a **plural** form in English, for example, *dog/dogs, woman/women, cat/cats, apple/apples.*
- If a word refers to a substance, it cannot be counted, so we cannot use *every*: **every milk, *every air, *every dirt, *every imagination, *every sincerity, *every anger.*
- But a substance can be measured, so we can use *a lot of* before it: *a lot of milk, a lot of air, a lot of dirt, a lot of wind.* This type of noun is called a **mass** noun.
- The type of noun that is the name of something unique, like *Paris,* or *Albert Einstein,* or *Christmas,* is called a **proper** noun.

Here is a summary:

Type	Use	Example
count	refer to things that can be counted	every dog, three books
mass	refer to substances	water, air
proper	refer to unique things, places, etc.	Albert Einstein, Paris, Frodo Baggins

Do Other Languages Have Nouns?

Anyone who has studied another language knows that other languages have nouns. But even if we haven't studied another language, we would guess that they do. Why? Because speakers of other languages have to be able to refer to the kinds of things that speakers of English refer to. Moreover, people need to be able to indicate whether the thing they are referring to is familiar or definite (expressed by *the* in English), unfamiliar or indefinite (expressed by *a* in English), singular or plural, and so on. Words that perform this function are what we call "nouns."

So all languages have nouns. However, the structure of the phrase that contains the noun varies among languages. And languages differ in how they express such things as definiteness and number. As we have seen, English uses *the* for definiteness. *The* is called a **determiner,** and more precisely, an **article.**

In many languages there are no words corresponding to *the.* Look at the following sentences from Mandarin Chinese (Jiang 2009:5).

(5) Lai   ren   le.
      come   person COMPLETED
      'Some person/people has/have come.'

      Ren   lai   le.
      person   come COMPLETED
      'The person/people has/have come.'

These examples show that when the noun *ren* 'person/people' is at the beginning of the sentence, it is interpreted as definite; that is, it refers to someone believed to be familiar to the participants in the conversation. But when the verb comes first, the noun is interpreted as indefinite; that is, it introduces someone or something new into the conversation.

Most significantly, there are no words in these sentences that correspond to English *the* and *some*. A literal translation of *Ren lai le* is 'Person come,' which is just like one type of error in English that we saw earlier: *Store on corner is closed.*

Another type of error in English has to do with marking singular and plural, as we saw in the example *Student in this class very friendly.* Notice that in the Chinese example in (5), the singular and plural have the same form. *Ren* can mean either 'person' or 'people.' This illustrates the fact that not all languages have singular and plural forms for nouns. It is natural for speakers of languages that do not have such forms to make errors when they speak a language that does have such forms. A speaker of a language that systematically distinguishes singular and plural needs to be accustomed to the fact that the number distinction has to be indicated by using a numerical expression (such as 'one,' 'many') or from context.

In some languages that have articles, whether the phrase is singular or plural is marked not by the noun but by the form of the article. Here are some examples from Māori and spoken French.

Māori	French	English
te ngeru	**le** chat	the cat
ngā ngeru	**les** chats	the cat**s**

The final *-t* and *-ts* are silent in the French words *chat* and *chats,* so the actual forms are [lə ʃa] and [le ʃa].

Let us look more closely at the function of determiners and how languages express these functions.

Determiners

WHAT IS A DETERMINER?

Determiners are the words and expressions that in English (but not all languages) precede the noun and that are used to express distinctions of quantity, uniqueness, and definiteness. Here are some common determiners in English.

- one, two, every, each, some, many, much, the, a

Some determiners are used to pick out objects from a group of objects of the same type.

- this, that, these, those

We already have mentioned one rule of English, which is that the determiner must precede the noun. This rule is what tells us that any word from column A can precede any word from column B in table 11.1.

Table 11.2 focuses just on determiners and nouns; it shows that there are a few other things that have to be said in addition to the relative order of the words.

We cannot simply combine a word from column A with a word from column B, even if we observe the ordering rule; we have to know something about the types of words we are dealing with. As we have seen, certain determiners go with mass nouns, and others go with count nouns. In addition, some determiners go only with plural nouns—

(6) these apples, those pigs, many cats, *these dog, *those imagination

—and some go only with singular nouns—

(7) this apple, that pig, every cat, *this dogs, *those rooster

—and others go with mass nouns—

(8) some wind, some anger, much dirt, much sincerity

—and others go with count nouns—

(9) some books, many books, several people

—and, finally, proper nouns do not have determiners.[1]

(10) *every Albert Einstein, *much Albert Einstein

● **TABLE 11.2**
Menu of Determiners and Nouns
. . . .

A	B
the	dog
a	cat
this	pig
that	rooster
these	apple
those	foot
one	moon
two	idea
every	sentence
each	milk
some	air
much	dirt
many	wind
	imagination
	sincerity
	anger
	aggressiveness
	Albert Einstein

1. To be precise, they do not have determiners that imply or require that there be more than one thing with the same proper name. Emphatic *THE* is quite possible with proper names, for example, *THE Albert Einstein*.

AGREEMENT

The idea that certain words "go with" certain words in terms of their form is what is called **agreement** in the description of languages. We see, for example, that *this* and *that* "agree with" singular nouns, while *these* and *those* "agree with" plural nouns. What *agreement* means in this case is that it is impossible to have *this* or *that* with a plural noun and *these* or *those* with a singular noun.

These observations suggest the following, which we call the Basic Noun Phrase Rule for English.

Basic Noun Phrase Rule (English)

Determiner precedes **noun.**

Restrictions:

- Count determiners go with count nouns.
- Mass determiners go with mass nouns.
- Singular determiners go with singular nouns.
- Plural determiners go with plural nouns.
- Proper nouns lack determiners.

The Basic Noun Phrase Rule describes how to create an expression in English that is based on a noun. Such an expression is called a **noun phrase.** All languages have noun phrases, but they may differ in various ways on how a noun phrase is made up. We'll look at some other examples of other ways of making noun phrases very shortly.

In the cases that we have been looking at, the determiner agrees with the noun in the property of **number**: singular determiners go with singular nouns and plural determiners go with plural nouns.

In some languages, agreement is quite pervasive, while other languages lack it entirely. Depending on the language, agreement may involve number and other properties of words. For example, if you look up the translation of 'this' in a French dictionary, it will tell you:

(11) ce (m), cette (f), cet (m) (before vowels)

What do (m) and (f) mean? We can figure it out if we see what happens when we put the determiners into column A and the nouns into column B for French, and start combining them freely, as shown in table 11.3.

If we take one word from column A we get some grammatical French expressions, as shown in (12).

(12) ce livre   'this book'
     cette maison   'this house'
     cet arbre   'this tree'
     cette table   'this table'
     cette chaise   'this chair'
     cette orange   'this orange'

These are French noun phrases. But other combinations don't work.

(13) *ce maison
     *cette livre
     *ce chaise
     *ce table
     *cet orange

● **TABLE 11.3**
Forms Expressing 'This' in French

A	B
ce	livre 'book'
ce	chien 'dog'
cette	maison 'house'
cette	table 'table'
cette	chaise 'chair'
cette	orange 'orange'
cet	arbre 'tree'

The reason that these don't work is that there are two classes of words in French, called "masculine" and "feminine," and the form of the determiner depends on which class the noun belongs to. These classes are called **gender** classes, and the determiner and the noun must **agree in gender.** So, *ce* is a masculine determiner that goes only with masculine nouns, and *cette* is a feminine determiner that goes only with feminine nouns. *Cet* is the form that *ce* takes when it precedes a vowel, as in *cet arbre* (similar to how *an* in English is the form of *a* before a vowel).

Another important observation is that determiners in these languages typically agree also in number with the nouns. So in French, for example, the form of the determiner is singular or plural depending on whether the noun is singular or plural. Table 11.4 lists all the French words meaning 'the,' 'this,' and 'that.'

● **TABLE 11.4**
French Determiners

Word	Gender	Number
le 'the'	masculine	singular
la 'the'	feminine	singular
les 'the'	masculine and feminine	plural
ce, cet 'this/that'	masculine	singular
cette 'this/that'	feminine	singular
ces 'these/those'	masculine and feminine	plural

French determiners show agreement for number, and they show agreement for gender in the singular forms. The same kind of pattern holds for other determiners in French and for related languages like Italian and Spanish.

Exercise 2

State the Basic Noun Phrase Rule for French, given the information in tables 11.3 and 11.4. We give you the first part below; say what the restrictions are.

Determiner precedes Noun.

GENDER AND SEX

It is important to recognize that gender is related to biological gender but is not the same as biological gender, or what we usually refer to as **sex.** There are two biological sexes for most living things, including humans, animals, and plants, namely, male and female. But inanimate things, and abstract things like ideas and beliefs, and substances like water and wood, do not have sexes per se, since they are not animate or even biological. But, amazingly, in languages like French, all nouns have **gender.** Everything is either "masculine" or "feminine."

Gender is a classification of the nouns into groups. It is not a necessary property of the object or substance that the word refers to. It is true that in French the nouns for females are typically feminine, and the nouns for males are masculine. This makes it easy to remember the gender for words like *homme* 'man' and *femme* 'woman.' But how can you figure out what the gender is of *livre* 'book' and *maison* 'house'? You can't, because gender is for the most part simply a classification of the nouns.

So for most nouns, you just have to learn what the gender is. The words are masculine or feminine, but the things that they refer to are neither male nor female. The properties that determine agreement are for the most part properties of the words, not of the objects. In fact, '(the) girl' in German is *(das) Mädchen,* which is neuter, not feminine, even though girls are females. And '(the) person' in German is *(die) Person,* which is feminine, even though some persons are female and some are male. Some additional examples that show that grammatical gender is really a linguistic distinction related to the biological distinction but not identical to it are given in table 11.5.

Grammatical Gender

Grammatical gender is not about biology; it is about the way that the language classifies the nouns for the purposes of agreement.

When we first encounter gender in another language we might say to ourselves, "Hey, these people are weird—they think of tables and houses as female and books and beds as male. What made them think of that?" But this is a mistake. The nouns have gender, but the inanimate objects that they refer to do not actually have sexes. Gender in the category of nouns is a way of classifying them. It is just as though we said, "OK, for the fun of it let's put the label RED on all apples and the label GREEN on all peppers" (with the labels in capital letters). It is true that many apples are red, but many are not, like Granny Smith apples. And many peppers are green, but many are not; some are red. And some apples and some peppers are neither red nor green. It is easy to get confused because the name of the classification label RED is related to the actual color red, and many objects classified as RED (that is, apples) actually have the color red. Similarly, we have gotten confused about gender in language because we have taken the classification scheme, using the labels "masculine" and "feminine," which correlate with some real biological property of some of the objects (those that are animate), and because we may have confused it with the biological property itself.

Making the situation a bit more complicated is the fact that some languages have three or even more noun classes based on gender. These languages do help to show that grammatical gender is primarily word classification, not biology. Typically, when there

● **TABLE 11.5**

Examples of Gender in Different Languages

English	French	German	Russian	Spanish
the house	la maison (f)	das Haus (n)	dom (m)	la casa (f)
the table	la table (f)	der Tisch (m)	stol (m)	la mesa (f) la tabla (f)
the boy	le garçon (m)	der Junge (m)	mal'chik (m)	el niño (m) el muchacho (m)
the idea	l'idée (f)	die Idee (f)	ideja (f)	la idea (f)
the problem	le problème (m)	das Problem (n)	problema (f)	el problema (m)
the bed	le lit (m)	das Bett (n)	post'el' (f)	la cama (f)
the tree	l'arbre (m)	der Baum (m)	derevo (n)	el árbol (m)
the water	l'eau (f)	das Wasser (n)	voda (f)	el agua (f)
the trash	le rebut (m)	der Abfall (m)	drjan' (f)	la basura (f)

are three classes, one is masculine, one is feminine, and one is neuter, as in German. This becomes odd to us when we discover that certain animates are grammatically neuter even though biologically they are either male or female. And as the number of classes gets larger, the connection with biological gender becomes less and less secure.

The arbitrariness of gender can be highlighted by considering the gender of some nouns referring to the very same thing in different languages. Usually, if the noun refers to something animate that has biological gender, the noun will be in the corresponding gender class. But if the noun does not refer to something animate, and the two languages are not related, the gender is really quite unpredictable. Table 11.5 shows some examples: (m) means "masculine," (f) means "feminine," and (n) means "neuter." There appears to be no pattern and nothing about the meanings of these words that would predict their gender, except perhaps for the case of 'boy,' which is masculine across all of these languages, and 'idea,' which is feminine.

English appears to express gender only in the words *he/him, she/her, his/her,* and *himself/herself*. But this is in fact not grammatical gender. We use *he/him, she/her,* and so on, to refer to people and animals, and the word that we use corresponds to the biological sex. *He* is used to refer to a single male individual, and *she* to a single female individual. English nouns do not have gender. We use *it* in English to refer to an inanimate object.

But because all French nouns must have gender, the French counterparts to English *he* and *she* must be used to refer to all things according to their gender. Compare the following sentences.

(14) J'ai   acheté   un   livre   et   il   était   cher.
     I have   bought   a   book   and   he   was   expensive
     'I bought a book and it was expensive.'

     J'ai   acheté   une   maison   et   elle   était   chère.
     I have   bought   a   house   and   she   was   expensive
     'I bought a house and it was expensive.'

The words *il* and *elle* are the same words that are used to refer to people, and when they are used in that way they are translated into English as *he* and *she*. So when we see the translation 'it (masculine singular),' we might be tempted to think that it is the same as *he,* and indeed we would use the word *il* in French to refer to a single male person. But *il* does not mean 'him'; it means 'him/it' and agrees with the gender class of the noun, not just the biological sex. So translating *il* as 'him' and *elle* as 'her' in these sentences would be a mistake; they correspond to 'it' in English.

NOUN CLASSES

To see that French gender is a simple example of what can be a more complex phenomenon in other languages, we consider the noun classes of Swahili, a Bantu language. In Swahili there are fifteen noun classes—therefore the form of a word in the singular and the plural is in part determined by what class it is in, and agreement takes into account the noun classes. For example, the form *m-* (class 6) is attached to the beginning of a noun that refers to a person.

(15) **m**-toto   '(a) child'
     m-tu   '(a) person'
     m-geni   '(a) guest'

To make the plural, the form *wa-* (class 7) is added to the noun.

(16) **wa**-toto   'children'
     wa-tu   'people'
     wa-geni   'guests'

However, if the word refers to a small thing, the singular has the form *ki-* attached to it, and the plural has the form *vi-*.

(17) **ki**-toto   '(an) infant'   **vi**-toto   'infants'
     ki-kapu   '(a) basket'   **vi**-kapu   'baskets'
     ki-ti   '(a) stool'   **vi**-ti   'stools'

Notice the use of the form *toto* for 'child/children' and 'infant/infants.'

WHERE DO DETERMINERS GO?

Essentially, the French noun phrase looks like the English noun phrase, at least as far as where the determiner goes. In some languages, though, the determiner follows the noun. In yet other languages, the meanings conveyed by English determiners are not expressed by distinct words but are understood from context and from the overall form of the sentence. Table 11.6 shows some simple noun phrases from other languages.

In Kwamera, Swedish, and Bulgarian, the word for *the* follows the noun; in the other languages illustrated here, it precedes the noun. Finally, as we have seen, some languages lack articles and use other devices, such as word order, to indicate definiteness and indefiniteness.

TABLE 11.6
Definite Articles across Languages

Language	Phrase	English translation
Chinese	pingguo apple	an apple, the apple
Kwamera[†]	kuri u dog this	this dog
Swedish	mus-en mouse-the	the mouse
Swahili	wa-toto class7-child	the children
Bulgarian	kuche-to dog-the	the dog
Italian	il cane the dog	the dog
French	le livre the book	the book
Russian	voda water	water, the water
German	das Wasser the water	the water

[†]From Tallerman 2011

LEARNING TO USE DETERMINERS

Part of the challenge of learning another language is to figure out in what ways it is different from the language or languages that you already know. This requires that you understand something about how your language works and that you pinpoint those areas in which the languages differ. The relationship between determiner and noun is one such area where differences can arise.

Having recognized that differences exist between noun phrases in different languages in terms of whether there is agreement and what the order of the noun and the determiner is, the next question that we have to consider is how to learn to produce and recognize the differences most effectively.

Being able to do this goes beyond knowing what the rule is. It even goes beyond knowing that the noun *maison* 'house' in French is feminine while the noun *lit* 'bed' is masculine. We have to get to the point where we automatically put the determiner in the right place and do the agreement without thinking about the rule. The essential step in learning how to get order, gender, and agreement right is to practice the forms together. That is, we do not want to simply memorize the words shown in (18).

(18) maison (f)
     lit (m)

Simply memorizing won't help us to handle the determiners *le, la, cette, ce*: we need to carry out an extra step. Here are the mental steps that we would have to go through:

1. Ask yourself: What is the word for 'house'?
1a. Answer: *maison*
2. Ask: What is the gender of *maison*?
2a. Answer: feminine
3. Ask: What is the feminine form for 'the'?
3a. Answer: *la*
4. Ask: Where does the determiner go?
4a. Answer: before the noun.
5. OK, *la maison*!

By the time we go through all of these steps, our audience will be lost, if we are speaking, or we will be lost, if we are trying to figure out what someone is saying. Here's another way to handle the determiners.

1. Ask your brain: How do you say 'the house'?
1a. Answer: *la maison*

1. Ask: How do you say 'this bed'?
1a. Answer: *ce lit*

In other words, we need to learn not just the gender and the rule for gender agreement, but the actual forms that are required in order for there to be proper agreement as part of the noun. Doing so will save us many costly steps.

Clearly, we must learn the rule in order to understand why some phrases are different from others. But once we know the rule, we must use it to construct the expressions, and then **we must learn the complete expressions so well that they become automatic.** When we want to say 'the house,' we don't want to have to waste time figuring out whether the proper form is *le* or *la*; we need to know that *la maison* means 'the house' and eliminate the extra mental steps. Learning the more complex forms reduces the amount of computational time that we have to go through, at those moments when time is precious.

Summary

We saw in this chapter that all languages have ways to refer to things. In any language, the main part of a phrase that refers to something is a noun. In some languages the noun has a fixed form, while in other languages the form of the noun is determined in part by the classification system of the language (such as gender). In some languages the status of what the noun phrase refers to in the discourse is marked by a determiner (such as *a* and *the*), while other languages use word order to accomplish this task.

We began this chapter with a few examples of typical errors that non-native speakers make. Here they are again:

(3) a. Sun is hot.
        Store on corner is closed.
    b. She lawyer.
    c. He lives in the Peru.
        The Professor Goldmund is very dynamic.
    d. Student in this class very friendly.
    e. I bought a book. He was very expensive.

These errors show us that some languages lack articles corresponding to *the* and *a*; that some languages use articles with proper nouns, unlike English; and that some languages make grammatical gender distinctions among nouns, while English does not.

When we are talking about two things of the same type, like apples or cars or dogs, using a determiner may not be enough to distinguish them. We could say "this apple" and "that apple" and point, but if we want to use language to distinguish them, we are going to have to describe them, for example, "the green apple" and "the reddish apple." In the next chapter, we look at how languages use adjectives and other descriptive devices to distinguish one thing from another in discourse.

References

Huang, C.-T. James; Y.-H. Audrey Li; & Yafei Li. 2009. *The syntax of Chinese.* Cambridge: Cambridge University Press.

Jiang, Wenying. 2009. *The acquisition of word order in Chinese.* Berlin: Mouton de Gruyter.

Tallerman, Maggie. 2011. *Understanding syntax.* Abington and New York: Routledge.

Describing Things

Describing Things

*L*et's take another look again at some examples of "foreign accent" in English.

(1) a. I gave her a rose red.
     b. I have helpfuls friends.
     c. The enrolled in community college student (is my friend).
     d. Here is the student which you met her last week.
     e. The book is on the table is mine.

What is wrong with these sentences? We can understand each of them, yet in some way each one is wrong. Let's compare them with how they would be expressed in grammatical English. Underlining shows where something should go, while strikeout shows something in the wrong place.

(2) a. I gave her a <u>red</u> rose ~~red~~.
     b. I have helpful<u>s</u> friends.
     c. The ~~enrolled in community college~~ student <u>enrolled in community college</u> (is my friend).
     d. Here is the student which you met ~~her~~ last week.
     e. The book <u>that</u> is on the table is mine.

As you can see, some of the differences are very subtle, but they have a considerable effect on whether a native speaker perceives the sentence as correct or not. Example (2a) shows that a word like *red* in English must precede the noun, not follow it. Example (2b) shows that only the noun is marked for plural; *helpful* is not. The words *red* and *helpful* are **adjectives.**

The remaining three examples illustrate properties of **relative clauses** in English. Example (2c) shows that the phrase *enrolled in community college* has to follow the noun (in contrast to *red,* which precedes it). Examples (2d) and (2e) are somewhat more complicated, and we'll come back to them later.

Adjectives and relative clauses in English have the function of describing things. All languages perform these functions. Languages differ in the form of adjectives and relative clauses, and in where adjectives and relative clauses are located in the noun phrase. We discuss how this works next.

Adjectives

ADJECTIVES IN ENGLISH

Adjectives are used to refer to properties of things and substances (physical and non-physical, and real and imaginary). Among the types of properties that can be referred to with adjectives follow:

- overall size; for example, *huge, big, little, small, tiny, enormous, middle-sized*
- size in a particular dimension; for example, *tall, short, fat, slim, elongated, stubby*
- shape; for example, *square, round, oval, squiggly, triangular, flat*
- qualities perceived by one of our senses; for example, *loud, quiet, shrill, squeaky, wet, melodious, rhythmic, shiny, dull, dark, scratchy, rough, red, black, green, polka-dotted*
- social or personal qualities; for example, *polite, rude, inquisitive, happy, sad, intelligent, silly, goofy*
- and many others

As we did in the case of determiners and nouns in chapter 11, we can say what the rule is for adjectives in English. Consider the examples in (3).

(3) huge dog   *dog huge
     the huge dog   *the dog huge   *huge the dog
     this huge dog   *this dog huge   *huge this dog
     every huge dog   *every dog huge   *huge every dog

We already know that the determiner has to precede the noun, so we have to look only at where the adjective goes. The examples in (4) show that the adjective also precedes the noun; moreover, the adjective has to follow the determiner. If there is more than one adjective, all the adjectives must follow the determiner and precede the noun.

(4) the huge gray dog
     the huge gray howling dog
     the huge gray happy howling dog
     and so on

Adjective Rule (English):
In a noun phrase, an
adjective precedes
the noun that it
modifies and follows
the determiner.

These observations allow us to formulate the English Adjective Rule. Using this rule, we can list the determiners in column A, the adjectives in column B and the nouns in column C. Table 12.1 gives a small sample of the members of the categories that produce possible noun phrases of English. If we take one word from column A, one from column B, and one from column C, we get sequences that look like English noun phrases, although some of them are nonsensical and others are simply bad English. For example, if the determiner and the noun do not obey the agreement restrictions of the Determiner Rule, the sequence is bad.

● **TABLE 12.1**
Menu for Simple English Noun Phrases

A	B	C
the	huge	dog
a	wet	water
every	square	idea
this	intelligent	sincerity
much	happy	foot
a lot of	stubby	proposal

Let us start at the beginning. *The, huge,* and *dog* combine according to the English Adjective Rule to form *the huge dog.* This is a proper expression of English, and we know what it means. Let us replace *dog* with the other nouns and see what we come up with.

(5) ☹the huge water
     ☺the huge idea
     ☹the huge sincerity

The first example, *the huge water,* sounds odd because it refers to a property of water that cannot be measured. Water can be heavy, or wet, or warm, but not huge. To indicate this type of oddness, we use the frowny face symbol ☹.

In comparison, an idea is a nonphysical object. It can be counted (e.g., *two ideas, every idea*) but because it is nonphysical, it does not have a physical size. But we can talk metaphorically of a nonphysical object as though it is physical, so we can use *huge* metaphorically to describe an idea. The smiley face symbol ☺ on *the huge idea* is used here to indicate this metaphorical usage.

Sincerity is a nonphysical "substance," so it is odd to use an adjective that measures physical dimension to describe sincerity, even metaphorically. It is as strange as talking about ☹*the huge air* or ☹*the huge water.* ☹*The huge sincerity* therefore gets the frowny face symbol assigned to it.

Notice that the sorts of things that we are describing here are not specifically about the English language but about how we understand the world as human beings. If we translated these expressions into some other language, they would be judged equally acceptable, metaphorical, or odd, to the extent that the words that we are using convey the same literal concepts. So ☹*la sincerité énorme* 'huge sincerity' should be as strange in French as it is in English, and in exactly the same way.

Exercise 1

As we have seen, table 12.1 gives rise to a number of perfectly good noun phrases and a number of less than perfect noun phrases, for example, ☹*much happy foot,* ☹*a lot of square water,* ☹*a stubby sincerity,* ☹*much wet idea.* For each of these bad combinations, say as precisely as you can why they're bad.

Notice also that there does not appear to be any agreement restriction between the adjective and the noun in English. While we found that we have to use *this* with singular nouns and *these* with plural nouns, the adjectives in column B can be used with either type of noun. For example, see (6).

(6)   this huge dog
      these huge dogs

This means that we do not have to add any restrictions to the Adjective Rule.

Descriptive and Restrictive Modification

An adjective is a word like the English *red, helpful, happy*. We can say

the happy dog
The dog is happy.

With stress on *dog*, the phrase *happy dog* means simply that the dog is happy. This is the **descriptive** or **attributive** use of the adjective.

- As an exercise, use the expression *the happy dog* in a sentence to simply say that the dog is happy. You should be able to hear that the stress falls on *dog.* Try this with other phrases.

With stress on *happy*, by contrast, the adjective is used to distinguish this dog from other dogs that are not happy. This is the **restrictive** or **contrastive** use of the adjective.

- As an exercise, use the expression *the happy dog* in a sentence to distinguish this happy dog from those that are not happy. You should be able to hear that the stress falls on *happy.* Try this with other phrases.

ADJECTIVES IN OTHER LANGUAGES

Now let us consider how a language might differ from English in regard to the counterpart of the Adjective Rule that says where to put adjectives in noun phrases.

- In some other language, the adjective could follow the noun.
- In some other language, the adjective might be required to agree with the noun.

Let us take a look at the examples in table 12.2. These examples show that the position of the adjective depends on the language. In Swahili, French, and Spanish, it follows the noun, while in the other languages, it precedes the noun. The determiner that means 'the' goes in different positions in different languages, as does the determiner that means 'every.' Each of these languages has a Determiner Rule and an Adjective Rule that says what the ordering requirements are and what the restrictions, if any, are. We illustrate shortly.

Remember that we have seen that in some languages there is agreement between determiners and nouns. Not surprisingly, in these very same languages, adjectives must also agree with the nouns. Let us look at some examples from a language that we have not talked about yet, namely, Italian. We indicate masculine agreement with M, feminine with F, singular with SG and plural with PL. First we look at noun phrases without adjectives, and then we throw some adjectives in. See if you can figure out what is going on in (7).

TABLE 12.2
Adjective Noun Order across Languages

Language	Phrase	English translation
French	un chien enorme a dog huge	a huge dog
German	der vernünftige Vorschlag the intelligent proposal	the intelligent proposal
Chinese	hao xuésheng good student	(a) good student
Swedish	den hungriga mus-en the hungry mouse-the	the hungry mouse
Spanish	cada hoja verde every leaf green	every green leaf
Russian	kazhdyje zelënyje list'ja every green leaf	every green leaf
Swahili	matunda mazuri fruit nice	nice fruit
Bulgarian	zeleni-te lista green-the leaves	the green leaves

(7) il   libro
     the-M.SG book-M.SG
     'the book'

    il   libro   piccolo
     the-M.SG book-M.SG little-M.SG
     'the little book'

    i   libri
     the-M.PL book-M.PL
     'the books'

    i   libri   piccoli
     the-M.PL book-M.PL little-M.PL
     'the little books'

    la   casa
     the-F.SG house-F.SG
     'the house'

    la   casa   piccola
     the-F.SG house-F.SG little-F.SG
     'the strange house'

    le   case
     the-F.PL house-F.PL
     'the house'

    le   case   piccole
     the-F.PL house-F.PL little-F.PL
     'the strange houses'

What do we see here? First, as (sometimes) in French, in Italian the adjective follows the noun. Second, the form of the adjective varies according to the gender and number of the noun, just like the form of the determiner does. In fact, we can even make a good guess about what the form is. Look at the difference between *piccolo* and *piccola*. They are the same as far as the *piccol-* part is concerned, and they differ just in whether they end in *-o* or *-a*. The four forms together suggest the picture shown in table 12.3.

TABLE 12.3. Italian Adjective Agreement

	singular	plural
masculine	-o	-i
feminine	-a	-e

But notice that these same endings appear on the nouns themselves. We have highlighted the endings in table 12.4 so that you can compare them with those for adjective agreement.

TABLE 12.4. Italian Nouns

	singular	plural
masculine	libr-**o**	libr-**i**
feminine	cas-**a**	cas-**e**

And we can make a nice chart for the determiners as well, as in table 12.5. It very closely resembles the chart for the adjectives and the nouns.

TABLE 12.5. Italian Determiners

	singular	plural
masculine	il	i
feminine	la	le

What these charts are telling us is that there is a pretty systematic way of indicating number and gender in Italian, and, moreover, the determiner and the adjective and the noun all have to show number and gender and agree with one another in number and gender.

So consider the following Italian vocabulary:

(8) ragazzo 'boy'
     ragazza 'girl'
     strano   'strange (m.sg.)'

How would we say 'the strange boy,' 'the strange boys,' and 'the strange girl,' 'the strange girls'? We just follow the rules.

(9) il ragaz**z**o stran**o**   'the strange boy'
     i ragaz**z**i stran**i**   'the strange boys'
     la ragaz**z**a stran**a**   'the strange girl'
     le ragaz**z**e stran**e**   'the strange girls'

And this is the general pattern that we find throughout Italian. (Maybe this one reason is why many people find Italian easy to learn.)

Exercise 2

Work out the Adjective Rule for Italian.

Exercise 3

What would you say is the best way to learn how to productively construct grammatical noun phrases in Italian?

Now let's look again at Swahili. As we discussed earlier, there are fifteen noun classes in Swahili, meaning that the form of a word in the singular and the plural is in part determined by what class it is in, and that agreement takes into account the noun classes. Consider again the examples we discussed, for example, the form *m-* (class 6) is attached to the beginning of a noun that refers to a person.

(10) **m**-toto '(a) child'
      m-tu '(a) person'
      m-geni '(a) guest'

And to make the plural, the form *wa-* (class 7) is added.

(11) **wa**-toto 'children'
      wa-tu 'people'
      wa-geni 'guests'

But if the word refers to a small thing, the singular has the form *ki-* attached to it, and the plural has the form *vi-*.

(12) **ki**-toto 'infant'   **vi**-toto 'infants'
     ki-kapu 'basket'   **vi**-kapu 'baskets'
     ki-ti 'stool'   **vi**-ti 'stools'

Here now are some examples of noun phrases containing adjectives.

(13) **ma**-tunda **ma**-zuri   'nice fruit'
     fruit   nice

     mi-tego **mi**-wili   'two traps'
     traps   two

     wa-tu   ha-**wa**   **wa**-zuri   'these nice people'
     people   these   nice

     vi-ti   **vi**-le **vi**-kubwa   'those big chairs'
     chairs   those   big

What we see is that the class marker that attaches to the noun also attaches to the adjective and the determiner. Just as in Italian and French, Swahili shows agreement throughout the noun phrase.

Exercise 4

Work out the Determiner Rule and the Adjective Rule for Swahili.

Relative Clauses

RELATIVE CLAUSES IN ENGLISH

A few errors produced by Japanese learners of English are shown in (14) (from Muto-Humphrey (2006)).

(14) a. Based on many informations of the daughter gathered, . . .
    b. But the mystery of behind the door still remained.

As we noted at the beginning of this chapter, one way to describe or restrict a thing in terms of its properties is to use an adjective; the other way is to use a relative clause. The examples in (14) are ungrammatical attempts to produce a relative clause. Let's look closely at what is missing that should be there, and what is there that should not be in these examples. In (14a), for instance, we find *many informations*. In English, *information* is not a count but a mass noun, so this phrase should be *much information*. But then there is *of the daughter gathered*, which should be *that the daughter gathered*, or *which the daughter gathered*, or simply *the daughter gathered*.

(15) Based on much information <u>that the daughter gathered</u>, . . .
Based on much information <u>which the daughter gathered</u>, . . .
Based on much information <u>the daughter gathered</u>, . . .

The Japanese learners of English use *of* to introduce a relative clause, because it follows the noun in English, while in Japanese a relative clause precedes the noun. The learners know that *of* can be used to separate phrases within a noun phrase, for example, *a picture **of** Sandy*, so they seize on *of* as the way to deal with this particular grammatical problem. The same strategy appears in (14b), which should be simply *the mystery behind the door*.

Let us consider more closely at how a relative clause is formed in English. We consider the relative clauses that we introduced earlier.

(16) The dog <u>that is happy</u> is eating my socks.
I chased the dog <u>that was eating my socks</u>.
My mother made me let go of the dog <u>that I caught</u>.

The first relative clause is *that is happy,* the second is *that was eating my socks,* and the third is *that I caught.* We call *dog* the **head** of the noun phrase. Its function with respect to the meaning of the phrase is to pick out the type of thing that the relative clause describes. We sometimes say that "the head is what the relative clause modifies."

What these examples suggest is that one way to form relative clauses in English is to take a complete sentence that says something about the head, like (17).

(17) the dog is happy

Strike out the phrase that corresponds to the head and its determiner, if there is one.

(18) ~~the dog~~ is happy

and put the word *that* in front of the clause.

(19) that is happy

This works for the other relative clauses in the examples, as shown in (20).

- - - - - - - - - - - - - - - -

(20) The dog was eating my socks   →
~~The dog~~ was eating my socks   →
That was eating my socks

(21) I caught the dog   →
I caught ~~the dog~~   →
that I caught

Striking out the phrase to form the relative clause means that a relative clause is **a sentence with a gap** in it that corresponds in meaning to the head—that is, there is a missing phrase in a particular position. It is for this reason that there is something strange about one of the "foreign accent" sentences, (1d), which was introduced at the beginning of this chapter.

(22) Here is the student which you met **her** last week.

Because the relative clause modifies *student* and expresses the relation of meeting the student, there should be a gap after *met*. But instead we find the word *her* in this position. Some languages use a variant of the construction illustrated in (22), but Standard English does not; the correct form is *which you met ___ last week*.

There are other ways to make relative clauses in English. One involves putting *who, which, where,* or *when* in front of the clause, instead of *that*.

(23) the man **who(m)** I saw
the dog **which** is happy
the place **where** I put the lasagna
the time **when** I first saw Paris

Some of these are not entirely colloquial for many speakers of English and are associated more with a written or formal style.

It is also possible to leave out *that*, but not when the left-out phrase is the subject of the relative clause.

(24) The dog that I caught ___ needed a bath. ~ The dog I caught ___ needed a bath.
the first time that I saw Paris ___ ~ the first time I saw Paris ___
I bought a dog that ___ was happy. ~ *I bought a dog ___ was happy.

Hence we have an explanation for what is wrong with another example, (1e), which was introduced at the beginning of the chapter.

(25) *The book ~~that~~ is on the table is mine.

The problem here is that the word *that* must appear in the relative clause, because the left-out phrase is the subject: *the book is on the table; the book **that** ___ is on the table*.

The other thing that we know about English relative clauses is that they follow the head of the noun phrase. Compare (26) with the grammatical sentences in (16).

(26) *The <u>that is happy</u> dog is eating my socks.
    *I chased the <u>that was eating my socks</u> dog.
    *My mother made me let go of the <u>that I caught</u> dog.

Thus, a third example of a relative clause error from the beginning of the chapter can be explained:

(27) *The enrolled in community college student (is my friend).

Here, *enrolled in community college* is a type of "reduced" relative clause that does not follow the noun; in a language like German, Japanese, or Korean, however, such a relative clause would precede the noun.

Relative clauses, like adjectives, have two functions. One is "restrictive," and the other is called "nonrestrictive" or "appositive." Consider the following examples.

(28) I saw the dog that/who was happy.
    I saw the dog, who was happy.

The first example is understood as picking the happy dog out from a group of dogs—hence its function is restrictive. The second example is simply stating that the dog was happy. It does not presuppose that there were any other dogs. Thus the nonrestrictive function is the same as the attributive function of the adjective that we discussed earlier. Typically the two types of relative clauses are distinguished in the written language, as shown in example (28): a comma separates the nonrestrictive relative from the noun, but no comma is used when the relative clause is restrictive.

RELATIVE CLAUSES IN OTHER LANGUAGES

The relative clause in French is similar to that of English in that it has a gap that corresponds to the head. The forms that appear at the beginning of the relative clause are selected on the basis of the structure in which the gap appears. If the gap is an object, the relative clause begins with *que*. If it is a subject, the relative clause begins with *qui*.

(29) l'homme **que** j'ai vu
    the-man that I-have seen
    'the man that I saw'

    l'homme **qui** m'a vu
    the-man that me-has seen
    'the man that saw me'

Notice that by making use here of the notions subject and object, we are able to state in a very simple way how the French relative clause is formed.

In contrast with English, it is not possible to drop *que* 'that' in the French relative clause. So the following is not a grammatical noun phrase of French.

(30) *l'homme j'ai   vu
     the-man I-have   seen
     'the man I saw'

In Italian the relative clause always begins with *che*.

(31) il   uomo **che**   ho   visto
     the man   that I-have   seen
     'the man that I saw'

     il   uomo **che**   mi   ha   visto
     the man   that me   has   seen
     'the man that saw me'

The relative clause in these languages follows the head noun, which makes it relatively easy for speakers of English to deal with them. But in other languages, the relative clause precedes the head noun. Look at example (32) from Korean.[1] The relative clause is underlined. (Notice that, in Korean, the verb comes at the end of the sentence.)

(32) John-un   <u>tomangka-nun</u>   **totwuk-ul**   cap-ess-ta.
     J.-TOPIC run.away-REL.IMPERF   **thief-ACC**   catch-PAST-DECL
     (lit. 'John <u>running away</u> thief caught.')
     'John caught a/the thief who was running away.'

     John-un   **totwuk-I**   <u>tomangka-nun</u>   <u>kes-ul</u>   cap-ess-ta.
     J.-topic **thief-NOM**   run.away-REL.IMPERF   kes-ACC   catch-PAST-DECL
     (lit. 'John <u>thief running away who</u> caught.')
     'John caught a/the thief, who was running away.'

The head that the relative clause modifies is in boldface in the Korean sentences and in the word-for-word translation. In the first example, the relative clause precedes the head. There is no Korean word corresponding to English *that* or *who,* but there is a marker *-nun* on the verb (*tomangka-nun*) indicating that it is in a relative clause. But Korean also has a construction in which the relative clause follows the noun. In this

---

1. Examples adapted from Kim (2008). REL marks the verb as being in a relative clause, IMPERF indicates that the action lacks a fixed endpoint, NOM marks the subject, ACC marks the object, and DECL indicates that the sentence is a statement.

case, there is a following pronoun *kes,* similar to the Italian *che,* but following the relative clause, not preceding it.

German also has two types of relative clauses, one that precedes the noun and one that follows it.[2]

(33) der   <u>in seinem</u>   Büro arbeitende   Mann
     the   in his   study working   man
     'the man working in his study'

     der   Mann <u>der</u>   <u>in seinem</u>   Büro arbeitet
     the   man   that in his   study works
     'the man who is working in his study'

Japanese is similar to Korean. The verb comes at the end of the sentence.

(34) Yamada-san ga   saru   o   kat-te   i-ru.
     Yamada-Mr NOM monkey ACC keep-PART be-PRES
     'Mr. Yamada keeps a monkey.'

In a noun phrase, the relative clause precedes the noun.

(35) <u>Yamada-san</u> <u>ga</u>   <u>kat-te</u>   <u>i-ru</u>   saru.
     Yamada-Mr NOM keep-PART be-PRES monkey
     'the monkey which Mr. Yamada keeps'

The relative clause also precedes the noun in Chinese.

(36) Zhāngsān mǎi   de   qich   hèn   guì.
     Zangsan   buy   NOM car   very expensive
     'The car that Zhangsan bought was very expensive.'

Summary

In this chapter we looked at two kinds of modifiers of nouns: adjectives and relative clauses. In some languages, adjectives precede the noun that they modify, and in some they follow. Like adjectives, relative clauses precede the noun in some languages and follow it in others.

(continued)

---

2. Examples from Andrews (2007).

A relative clause is a sentence whose function is to modify a noun. Relative clauses show a number of variants of form as well, in terms of whether they have something introducing them (like *that* or Italian *che*) that marks them as relative clauses, or something following them (like Korean *-nun*), or nothing at all, as in Chinese.

Additional Exercises

1. Pick a language that you are familiar with other than English. Do adjectives precede or follow the head noun? Is there agreement? Can you state the rule for the noun phrase in this language?

2. Pick a language that you are familiar with other than English. How do you construct the counterparts of the following underlined relative clauses in this language?

   (1) a. the book I bought
       b. the salesperson that I bought the book from
       c. the salesperson who sold me the book

Discuss the differences between the rules for forming relative clauses in your language and in English. Also state clearly where the relative clause appears in the sentence with respect to the noun that it modifies.

References

Andrews, Avery. 2007. Relative clauses. *Language Typology and Syntactic Description,* ed. Timothy Shopen. Online: arts.anu.edu.au/linguistics/People/Avery Andrews/Papers/ typrc2_june.pdf.

Kim, Min-Joo. 2008. Internally-Headed Relatives Instantiate Situation Subordination. *Japanese-Korean Linguistics 13*, ed. Mutsuko Endo Hudson, Peter Sells, & Sun-Ah Jun. Online: people.umass.edu/minjoo/papers.

Muto-Humphrey, Keiko. 2006. Frequent Errors in English Grammar: Articles and Possessive Markers. *Journal of School of Foreign Languages 31.* Online: library.nakanishi.ac.jp/ kiyou/gaidai(31)/05.pdf.

13

Talking about Events

Introduction

*I*n the preceding two chapters we looked at noun phrases, which are used to refer to things. Generally speaking, sentences express properties of the things that the noun phrases refer to, as in *This book is interesting,* or relationships between them, like *Sandy is reading a book.* The precise literal content that a sentence expresses and the communicative function that it performs are dependent on its form. As we have seen, form includes the order in which the words appear and on whether and how they show particular grammatical markings.

For example, both factors are involved in an English sentence like *I saw Chris.* The words must be in the order shown in order to convey the intended meaning—we can't say **Saw I Chris*—and we can't say **Me saw Chris* to express this meaning, even though *me* refers to the same person as *I* does.

We focus in this chapter on the two main contributions of form in sentences: (a) the literal content of a sentence, that is, the relationships that the sentence expresses and the properties that are attributed to the participants; and (b) the function of the sentence, that is, whether it is a statement, a question, or a request or command.

Some Errors in English

As before, we begin with some typical errors that learners of English make because the rules of their language are different from those of English. These errors highlight the differences.[1]

Dutch
(1) I must at once my sister see.

German
(2) You speak very well German.
(3) On Tuesday have we a holiday.

French
(4) She lives not in Paris.
(5) The telephone they repaired it?
(6) She is the woman the most beautiful that I know.

Italian
(7) Can you suggest us a good restaurant?
(8) Say me the truth.

Spanish
(9) Do you can swim?
     Maria cans swim.
(10) I no understand.

Russian
(11) At what are you looking?
     With whom were you talking when I saw you?
(12) New house is building near cinema that is near us.
(13) I have many money.

Polish
(14) Tell me where are they.
     She wants to know what do you want.

Persian
(15) The man, which I saw him, . . .
     The book, which I gave it to you, . . .

---

1. These errors are taken from the book *Learner English,* by Michael Swan and Bernard Smith, a rich compendium of errors that native speakers of languages other than English make when learning English.

Arabic

(16) I went to the store for buy some clothes.

(17) He was soldier.

Chinese

(18) This is a very difficult to solve problem.

Korean

(19) Many foreigners exist in Seoul.

(20) Tomorrow will hot.

These examples demonstrate that there are two basic factors that go into expressing an idea in a language: the particular words that are used and the order in which they appear. For example, in the Dutch example (1), the words are well chosen, but the order is wrong—the verb *see* should come before *my sister,* which should come before *at once.* The order should be *I must see my sister at once.* This error reflects the fact that the order in the Dutch verb phrase is the reverse of the order in the English verb phrase. In particular, the verb appears at the end of the verb phrase in this kind of sentence in Dutch, while it begins the verb phrase in English.

On the other hand, in the Italian example (8), the error consists of the fact that the verb *say* does not function like *tell. Tell me the truth* is grammatical but **Say me the truth* is not. This error reflects the fact that Italian uses the same word to express both 'say' and 'tell.'

Let's look more closely at how an English sentence is constructed and at some of the ways in which other languages differ from English.

Verbs and Verb Phrases

The key to expressing a property or relation is the verb, so we will begin with verbs and the phrases that are built around them. With each verb are associated a number of **roles,** which distinguish the various participants in a relation. The participants are typically indicated by the noun phrases. For example, in a sentence like *The dog gave its owner the ball,* there are three roles: the thing given (the ball), the giver (the dog), and the recipient (the owner).

(21) dog   GIVER
     ball   THING GIVEN
     owner RECIPIENT

These roles are associated with the verb and form a central part of the verb's meaning. There may be several verbs in the language that express the same general type of event; in this case, for example, similar verbs are *send, sell, lend,* and so on. Each verb refers to a relation in which something is going from one individual to another. What differs from one verb to another are the fine details of how this transmission takes place and the nature of possession involved. So, for example, *lend* is a nonpermanent transfer of possession, *sell* involves money, *send* involves some medium of transmission (such as the Internet), and so on. What is fundamentally important is that every language is able to express these relations, and it does so by distinguishing the participants in terms of what we have called 'form'—the order of words and their grammatical marking.

Grammatical Structure and Roles

The grammatical structure of the sentence serves to distinguish the participants in a relation from one another and specifies which one is playing which role.

Let's look closely at verbs and consider how they are used in sentences to express specific meanings. We begin with a few simple sentences that we have already discussed. We can create them from the familiar table 13.1.

● **TABLE 13.1**
A Menu for Making Simple English Sentences

A	B	C
The	dog	barked
A	cat	hissed
This	pig	grunted
That	rooster	crowed

(22) The dog barked.
⊗The dog hissed.
The dog grunted.
⊗The dog crowed.

As before, we use the symbol ⊗ to indicate that a sentence like *The dog crowed* has an odd meaning. The form of these sentences is not a problem—they have the same basic form as the good sentences, like *The dog barked*. This distinction between whether the meaning is good or not and whether the form of the sentence is good or not is an important one.

Table 13.1 indicates the order in which words may appear so that they constitute a grammatical English sentence. (This is part of what we have called *form*.) We already know something about the noun phrase *the dog*; it is an expression that refers to some dog that we are aware of or have been talking about. It satisfies the Determiner Rule, so it conforms to a rule of English. Since the words of column C appear to function in more or less the same way to help form sentences, it is reasonable to conclude that they form a category. This category, **verb**, is distinct from the category **noun**: you can't put a verb into the position occupied by a noun and get a good sentence: *The hissed grunted.*[2]

Since all of these sentences have certain things in common, it is possible to say in a more general way what a simple English sentence looks like. Consider the sentences *The dog barked* and *The dog chased the cat*. Regardless of what follows the verb in these examples, there is a noun phrase preceding the verb. This is true no matter what form the noun phrase takes; we could use *the huge dog* or *the huge howling dog* or whatever, and it wouldn't matter.

(23) The huge dog barked.
      The huge dog chased the cat.
      The huge howling dog barked.
      The huge howling dog chased the cat.
      and so on.

Our intuition as native speakers is that the thing this phrase refers to is playing the same role with respect to the action described by the verb. This role, which is that of the initiator or causer of a voluntary act, is called the **agent** of the act. We will have more to say about roles in the next section.

Since we have rules that say how to make a noun phrase in English, we do not need to list all of the possible components in separate columns. We can just use one column for all of the noun phrases, as shown in table 13.2. What this says is that we can create any noun phrase we want, and then follow it with a verb, and so on, and we will get a sentence.

● **TABLE 13.2**
Preliminary Rules for Forming an English Sentence

A	B	C	D
[**noun phrase**]	barked		
[**noun phrase**]	chased	the	cat
[**noun phrase**]	grunted		
[**noun phrase**]	hissed		
[**noun phrase**]	opened	the	door
[**noun phrase**]	crowed		

---

2. A notable property of English is that many words can be used both as nouns and as verbs. Only the context in which the word appears tells us what its category is. For example, we can have *the chair* and *chair a meeting*, *a hand* and *hand me the hammer*, *a ferocious kick* and *kick the ball*. In some other languages, nouns and verbs have distinctive forms that reflect their categories.

You may have also noticed that what follows the verbs *chased* and *opened* looks like a noun phrase, too. In fact it is true that because of their meanings, some verbs must or may occur with a second noun phrase; these are called **transitive** verbs. Other verbs, because of their meaning, cannot have a noun phrase following them. These are called **intransitive** verbs. In English, the second noun phrase typically follows the transitive verb.

(24) The dog chased the cat.
     The dog chased the rooster.
     ☹The dog chased the door.
     *The dog grunted the cat.
     *The dog hissed the door.

We have called the noun phrase that follows the verb the **object**; it is sometimes called the **direct object**; we say that some verbs, like *chase*, **select** direct objects while others, like *hiss*, do not.

Transitive and Intransitive

- An **intransitive** verb refers to an event or state that has only one participant, for example, *grunt*.
- A **transitive** verb refers to a relationship between two or more participants, for example, *chase*.

But notice that if a verb selects an object, the object cannot precede the verb, as shown in (25).

(25)

Object before verb	*Object after verb*
*The huge dog <u>the cat</u> chased.	The huge dog chased <u>the cat</u>.
*The huge howling dog <u>the cat</u> chased.	The huge howling dog chased <u>the cat</u>.
*The cat <u>the door</u> opened.	The cat opened <u>the door</u>.
*My roommate <u>the beer</u> drank.	My roommate drank <u>the beer</u>.
*The fire <u>the house</u> destroyed.	The fire destroyed <u>the house</u>.
and so on.	

Notice also that where the noun phrase goes determines what role the thing that it refers to plays in the event. In *The dog chases the cat,* the agent is *the dog,* and the thing chased is *the cat,* not the other way around. *The cat chases the dog* describes a very different scenario. This is a very simple but important illustration of how form is used in a language to convey meaning.

These observations suggest several things. First, like the noun, the verb appears in a phrase, and it is the verb phrase (i.e., the verb plus the object, if it selects one) that describes the type of action. We can use the method of columns to summarize the form of a verb phrase in English, as in table 13.3. What this says is that verb phrases can be formed from intransitive verbs alone (like *hissed* and *grunted*) or by combining a transitive verb with a following noun phrase (like *chased the cat*).

Second, whether a verb phrase can consist of an intransitive verb alone or a transitive verb and an object depends largely on the meaning of the verb.[3] Let's state the rule for the verb phrase now.

● **TABLE 13.3**
English Verb Phrases

A	B
hissed	
grunted	
chased	[noun phrase]
opened	[noun phrase]

Verb Phrase Rule (English)

A verb phrase consists of a verb, possibly followed by a noun phrase (the Direct Object).

Restrictions:

- A verb has a direct object in the verb phrase only if the meaning of the verb allows for a direct object.
- A verb cannot have a direct object if its meaning does not allow for a direct object.

Identifying the Participants in an Event or State

As we have noted, an important function of grammar concerns the roles played by the participants in an action expressed by a sentence, that is, how they match up with the phrases in the sentence. Let's now look at this function in more detail.

To see how important it is to get the roles of the various individuals right, consider the automatic translation from English to German and back to English in table 13.4. The German sentences correspond word for word to the English ones: *die* 'the,' *Kinder* 'children,' *Kartoffeln* 'potatoes,' *bereit* 'ready,' *zu* 'to,' *essen* 'eat, have dinner.'

---

3. There are some verbs, like *eat* and *drink,* that may be either transitive or intransitive, with essentially the same meaning.

- **TABLE 13.4**
  A German-to-English-to-German Translation

English	To German	Back to English
1. The children are ready to eat.	Die Kinder sind bereit zu essen.	The children are ready to have dinner.
2. The potatoes are ready to eat.	Die Kartoffeln sind bereit zu essen.	The potatoes are ready to have dinner.

The bad translation of *The potatoes are ready to eat,* and the comparison of the examples, illustrate this very central function of verbs. The difference between numbers 1 and 2 is that the children are the ones who will be performing the action of eating in 1 (they are **agents**), and the potatoes are, by contrast, the things that will be eaten in 2; they will have something done to them (we say that the potatoes are the **theme** of the eating event). But the automatic translation software does not pick up this distinction and treats potatoes as though they were performing an action.

Roles

There are many verbs that involve only one participant. In these cases, we find that the phrase which refers to the participant occupies the subject position in the English sentence.

(26) Robin is snoring.
      Someone called.
      Albert fell.
      The bomb exploded.
      My goldfish died.

When a sentence describes an event that is caused by a living creature, such as a person or an animal, the cause is the **agent**. *Robin* is an agent in *Robin is snoring,* and *someone* is an agent in *Someone called.* But as the examples in (26) show, there are many sentences where the cause is not mentioned in the sentence, yet something happens. Albert falls, moving from a higher position to a lower position (ouch!). The bomb explodes, changing from an intact bomb into a bunch of pieces. My goldfish goes from the state of being alive to the state of being dead. The thing that changes state in sentences like these is also called the **theme**.

In addition, actions can be caused by inanimate things. For example, we can say *The rock broke the window.* In this case, the rock was the **instrument** that caused the breaking of the window, but it was not an agent because it did not act on its own to break the window.[4]

Basic Roles

Agent: The individual (animate thing) that causes or initiates an action.
Theme: The entity that undergoes a change of state or is acted on by an agent.
Instrument: Typically an inanimate thing that brings about a change.

In English, the positions to the left and the right of the verb are special. The phrase to the left is what we have called the **subject** and the one to the right the (direct) **object.** These are called the **grammatical functions.** We see that the subject of the sentence plays the agent role in the event of *chasing,* while the object plays the theme role in this event. By distinguishing subject and object, speakers of English are able to keep track of the participants in a direct action: the agent of chasing is expressed as the subject, and the theme is expressed as the object.

This **matching up** of subject with agent and object with theme holds for the vast majority of English verbs that express direct actions. But the positions in a sentence are used to keep track of other roles as well, that is, for verbs that express not direct actions but rather states and various types of events. So, for example, in the sentence *I received a letter,* the subject does not cause the action and is not an agent. It has the same word order and structure as *I wrote a letter,* but the role of *I* is different in the two sentences.

For this reason, we have to distinguish the positions and the grammatical relations from the roles. Being a subject has to do with the form, while being an agent or having some other role has to do with the meaning. The subject in English is simply the noun phrase that precedes the verb and agrees with it. Its role depends on the particular verb.

Similarly, if you feel the rain on your face, you are not initiating any action, but you know that the subject of *feel* refers to the individual that is experiencing the sensation.

(27) I feel the rain on my face.

So you are not an agent in this case, but an **experiencer.** But the verb is transitive; it has a subject *I* and a direct object *the rain.*

Finally, some verbs describe transfer of possession from one individual to another, for example, *Sandy gave Chris the money.* In such cases, what is being transferred is the theme, while the destination of the transfer is the **goal** (or **recipient**).

---

4. An animate entity can be an instrument if it is a cause but does not act with intention. For example, if you lose your balance and knock over a glass of water, you are the instrument of spilling the water, but not the agent.

Notice that in *Sandy gave Chris the money,* there are two noun phrases following the verb. Only one can be the direct object; in this case, it is *the money,* which is the theme, because it undergoes the change of possession. The noun phrase that refers to the goal is typically called the **indirect object.** Notice also that the indirect object precedes the direct object in English.

Other Roles

Instrument: A cause that lacks intention.
Experiencer: Animate entity that undergoes a feeling, perception, or emotion.
Goal: The recipient of a change of possession.

We say that the verb **governs** the roles that depend on it. Some verbs, like *snore,* govern one role, that of agent. Some verbs, like *bite,* govern two roles. In the simple case, one role is associated with the subject and a second role is associated with the object, as we have seen. But we have seen that the situation can be more complicated: in some cases, a verb governs more than two roles. And when this occurs, one of the roles is associated with a phrase that is neither the subject nor the direct object, but something else.

Roles and Grammatical Functions

- An English sentence typically has a **subject.**
- A sentence with an **intransitive** verb has a **subject**; a sentence with a **transitive** verb has a **subject** and an **object.** Certain verbs take an **indirect object** as well.
- The **roles** associated with subject, object, and indirect object depend on the **meaning** of the verb.

Subject and Object across Languages

The roles assigned to the participants referred to in a sentence are part of the literal content of the sentence. How each role gets assigned depends on the form of the sentence. The need to express the roles of individuals in an event or a state is not a special property of English. It is something that all languages do, because talking about events, relationships, properties, and states is what people use language for (among other things). So all languages must have a way of indicating in a sentence which participant is the agent, which is the theme, and so on. Typically, languages do this by distinguishing the noun phrases in terms of their form or position in the sentence.

There are three main ways in which languages distinguish subject and object. As we have just noted, English does it by position (also called **word order**). Other languages do it by **case,** which is a marking on the noun phrase, or by **agreement** with the verb. We illustrate each of these below.

WORD ORDER

French is similar to English in the way it uses word order to distinguish subject and object. But in French, there are no indirect objects like there are in English. (As before, the asterisk indicates that the sentence is not grammatical in the language.)

(28) Je donne le livre   à Marie.
     I give the book to Mary.

     *Je donne Marie   le livre.
     I give Mary   the book.

In French, the goal role is marked by the preposition *à*.

(29) Je donne   le livre à   Marie.
     agent   **theme**   **goal**

In Ojibwa, the direct object comes before the indirect object. (The subject is incorporated into the verb in this example.)

(30) **Ojibwa (Algonquian)**
     Ngi:mina: mzinhigan   Ža:bdi:s.
     I-gave-it book   John
     agent   **theme**   **goal**
     'I gave John a book.'

And in Palauan and Kinyarwanda, the indirect object comes before the direct object, just like in English.

(31) **Palauan**
     Ak   milstęrir   a ręsęchęlik a hong.
     I   give   my friends a book
     agent   **goal**   **theme**
     'I give my friends a book.'

(32) **Kinyarwanda**
     Umugóre aréereka ábáana   amashusho.
     woman   shows   children   pictures
     agent   **goal**   **theme**
     'The woman is showing the children pictures.'
     (Examples from Y. N. Falk (n.d.))

Notice two important things about these examples. First, the roles associated with the verb are the same to the extent that the verbs mean the same things in the different languages. This is because these verbs express typical relationships that exist in all human societies, such as giving and showing, and all languages have words for these relationships. But different languages use different word orders to designate which part of the sentence corresponds to which role. As we see in the next section, there are languages in which word order is not used for this function; rather, it is done by marking the noun phrases to indicate their grammatical functions.

CASE

Case is used to mark the function of a noun phrase in a sentence, regardless of where it is located. Consider again these examples from Japanese.

(33) John   ga   sono tegami   o   yon-da.
     John   NOM   that letter   ACC   read-PAST
     'John read that letter.'

     John   ga   sono tegami   o   yon-da-ka.
     John   NOM   that letter   ACC   read-PAST-QUESTION
     'Did John read that letter?'

Notice that we did not say earlier what the meanings of *ga* and *o* are. That is because they have no meanings—they have grammatical functions. The particle *ga* indicates that *John* is the subject of *yon-da* 'read,' while the particle *o* indicates that *sono tegami* 'that letter' is the object. Therefore, *John* gets the agent role, and *sono tegami* gets the theme role.

Because of this fact, the Japanese subject and object can be in a different order with respect to one another in the sentence, and it is still possible to figure out who is causing the action, and what is undergoing it.

(34) Sono   tegami   o   John   ga   yon-da.
     that   letter   ACC   John   NOM   read-PAST
     'John read that letter.'

     Sono   tegami   o   John   ga   yon-da-ka.
     that   letter   ACC   John   NOM   read-PAST-QUESTION
     'Did John read that letter?'

Similarly, when there is a direct object and an indirect object, either order of objects is possible.

(35) John **ga**   Mary ni sono hon   **o**   miseta.
John NOM   Mary to that   book ACC   showed
'John showed that book to Mary.'

John **ga**   sono hon   **o**   Mary ni miseta.
John NOM   that   book ACC   Mary to showed
'John showed that book to Mary.'

Notice here that the noun phrase that refers to the goal is marked with the case marker *ni*, which we translate as 'to.'

This flexibility of word order is found in many other languages that use case, like Russian and German. In such languages, case is indicated not by particles, as it is in Japanese, but by modifications in the form of words, or **morphology.** For example, here are some forms used in Russian for the subject and object.

(36) **Russian**

	subject (nominative case)	object (accusative case)
'book'	kniga	knigu
'man'	ot'ets	otsa
'beer'	pivo	pivo

So if you say *The book fell* in Russian, you use the form *kniga* to refer to the book, since it is the subject, but if you say *I read the book*, you use the form *knigu*, since it is the direct object. Similarly, for *The man fell* you use the form *ot'ets*, but for *I saw the man* you use the form *otsa*. But some words do not show this particular variation in form, as seen with *pivo*.

In addition to nominative (NOM) and accusative (ACC) case, Russian has other cases, including dative (DAT), instrumental (INSTR), and genitive (GEN). All of these have many uses. Dative case is a typical way to indicate the goal of giving, instrumental case can be used to indicate that some action was accomplished, and genitive case is used to express possession, among other things. Here's an example in which all five cases are used. We give the Russian sentence using the Russian alphabet and then transliterate it into the Roman alphabet, just for fun.

(37) Анна   руками   дала Ивану   голубую   книгу   Игоря.
Anna   rukami   dala Ivanu   golubuju knigu   Igor'a
Anna-NOM hands-INSTR gave Ivan-DAT blue-ACC book-ACC Igor-GEN
'Anna gave Igor's blue book to Ivan with her hands.'

Notice that both *golubuju* 'blue' and *knigu* 'book' are marked with the accusative case. We say that they must **agree** with one another in case. This type of agreement is similar to what we saw in chapter 11 with respect to gender and number agreement in French and Italian noun phrases.

Exercise 1: English Case

English shows a remnant of an earlier case system in the form of the pronouns, such as *I, me, she, her, he, him, his, we, us, they, them, who, whom, whose,* but nowhere else in the language. Which of these words are nominative case forms (used for subject), which are accusative (used for object), and which are genitive (used for possession)? Using your answer to this question, explain why the following sentences are ungrammatical.

　　*Me like you very much.
　　*Please give it to I.
　　*Whom is hungry?

AGREEMENT

Agreement between the noun phrases and the verb is yet a third way to indicate the function of a phrase.

In a language that uses this type of agreement, the form of a noun is the same regardless of whether it is subject or object, just as in English. But the verb has a form that is determined by particular properties of the subject and, in some languages, the object.

Consider the following examples from Swahili. As we noted in chapter 11, Swahili has fifteen noun classes. Interestingly, in a sentence, the verb typically displays a marker that is the same as the class marker of the subject and another marker that is the same as the class marker of the object. The verb is said to agree with subject and object. *Agreement* means that the forms match according to specific rules of the language.

Here are some examples. The class marker is indicated by a number. SG means 'singular' and PL means 'plural.' INDIC abbreviates 'indicative,' meaning roughly that the sentence is about a concrete reality and is not a hypothetical or an imperative, and PP means 'present progressive.'

Swahili

(38) Juma a-li-mw-on-a　　　　　Mariam.
　　Juma 3SG-past-3SG-see-INDIC　Mariam
　　'Juma saw Mariam.'

　　M-toto　　　a-ni-ki-soma　　ki-tabu.
　　1SG-child　1SG-PP-7SG-read　7SG-book
　　'The child is reading the book.'

　　Ki-tabu　　wa-na-ki-soma　　wa-toto.
　　7SG-book　2PL-PP-7SG-read　2PL-child
　　'The children are reading the book.'

While the precise shape of the class markers attached to a verb may be different from that attached to a noun, the class marker attached to the verb is specifically chosen for the class of the noun that it agrees with.

PREPOSITIONS

In English some roles may be expressed by another type of phrase, called a **prepositional phrase.** Some examples are given in (39). The words marked in boldface are members of the category **preposition.** The prepositional phrases are underlined.

(39) a. Sandy sailed   **to** <u>Salem</u>.
         agent   **goal**

b. Sandy smashed   the window   <u>**with** a hammer</u>.
    agent   **theme**   **instrument**

Here is another example with three roles.

(40) I borrowed this book <u>**from** the library</u>.

In this sentence, the role of one of the participants in the scene, the library, is identified by using a preposition. The preposition in this sentence identifies the source of the book. The source is the origin of the change. Notice that this role is associated with neither subject nor object, but with a preposition.

The reason why this example is important is that it shows that verbs and prepositions can work together to identify certain roles in the sentence. The verb governs certain roles directly, through the subject and object, and the prepositions supply the others.

We have seen that the position of a noun phrase can perform this function in English; for example, the subject of *give* is the agent, and there can be two objects. But while the concept of borrowing involves three roles—an agent, a theme, and a source—*borrowed* in (40) does not appear with two objects.

(41) *I borrowed the library the book.

The proposition *from* has to be used to mark the source on behalf of the verb *borrow.*

The phenomenon that we see here is very widespread. It is so important because in order to use a verb correctly, we must know how to identify all of the participants in the scene described by the verb.

Actives and Passives

In most languages there is more than one way to identify the roles governed by a verb. Thinking about the English sentences that we have discussed thus far, we see that there is one general pattern, which we will state as a rule. First, let's consider the pattern illustrated by these examples.

(42) a. Robin was snoring
     b. The dog bit the cat.
     c. The bomb exploded.

In the first example (42a), the subject refers to the agent, and there is no theme. In the second example, the subject refers to the agent, and there is a theme. In the third example, there is no agent, and the subject is the theme.

These examples illustrate a general pattern, which is that the subject is reserved for the agent if there is one; if there is not, the subject can identify other roles. So we do not expect to find a simple sentence of English with an agent where the agent is not the subject. We summarize our observations in the form of the Agent/Theme Rule.

Agent/Theme Rule (English)

1. If a verb governs the agent role, this role is expressed by the subject.
2. If a verb governs the theme role, and if there is an agent, this role is expressed by:

    a. the direct object, or
    b. the object of a preposition, depending on the verb.

3. If there is no agent, the theme role is expressed by the subject.

Restriction: Clause 3 has exceptions.

One type of exception to clause 3 involves verbs such as *receive,* which expresses its theme as direct object and a role other than agent as subject.

(43) I | received | some email | today   (from Pat).
     goal   **theme**   **source**

These exceptions have to be learned as part of the meaning of the particular verb.

The Agent/Theme Rule seems a bit rigid because it says that if there is an agent, it must be the subject. Fortunately, many languages, including English, have ways to get around such rigid rules and introduce some flexibility and variety in how the roles are identified. In English this flexibility is achieved through the use of the **passive** construction, illustrated by the following pairs of sentences.

(44) The dog bit the cat.
　　　The cat was bitten by the dog.

　　　Pat opened the door.
　　　The door was opened by Pat.

In the first pair of sentences, the agent is the dog; in the second pair, the agent is Pat. But in *The cat was bitten by the dog*, the subject is not the agent, but the theme. And the agent is the object of the preposition *by*. A similar observation can be made about the second pair of sentences.

　　　Looking closely at these sentences, we see that there is a pattern. We use figure 13.1 to pick out the significant features that participate in this pattern. What we see here is that we can put the direct object into the subject position, and the subject into the preposition phrase with *by*, if we also change the verb *chased* into *was chased*. (The present tense form *chases* is changed into *is chased*.) These two ways of identifying the roles governed by a verb are called **active** and **passive.**

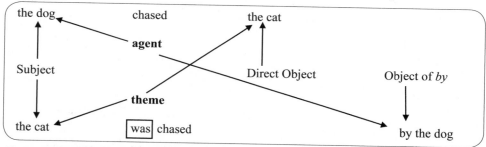

Figure 13.1. Roles of the Passive Construction

　　　The form of the verb in the passive is that of the past tense in English for regular verbs and a special form for irregular verbs. We call this form the **passive participle.**

(45)　　**Present**　　　Past　　　　　**Passive Participle**
　　　Regular
　　　　chase　　　　chased　　　　chased
　　　　deliver　　　delivered　　　delivered
　　　　carry　　　　carried　　　　carried
　　　　toss　　　　　tossed　　　　tossed
　　　　cook　　　　　cooked　　　　cooked
　　　Irregular
　　　　eat　　　　　ate　　　　　　eaten
　　　　see　　　　　saw　　　　　　seen
　　　　write　　　　wrote　　　　　written
　　　　know　　　　knew　　　　　known
　　　　give　　　　　gave　　　　　given

Active and passive are very general constructions. For almost every active there is a passive, and vice versa, with some limited exceptions. The subject does not have to be an agent; it can be a recipient, as with *receive*, or an experiencer, as with *see, hear,* and so on.

(46) Robin received some email.
Some email was received by Robin.

Leslie saw the dog.
The dog was seen by Leslie.

Pat heard the music.
The music was heard by Pat.
and so on.

Now here is something very important to observe about the passive. Suppose that you wanted to express the idea that something chased the cat, but you didn't know who or what the agent was. You could say

(47) Something chased the cat.

but you couldn't say

(48) *Chased the cat.

as a full sentence. This is because of the requirement that every nonimperative sentence in English has a subject.[5]

The passive gives us another way to avoid mentioning the agent in this type of case, because in the passive, the requirement that there is a subject is satisfied by the noun phrase that expresses the theme (in the case of *chase*), that is, the direct object. We can leave out the prepositional phrase and express just the idea that we want, namely, that we don't know or don't care who or what the agent is.

(49) The cat was chased.

Because a different role is identified by the subject, the sentence has a somewhat different emphasis than the active and can be used for stylistic variety.

Notice that this trick can be used regardless of what role the direct object of the active expresses. We can say

(50) The door was opened.
Some email was received.

---

5. Some would say that the imperative, as in *Eat your vegetables!,* has a subject, namely, *you,* but it is invisible.

The dog was seen.
The music was heard.
and so on.

The role that is associated with the direct object in the active is associated with the subject in the passive. This observation gets us to our next rule, the Active/Passive Rule.

Active/Passive Rule (English)

A statement can be

1. active, with roles expressed by subject and object, or
2. passive, with

   a. a form of the auxiliary verb *be* followed by the passive participle,
   b. the direct object role expressed by the subject, and
   c. the subject role expressed by the object of *by*, or not expressed at all in the sentence.

Exercise 2: Passives

In the following groups of three sentences, there is an active, a passive, and a third type of sentence. While the roles expressed are the same, the grammatical properties of the sentences differ. Describe the grammatical differences between the first, second, and third sentences in each group of three. Which one is passive? Why?

[1] The storm sank the boat.
    The boat was sunk by the storm.
    The boat sunk in the storm.

[2] The wind opened the door.
    The door was opened by the wind.
    The door opened in the wind.

[3] Sandy sent Leslie a letter.
    Leslie was sent a letter by Sandy.
    Leslie got a letter from Sandy.

Summary

In this chapter we looked at the content of a sentence—in particular, the relationships that the sentence expresses and the properties that are attributed to participants. We discussed how roles such as theme, agent, and goal can be expressed by case, particles, word order, or verbal agreement in different languages. Then we looked at how the form of a verb plays a role in determining the content and function of the sentence. We compared how this is done in English with how it is done in other languages. Verbs in some languages use inflection to mark distinctions of time and aspect. The verb is also typically involved in marking whether a sentence is a statement, an imperative, or a question.

Additional Exercises

1. Choose a language that you are familiar with other than English. What is the basic form of the verb phrase in this language? Where does the direct object go in a transitive sentence, and if there are two objects, where do they go with respect to the verb?

2. Choose a language that you are familiar with other than English. How are subject and object distinguished in this language? Do the rules involve word order, morphological form, or both?

3. Choose a language that you are familiar with other than English. Are there alternative ways of expressing the same roles in this language that are similar to the active/passive alternation in English? How is the passive distinguished from the active?

4. The examples in (1)–(20) in the text illustrate some typical errors that non-native speakers of English make in English. We have already discussed (1) and (8). For the remaining errors, say what the error consists of (that is, what the speaker did wrong), how to correct the error, and why you think that the error occurred. In some cases, the error may show something about the speaker's language, while in other cases, the speaker may be misapplying a rule of English. Try to describe what aspect of English is being modified by the non-native speaker and what the differences are in the way that English and the other language carry out the same function. (You can say what the grammatical English variant would be, but also try to describe what the difference is in a general way.)

5. Choose a language other than English that you are familiar with. How is the relation expressed by the English word *afraid* expressed in this language? Does the language designate who is afraid and what that person is afraid of in the same way as English does?

6. Choose a language other than English that you are familiar with. How is the relation expressed by the English word *likes* expressed in this language? Does the language designate who does the liking and what that person likes in the same way as English does?

7. Choose a language other than English that you are familiar with. How are the roles expressed by the arguments of words such as *give, tell, sell, send* in English designated in this language? Compare this with how English designates these arguments.

8. Many verbs in English combine with prepositions to express specific meanings. For example, *look for* means 'seek,' *look at* means 'observe,' *look after* means 'guard' or 'oversee,' and so on.

    a. How many other prepositions can you find that combine with *look* to express special meanings?

    b. Find other verbs in English that combine with a range of prepositions in this way, and say what the different meanings are.

    c. Choose a language other than English that you are familiar with. To what extent do the verb + preposition pairs in English in parts (a) and (b) translate literally into this language? Does this language use verb + preposition pairs in the same way that English does? If not, what are the differences?

References

Falk, Y. N. (n.d.) Ditransitive constructions. Online: pluto.mscc.huji.ac.il/~msyfalk/Typology/English/Ditransitives.pdf.

Swan, Michael, and Bernard Smith. 2001. *Learner English: A teacher's guide to interference and other problems,* 2nd ed. Cambridge: Cambridge University Press.

Talking about Time

Introduction

As we have seen, a typical sentence of a language expresses a relationship between entities or a property. We have not yet discussed another important aspect of sentences that many languages also express, which has to do with the time of such a relationship or property. As a language learner, you will have to come to terms with the different ways in which your native language and the language you are learning deal with time.

To get a feel for how this part of language works, let's take a look at some more examples showing a "foreign accent" in English.

(1) a. They still discuss the problem.
     b. I study here for a year.
     c. She avoids to go.
     d. I want that you stay.
     e. I can't to fix that!

Compare these to the correct forms.

(2) a. They <u>are</u> still discuss<u>ing</u> the problem.
     b. I <u>have</u> <u>been</u> study<u>ing</u> here for a year.
     c. She avoids ~~to~~ go<u>ing</u>.
     d. I want ~~that~~ you <u>to</u> stay.
     e. I can't ~~to~~ fix that!

Example (2a) shows that in order to talk about an ongoing event, it is necessary to use a form of the auxiliary verb *be* and a main verb with *-ing*. For something spanning a period of time that began in the past and includes the present, *have been . . . -ing* is necessary, as shown by example (2b).

The other three examples illustrate other subtle details about what form of the verb appears in various contexts. The verb *avoid* occurs only with a verb in the *-ing* form, as contrasted, for example, with the verb *try,* which occurs either with *-ing* or *to,* and *want,* which only occurs with *to.*

(3)   a.   She tried to go.
     b.   She tried going.
     c.   She wanted to call.
     d.   *She wanted calling.

The verb *want* occurs only with *to,* and not with a full clause that begins with *that.* In other languages, such as German, the literal translation of (1d)—*I want that you stay*— would be the way to say this.

(4)   Ich   will,   dass   du   bleibst.
     I   want   that   you   stay
     'I want you to stay.'

And the verb *can't* must appear with the 'bare' form of the verb, that is, one that lacks 'to.' In many languages, such as German, the form of the verb that appears with the counterpart to *can* is translated as the English infinitival *to.*

(5) Ich   kann   das   nicht   reparieren!
   I   can   that   not   to-repair
   'I can't fix that!'

Getting this aspect of the grammar right, in English and in other languages, is an important part of speaking without an "accent." Moreover, it is one of the most difficult areas of grammar for non-natives to master. Let's take a look at the kinds of meaning differences that are expressed by differences in verb form.

Tense and Time

When the sentence is a statement, the verb can have different forms. We will use the most extreme English case to illustrate this phenomenon, that of the verb *to be.*

(6)   I <u>am</u> here now.   I <u>was</u> here yesterday.
     You <u>are</u> there now.   You <u>were</u> here yesterday.

He <u>is</u> here now.   He <u>was</u> here yesterday.
We <u>are</u> here now.   We <u>were</u> here yesterday.
They <u>are</u> there now.   They <u>were</u> there yesterday.

There are five different forms of the verb that are used in sentences like the ones above: *am, was, is, were,* and *are.* Notice that while we say that the verb is "(to) be," the form *be* does not actually appear in this list. Moreover, some of the verb forms are used to refer to a situation in the present (*am, is, are*), while others are used to refer to a situation in the past (*was, were*).

The different forms of a word make up its **inflections.** The inflections of a verb make up its **conjugation.** The part of the conjugation (i.e., the particular verb form) that plays a role in expressing the time is called **tense.** In these examples we have illustrated **present tense** and **past tense.** Present tense of the verb *be* is expressed by *am, is,* and *are.* Past tense is illustrated by *was* and *were.*

The reason to focus on English conjugations is of course not to teach you about how English works, but to highlight the fact that verb form can be a critical part of what makes up a grammatical sentence in a language. Other languages have conjugations too, and they can be more elaborate than those of English. Here's the English conjugation in (2) translated into French. (The verb forms are underlined; *vous* means 'you,' *il* means 'he,' *nous* means 'we,' *ils* means 'they,' *maintenant* means 'now,' and *hier* means 'yesterday.')

(7) Je <u>suis</u> ici maintenant.   J'<u>étais</u> ici hier.
'I am here now.'   'I was here yesterday.' and so on
Vous <u>êtes</u> ici maintenant.   Vous <u>étiez</u> ici hier.
Il <u>est</u> ici maintenant.   Il <u>était</u> ici hier.
Nous <u>sommes</u> ici maintenant.   Nous <u>étions</u> ici hier.
Ils <u>sont</u> ici maintenant.   Ils <u>étaient</u> ici hier.

And some languages are more complex in cases where English is simple. Here is the present tense of *sourire* 'to smile.' Notice how the French verb takes five different forms, while the English verb takes only two forms.

(8) **French**   **English**
Je sour<u>is</u>.   I smile.
Tu sour<u>is</u>.   You (singular) smile.
Il sour<u>it</u>.   He smile<u>s</u>.
Nous sour<u>ions</u>.   We smile.
Vous sour<u>iez</u>.   You (plural) smile.
Ils sour<u>ient</u>.   They smile.

It is important to recognize that tense has to do with the **form** of a verb. This formal aspect of the verb must be distinguished from **time,** which has to do with **meaning.** In

English we can refer to many different times, including the future, but we do not use different forms of the verb in every case. For example, to express the future time of the event 'I see my friend' we could say

(9)   a.   I <u>will</u> see my friend tomorrow.
      b.   I <u>am going</u> to see my friend tomorrow.
      c.   I <u>am</u> see<u>ing</u> my friend tomorrow.

or even

      d.   I see my friend tomorrow.

or

      e.   I <u>am about to</u> see my friend tomorrow.
      f.   I <u>am to</u> see my friend tomorrow.

As example (9a) shows, it is possible to refer to the future in English using the verb *will*. *Will* is an **auxiliary** verb (see later discussion) and is also in the present tense. The examples in (9) show that *will* + verb and expressions like *am/is/are going to* + verb, and the verb alone, all used in the present tense form, can express reference to the future. But, importantly, they do not do it by using future tense—from the perspective of verb inflection, English does not have a future tense per se. It has only two tenses, present and past.

The difference between tense and time is a very important one, and it is important not to confuse them.

The Relationship between Time and Tense

Tense has to do with the form of a verb; reference to time has to do with the meaning of a sentence. The meaning may depend on the tense, but it may depend on other things as well, such as expressions that refer to actual times and auxiliary verbs.

As we will see, all languages can refer to time, but not all languages use tense in order to do this. Or they may use tense in some cases (e.g., present tense *see*, past tense *saw*), as in English, but may use another means in other cases (e.g., future reference but present tense *will see, am seeing*). We emphasize once again: **English has no future tense inflection.**

Exercise 1: Time and Tense

For each of these sentences, say what the time is and what the tense is. Is there an exact match between tense and time? If not, what kinds of mismatches are there?

> We welcome your inquiries.
> Did you hear that?
> How long have you lived here?
> When are you going to stop smoking?
> (Phone rings "Ring Ring") That will be the cable guy.
> So then he goes, "Yuck!" And I say, "What's your problem?"
> Can you stop by tomorrow at around 3 PM?
> Dogs bark.

English Auxiliary Verbs

Let's look more closely now at how English uses **auxiliary** verbs to express properties of the time of an event. Example (10) shows the auxiliary verb *will* followed by the main verb *see.*

(10) I will see my friend tomorrow.

Will is a member of the special class of auxiliary verbs called "modal." English has a number of modals that express such notions as future time, necessity, obligation, and possibility: *will, would, must, shall, should, can, could, may, might.* (Notice that all of these can be used to refer to a future event.)

Auxiliary verbs precede the verb in a typical statement in English. The exact position of the auxiliary verb in the sentence is an indicator of the communicative function of that sentence, that is, whether it is a statement or a question; other languages use other formal devices for expressing the function, as we will see in the next chapter.

The next example illustrates the use of auxiliary verbs in the **progressive.**

(11) I am eating a pizza.

The progressive is complex in form; it is a **verbal cluster** made by adding *-ing* to the bare form of the main verb and placing this verb after a form of the auxiliary verb *be.* The *-ing* form is called the **present** (or **progressive**) **participle.** In this particular example, the verb *be* is inflected for present tense, so we get

(12) am eating, is eating, are eating
      and so on.

One key meaning expressed by the progressive is that of an event under way or in progress (which is why it's called the progressive).

The progressive can also be used with past tense to refer to an action that was under way at some time in the past, for example,

(13) I was going, they were going,
       and so on.

Exercise 2: English Auxiliary Verbs

Suppose that you are teaching English to a group of non-native speakers. How would you explain the order in which the following words may appear in two-word sequences in a grammatical English sentence: *must, can, has, have, is, be, been, speak, speaking, spoken.* (For example, *must* and *can* cannot appear together: **must can, *can must,* but *must speak* is possible, and **speak must* is not.) Rather than list all of the possible sequences, try to find the simplest way to explain what makes a two-word sequence grammatical.

Future Tense Inflections in Other Languages

While English has only two formal tenses, present and past, other languages have future tense inflections as well. Here's an illustration, using Spanish next to English.

(14) 'The dog barked at the cat.'   El perro **ladró**   en el gato.
                                        the dog barked to the cat
       'The dog barks at the cat.'   El perro **ladra** en el gato.
                                        the dog barks to the cat
       'The dog will bark at the cat.' El perro **ladrará**   en el gato.
                                        the dog will-bark to the cat

You can see that where English uses an auxiliary verb, Spanish simply uses another form of the verb (and thus does inflect for and have future tense). This is one of the main differences between English and other languages.

Let us see how things work in Russian.

(15) 'The dog barked at the cat.'   Sobaka <u>lajala</u>   v kote.
                                        dog   barked at cat
       'The dog barks at the cat.'   Sobaka <u>laet</u> v kote.
                                        dog   barks at cat
       'The dog will bark at the cat.' Sobaka <u>budet</u> <u>lajat'</u>   v kote.
                                        dog   is   to-bark at cat

Russian uses a present tense form of the verb *be* plus the verb to refer to the future in this case, and it is thus similar to English in not having a future tense, using other means to refer to future time. For another class of verbs (the "perfectives"), Russian expresses the future by using the present tense of the verb itself.

(16) Sobaka zalajet v kote.
     dog   barks   at cat
     'The dog will bark at the cat.'

There are other languages that do not have tense inflections at all. Here is how we would translate reference to different times in Chinese. The form *le* is a particle that denotes completion of the event or what is called "perfective aspect."

(17) Wo zuotian   qu kand ian ying   le.
     I   yesterday go watch movie   PERF
     'I went to the movies yesterday.'

     Wo xianzai   qu kan   dian ying.
     I   today   go watch movie
     'I am going to the movies now.'

     Wo mingtian yao qu kan   dian ying.
     I   tomorrow   go watch movie
     'I will go to the movies tomorrow.'

These examples show that there is no inflection for tense in Chinese—the same form of the verb *qu kan* 'go watch' is used regardless of the time referred to, and the time is expressed directly by an adverb.

What these examples also show is that languages can refer to the present, the past, and the future, whether they have a specific verb form, that is, tense inflections, that pick out a certain time or not. The commonly held notion that some languages cannot express the future because they lack future verb inflection, and that speakers of those languages therefore are unable to think about the future, is mistaken. All people can think about and refer to the future, but different languages provide different grammatical means of doing this. Some use inflectional forms, and some do not.

Aspect

In addition to the time of an event, the form of a verb in some languages can indicate whether the event has been completed or not with respect to a particular time and whether it occurred at a particular point of time or extended over a period of time. These properties are called **aspect.** A event that is marked as completed with respect to some particular time is said to have **perfect** aspect, and an ongoing event is in the **progressive** aspect, as we saw in our discussion of *I am eating a pizza.*

We saw some aspect errors earlier, in (1). Here are some more, with the correct forms in brackets.

(18) a. I have seen him yesterday.   [saw]
      b. All my nineteenth-century ancestors have lived here.   [lived]
      c. I know him for five years.   [have known]
      d. I live in Amsterdam since I was a child.   [have lived]
      e. I have a lot of trouble with John at the moment.   [am having]
      f. This house is belonging to my father.   [belongs]
          (From Swan and Smith 2006)

This area of grammar is a very difficult one for the language learner in every language. It is difficult for learners of English, and it is difficult for English speakers trying to learn other languages. Either the other language doesn't mark the distinctions in the same way as the learner's language does, or it doesn't mark them at all. Boiling the problem down to its essentials, it is the "problem of aspect."

The Problem of Aspect

In English,

- When do we use the simple present: I wash
- When do we use the progressive: I am washing
- When do we use the simple past: I washed
- When do we use the perfect: I have washed
- How do we express the differences between these sentences in languages that do not have exactly the same distinctions?

Consider an event that uses the verb *wash,* for example, washing a window. If you say what is happening at the moment that it occurs, you might say *I am washing the window.* This conveys the idea that the action is ongoing—it has already started, it is occurring now, and it will continue for awhile. If, however, you are speaking now of what happened in the past, you might say *I washed the window.* If there is a question of whether it has been completed with respect to the time of speaking, you might say *I have washed the window (already).* If you shift your perspective into the past and describe your ongoing action from your current position, you might say *I was washing the window.* But if you say simply *I wash the window,* this must mean that you do it habitually.

Given all of this, what must *I have been washing* mean? Why? (All of the forms in the present and past tense are summarized in table 14.1.)

● **TABLE 14.1**

The Aspects of *Wash*

Form	Aspect	Use
I wash	simple present	habitual
I am washing	present progressive	ongoing now
I have washed	present perfect	completed in the past, relevant to the present
I washed	simple past	some time in the past, or habitual in the past
I was washing	past progressive	ongoing in the past
I have been washing	present perfect progressive	ongoing in the past extending into the present
I had been washing	past perfect progressive	ongoing in the past extending into a later time in the past

Aspect in English is expressed by combining *be* and the verb with *-ing* added to it (this is called the **progressive** form of the verb because it expresses an ongoing event) or by combining *have* and the verb with *-ed* or *-en* added to it (this is called the **perfect** form because it expresses a completed event).

Exercise 3

The verb *go* is used in colloquial English to refer to speaking: "So she goes, what did you do with my notebook?" Can all forms of *go* be used in this way, or are there restrictions? If so, what are they? Give examples using the simple past, the present perfect, and so on.

Other languages mark tense and aspect using form, but not all of them do it like English does. For example, Arabic does not mark tense and aspect by adding forms to the beginning or the end of the basic verb. Rather, it changes the pattern of vowels in the word while holding the consonants constant. The following examples illustrate.

(19) **katab** 'write'   **aktub** 'write (completed)'

The basic form of the verb is *k-t-b*, and the various tenses and aspects (and other forms as well) are made by putting particular vowels in the slots before, after or between consonants.

Russian also marks aspect differently than English does. As mentioned above, verbs in Russian come in two varieties, called "imperfective" and "perfective."[1] The same basic meaning may be expressed by two verbs—an imperfective verb and a perfective verb—and the two verbs would be translated the same into English. For example, the verbs *pisat'/na-pisat'* both mean 'to write.'

Typically, an imperfective verb in Russian is used in the present tense to express a habitual or ongoing action in the present, while the perfective is typically used to refer to future time when it is in the present tense. Used in the past tense, the imperfective indicates a habitual or ongoing action in the past, while the perfective is used in the past tense to indicate a completed action. The present tense forms of the verbs meaning 'to write' are in (20), and the past tense forms are in (21).

(20) pisat   '(s/he) writes, is writing'
      napisat   '(s/he) will write'

(21) pisal   'wrote, was writing'
      napisal   'wrote (once)'
      (Examples from Unbegaun 1957:229–32)

Here are a few more pairs of Russian verbs. You can see from these examples not only that the perfective is related to the imperfective in form but also that the relationship is not a regular and predictable one.

(22) **Imperfective**   **Perfective**
     delat'   s-delat'   'to do'
     prosit'   po-prosit'   'to ask'
     davat'   dat'   'to give'

     Ja delaju   'I do, I am doing'
     Ja sdelaju   'I will do'

Exercise 4

Why do you suppose the present tense form of the Russian perfective refers to future time?

---

1. The terms 'perfective' and 'perfect' both have to do with the completedness of an event. There are two terms in part because they arose in different grammatical traditions and in part because different grammars mark completedness in different ways.

Additional Exercises

1. One of the most difficult challenges in any language is to convey the relationship between the time of speaking and the time of an event. Choose a language other than English that you are familiar with. How does this language express the future with respect to the time of speaking? Does it systematically distinguish the near future and the more distant future using grammatical form? Does English make this distinction and, if so, how?

2. Choose a language other than English that you are familiar with. Does the language use the form of the verb to distinguish an activity in the past that extends into the present from one that occurs only in the present? Is there a way to distinguish an event that occurs frequently or habitually from one that is occurring just now?

3. The progressive in English can be used to refer to a future event, as in the following example:

   (i) I am seeing my friend tomorrow for lunch.

   Can you think of a possible reason why the form that indicates an ongoing event can be used to refer to an event in the future?

References

Swan, Michael, and Bernard Smith. 2001. *Learner English: A teacher's guide to interference and other problems,* 2nd ed. Cambridge: Cambridge University Press.

Unbegaun, Boris. 1957. *Russian grammar.* Oxford: Clarendon Press.

The Work That Sentences Do

*I*n this chapter we explore how the form of a sentence is related to how it is used. In order for us to understand how a language works, we must recognize the relationships between the grammatical form of sentences, their literal meaning, and how they function in written and spoken communication.

Expressing Sentence Function

THE MAJOR FUNCTIONS

The major functions of sentences are making statements (declaratives), asking questions (interrogatives), and making requests or issuing orders (imperatives). The form of the sentence typically indicates what its function is.

Sentence Form and Function

FORM	FUNCTION
Declarative Example: You are sitting down.	Makes a statement.
Interrogative Example: Are you sitting down?	Asks a question.
Imperative Example: Sit down.	Makes a request or issues an order.

There are particular rules of English that govern the form that a sentence must have in order to be understood as having a particular function. Here are some typical errors that German learners of English make that highlight how important these rules are.

(1)   a.   When begins the class?
         b.   Bought you the textbook?
         c.   Where goes this train?
         d.   Speaks Ted English?
         e.   Why said you that?

What is happening here? Compare these questions with the correct English forms.

(2)   a.   When does the class begin?
         b.   Did you buy the textbook?
         c.   Where does this train go?
         d.   Does Ted speak English?
         e.   Why did you say that?

In each of the "German" sentences, the main verb, that is, the verb that expresses the relation or action, precedes the subject of the sentence.

(3)   when   begins   the class
         1   2   3

But in the correct English sentence, the main verb follows the subject, and an auxiliary verb precedes the subject.

(4)   when   does   the class   begin
         1   2   3   4

Notice also that auxiliary *does/do/did* appears only if there is no other auxiliary verb, like *have* or *be* or a modal.

(5)   when   will   the class   begin
         1   2   3   4

We cannot say *When does the class will begin?* or *When does will the class begin?*

Rules such as these are challenging for learners of English. Correspondingly, English speakers learning a language such as German have to recognize that there is no form of *do* in German questions. (In fact, very few languages have the counterpart of the English auxiliary *do*.) The word orders in (1) reflect the normal order of German, for example. This is exemplified in (6).

(6) a. Wenn   beginnt   die Klasse?
         when   begins   the class
         'When does the class begin?'
     b. Kauftest   du   das Lehrbuch?
         Bought.2SG   you.SG   the textbook
         'Did you buy the textbook?'

QUESTIONS

There are two types of questions, yes-no (YN) questions like *Are you hungry?* and wh-questions. A competent speaker of English knows implicitly how these functions are expressed in English. As an exercise, before going on see if you can state explicitly what the basic differences in form are between these sentence types (we have already discussed some of these differences previously).

As we have seen, a statement in English has the following basic form: First, there is a phrase that (usually) refers to something, which is typically called the **subject** of the sentence. It is followed by one or more verbs, like *can, am, is, drinks, drank,* and *drinking.* One of these verbs expresses some kind of relationship or property involving the subject (like *drinks*). The verb that expresses this relationship may be followed by other things, depending on the verb and the meaning to be expressed. And there may be auxiliary verbs that express possibility, necessity, and so on, and inflections that express tense and aspect. Hence we may have examples such as those in (7).

(7) I can drink that cup of coffee.
     I am drinking.
     She is drinking quickly.
     A fish drinks water in the lake.
     We drank it all.
     and so on.

In order to keep track of our observations about what we know about English sentences, we introduce table 15.1. What appears between parentheses indicates material that is possible but not necessary in a sentence of this type.

● TABLE 15.1
Form of an English Statement

Function	English Form
Declarative	Subject—(Auxiliary Verb)—Main Verb—(Other stuff)

Now we see that an English question has a form that distinguishes it from the corresponding statement. While the auxiliary verb follows the subject in the statement, it precedes the subject in the question, as we saw in our discussion of errors in questions. So we have the following questions corresponding to the statements just above. Notice again that if the statement does not have an auxiliary verb, the corresponding question has the auxiliary verb *does/do/did*.

(8) Can I drink that cup of coffee?
     Am I drinking?
     Is she drinking quickly?
     Does a fish drink water in the lake?

So let's add questions to table 15.1 to obtain table 15.2.

● **TABLE 15.2**
Form of English Statements and Questions

Function	English Form
Declarative	Subject—(Auxiliary Verb)—Main Verb—(Other stuff)
YN-Question	Auxiliary Verb—Subject—Main Verb—(Other stuff)

Now, as we have said, other languages must express the same functions, but they may use different forms. We have already looked at German. Table 15.3 summarizes the forms of statements and questions in German. (Can you see what the main difference is between German and English?)

● **TABLE 15.3**
Form of German Statements and Questions

Function	German Form
Declarative	Subject—Verb—(Other stuff)
YN-Question	Verb—Subject—(Other stuff)

For further comparison, here are some YN-questions from Japanese; they are very different in form from those in English and German.

(9) Eigo   o   hanashi-masu.
     English   ACC   speak-POLITE
     'You speak English.'

     Eigo   o   hanashi-masu-ka?
     English   ACC   speak-POLITE-QUESTION
     'Do you speak English?'

     Eigo   o   hanas-e-masu.
     English   ACC   speak-can-POLITE
     'You can speak English.'

     Eigo   o   hanas-e-masu-ka?
     English   ACC   speak-can-POLITE-QUESTION
     'Can you speak English?'

We notice four main characteristics of these Japanese sentences.

- First, the subject is not explicitly mentioned. In Japanese, the subject and other things that are under discussion do not have to be mentioned if they are known from the conversation or the context. Since the subject is 'you,' it is known from the context.
- Second, the verb always comes at the end of the sentence.
- Third, the auxiliary verb and the main verb are not separate verbs; they form a single complex verb.
- And fourth, the YN-question is formed by adding -ka to the verb.

The points are summarized in table 15.4.

● TABLE 15.4
Basic Japanese Sentence Structure

Function	Japanese Form
Declarative	(Subject)—(Other stuff)—(Complex)Verb
YN-Question	(Subject)—(Other stuff)—(Complex)Verb—*ka*

WH-QUESTIONS

Finally, there are questions that ask about the identity of a participant in a relation, or about such things as the manner, reason, time, or place. For example, suppose there used to be some ice cream in the freezer, and now there is an empty ice cream container on the kitchen table. We may be pretty certain that someone ate the ice cream. And "Someone ate the ice cream" is the content of a declarative sentence that we can express. But we have a particular way of phrasing a question in English to determine the identity of the person who ate the ice cream:

(10) Who ate the ice cream?

This type of question (as mentioned previously) is called a **wh-question,** because it is formed with question words that all begin with *wh-,* except *how.*

Every language has a means for eliciting the specific content of a relation whose general outlines are known (or suspected). That is, every language has wh-questions. But the form of a wh-question varies from language to language. The major variable is whether the wh-word or wh-phrase is in the initial position in the sentence or whether it remains in place.

Here for comparison are some wh-questions from other languages with their English translations. Note where the wh-phrases appear.

(11) **Chinese**
hufei   mai-le   **shenme**   (ne)?
Hufei   buy-PERF   what   PRT
'What did Hufei buy?'

Lisi **weishenme**   cizhi?
Lisi why   resign
'Why did Lisi resign?'

Ni   renwei   Lisi   **weishenme**   cizhi?
you   think   Lisi   why   resign
'Why do you think Lisi resigned?'

(12) **French**
Jean a   acheté   **quoi**?
Jean has   bought   what
'What has Jean bought?'

Quel livre   Jean   a-t-il   acheté?
which book   Jean   has-he   bought
'Which book did John buy'?'

(13) **Korean**
Chelswu-ka   **mues-ul**   po-ass-ni?
Chelswu-NOM   what-ACC   see-PAST-Q
'What did Chelswu see?'

(14) **Japanese**

John	ga	**nani**	o	kaimasita-ka?
John	NOM	what	ACC	bought-POLITE Q

'What did John buy?'

In French, there are two ways to make wh-questions, including one similar to English in that the wh-phrase appears at the front of the sentence, while in the other languages illustrated, the wh-phrase does not appear at the front of the sentence.

Exercise 1

Give an explicit statement of the rule for forming wh-questions in English.

IMPERATIVES

The last basic sentential form is the imperative, which has the function of making a request or giving an order.[1] Before continuing, try to say explicitly what the general form of the English imperative is—just keep in mind that there are no auxiliary verbs in the imperative. Table 15.5 provides the imperative forms.

> ● **TABLE 15.5**
> **Forms of Major English Sentence Functions**
>
> | Function | English Form |
> |----------|-------------|
> | Statement | Subject—(Auxiliary Verb)—Main Verb—(Other stuff) |
> | YN-Question | Auxiliary Verb—Subject—Main Verb—(Other stuff) |
> | Imperative | Main Verb—(Other stuff) |

The imperative in many other languages is similar in form to that of English. Here are a few more examples of imperatives from other languages—for each one, try to identify the particular form that indicates that it is an imperative.

---

1. Imperatives have other functions, but these are the main ones.

(15) **French**

Vous	me	donnez	la bière.	Donnez-moi	la bière.
you	to-me	give	the beer	give-me	the beer

'You give me the beer.'   'Give me the beer!'

Vous	lisez	le	livre.	Lisez	le	livre.
you	read	the book		read	the book	

'You are reading the book.'   'Read the book!'

(16) **Polish**

pytać	pytam	pytasz	pyta
'to ask'	'I-ask'	'you-ask'	'he-asks'

Pytaj!
'Ask!'

(17) **German**

Sie	rauchen	nicht.	Rauchen	Sie	nicht!
you (polite)	smoke	not	Smoke	you (polite)	not

'You don't smoke.'   'Don't smoke!'

Du	rauchst	nicht.	Rauch nicht!
you (familiar)	smoke	not	smoke not

'You don't smoke.'   'Don't smoke!'

Exercise 2

Suppose you are trying to explain to someone who is learning English how to make statements, questions, and imperatives. Fill in the blank for each of the following:

1. In order to form a statement, _____.
2. In order to form a YN question, _____.
3. In order to form an imperative, _____.

Hint: Start with the statement, and describe the question and imperative in terms of it. (Your explanation will probably take up more space than the blanks here do.)

Using Sentence Form to Communicate Ideas

We conclude our survey of the basic functions of sentences with some observations about the relationship between the form of a sentence and its function. It turns out that while there are certain forms that are typically associated with the functions declarative, interrogative, and imperative, the meanings that such sentences express can often be conveyed using other forms.

Suppose that you are in a restaurant and you want a cup of coffee and you want the waiter to give you one. You could say:

(18) Give me a cup of coffee.

(19) Can you give me a cup of coffee?

Of course there are many other things that you could say that you could reasonably expect would have the effect of the waiter giving you a cup of coffee, which we will get to shortly.

What do these two sentences have in common? They are about some event of the waiter giving you a cup of coffee. Examples (18) and (19) in part have the same **literal meaning,** or what we refer to as **content,** which is this idea of the waiter giving you a cup of coffee.

Moreover, they both communicate the same more complex idea: you want a cup of coffee and you want the waiter to give you one. We call this more complex idea the **force** of the sentence.

Notice that neither sentence literally says that you want a cup of coffee. You could say this, though:

(20) I want a cup of coffee.

And this sentence, like (18) and (19), has the same force. But it has a different content, since it doesn't actually refer to an event of the waiter giving you a cup of coffee.

Each of these three sentences has a different form, and each literally expresses a different (but related) meaning.

- Sentence (18) is in the **imperative form,** marked by the fact that it lacks a subject. That is, it does not literally say who should perform the act of giving the cup of coffee. What this sentence does is express a command (or make a request, particularly with the addition of the politeness marker *please*). It literally and directly expresses your request that the person that you are talking to, in this case, the waiter, give you a cup of coffee.
- Sentence (19) is in the **interrogative** form, marked by the fact that *can* precedes *you.* This sentence asks a question. It is literally a question about whether the waiter has the **ability** to give you a cup of coffee. It expresses neither your desire nor your inten-

tion. But you can ask for a cup of coffee this way because you can reasonably expect the waiter to draw the intended conclusion, again by recognizing that this is the sort of thing that people say in restaurants when they are ordering a cup of coffee.

- Sentence (20) is in the **declarative** form. It makes a statement. It expresses your desire for a cup of coffee, but does not express your intention that the waiter should do anything. The literal meaning is that you want a cup of coffee. The waiter must draw the conclusion that he should give you a cup of coffee because you expressed your desire for a cup of coffee and because of the context (after all, you are in a restaurant).

The differences between these sentences highlight the difference between (a) the form of the sentence, what we call its structure or its grammar or grammatical form; (b) the literal meaning (content) that depends on this form; (c) the function of the sentence, that is, whether it makes a request, asks a question, or makes a statement; and (d) the force of the sentence, that is, the more complex idea that it communicates.

Exercise 3: Form, Function, and Force

To be sure that you understand the distinctions being made here, stop now and write down what the form, function, and force are of sentences (24) and (26). The answers follow below.

An example like (20) also shows that it is possible for a sentence to express literal content and at the same time to communicate a more complex idea indirectly, because speakers are able to draw conclusions about what other speakers have in mind when they say certain things. The direct idea is that the speaker wants a cup of coffee; the indirect idea is that the waiter should give it to him or her.

In fact, you could express your desire for a cup of coffee by simply saying:

(21) A cup of coffee, please.

or even:

(22) Coffee, please.

These are not even complete sentences, yet they have the same force as the other ways of asking for a cup of coffee. Again, this is because of the context.

Just as the same idea can be expressed in a number of different ways, so can the same form express a number of different ideas. Take a look again at sentence (19) (*Can you give me a cup of coffee?*). This sentence has the form of a question, but it is used to express a request. The following sentences are all questions, but not all have the interrogative function of asking for information.

(23) **Is** it time to leave yet?

(24) What kind of dog **is** that?

(25) **Do** I look like a maid to you?

(26) What kind of idiot **do** you take me for?

Sentence (23) appears to ask a very straightforward question—it is asking whether it is time to leave yet. The expected answer is either yes or no. Sentence (24) is a different kind of question as far as its form is concerned, but again it seems to be very straightforward: it is asking the hearer to identify the type of dog that is being observed.

Sentence (25) has the same form as sentence (23), but it does not seem to invite a YN answer—a normal interpretation is that the speaker is objecting that he or she is definitely not a maid (and should not be treated like one, perhaps). Similarly, sentence (26) suggests that some idea that has been expressed in the conversation is stupid. Both of these last two sentences have the indirect force of a statement, not a question, even though they have the form of a question.

Finally, consider sentences (27)–(29).

(27) The waiter gave me a cup of coffee.

(28) I got a cup of coffee from the waiter.

(29) This is the cup of coffee that the waiter gave me.

These sentences express a relation between the speaker, the waiter, and a cup of coffee. It is the same relation expressed literally by sentences (18) and (19), namely. the relation "waiter gives me a cup of coffee." Notice that this relation is a constant whether the sentence makes a request, makes a statement, or asks a question. As seen, this relation forms part of the content of the sentence. The total content of a sentence consists of the relation or relations that the sentence expresses between the people and things referred to in the sentence, as well as less concrete things like times, places, reasons, and events.

Let's look again at sentence (19) (*Can you give me a cup of coffee?*) to distinguish these aspects of form, content, function, and force. The sentence has interrogative form: the verb *can* precedes the word *you*. In contrast, in a declarative statement, the order would be the other way around: *You can give me a cup of coffee.* The content, as we have seen, is the relation "give" between the hearer (in this case the waiter), the speaker, and a cup of coffee. The literal meaning of the question is to ask whether the hearer is able to give the speaker a cup of coffee. And the intended force is that the waiter should give the speaker a cup of coffee.

Let's look at another example, sentence (23) (*Is it time to leave yet?*). Again, the sentence has the form of a question: *is* precedes *it*. The content concerns the time of an event, that of leaving. The function is to ask whether it is time to leave yet. And the intended force is that the hearer should answer the question yes or no.

Answer to Exercise on Form, Function, and Force

Sentence (24) has the form of a question, in particular, a wh-question. It has the function of asking what kind of dog that is. The force is that the hearer should provide the answer to the question. Sentence (26) is also a wh-question. It has the function of asking the hearer what kind of idiot the hearer takes the speaker for. But it has the force of saying that the speaker thinks that the hearer is an idiot.

Summary: Form, Content, Function, and Force

Summarizing, we have seen that we need to distinguish four key properties of sentences. First, there is the form of the sentence—what is the arrangement of the words and phrases? Second, there is the literal content of the sentence, which expresses the relationships between the people and things referred to. Third, there is the function of the sentence, for example, to make a request, to make a statement, or to ask a question about that content. Fourth, there is the intended force of the sentence, the meaning that the speaker intends for the hearer to understand, perhaps by inferring what the speaker has in mind from the literal content and the form of the sentence.

When we talk about "the work that sentences do," we are referring both to the capacity of language to express functions and forces like those that we have just examined and to know precisely how the form of the language is used to do this.

Language Meaning

All human languages provide their speakers with the resources to express and communicate exactly the same basic contents, functions, and forces.

SECTION IV

Acting like a
Native Speaker

The Link between Language and Culture

Introduction

*I*n the preceding chapters we considered a number of factors that come into play in determining how a sentence of a language is understood. As we saw, the form of a sentence, along with the context in which it is spoken, provides a sentence with its literal and implied meaning. In the remaining chapters, we look at another type of meaning that is conveyed by a sentence: **social meaning.** Acquiring the ability to understand the social meaning of an utterance is also an important part of learning a new language.

Language is inherently social since we use it to interact with other people. It is also an important part of how we establish and maintain social relations and generally define ourselves in a culture. In other words, language is more than just a way to communicate; it is also a way of defining social relationships and projecting our social identity. As a result, what we say and how we say it conveys a great deal of information about our social status, gender, age, relationship to the listener, formality of the situation, and so on. This type of information can be revealed in a number of ways, such as by the pronunciation of particular words. Hearing someone pronounce the word *car* as [kɑ] rather than [kɑɹ], for example, may be a cue to the listener that the person grew up in the Boston area of the United States. The choice of grammatical construction that an individual uses can also reveal social meaning, as in the use of *May I have a coffee?* as opposed to *Give me a coffee!* or *Gimme a cup of coffee!* in making a request. Depending on the situation, the use of the command/request form as opposed to interrogative form can reflect, for example, a person's level of education, emotional state, or degree of familiarity with the recipient of the command/request.

Given the interweaving of language and culture, social meaning in language can also give us information about a society's traditions, norms, and values, and, as such, it provides a window into the culture of the people who speak the language. This means that learning a foreign language means more than learning new sounds, words, and grammar. It also means learning a new culture and, with it, how social meaning is expressed in that culture. The better you understand the culture of the language you are learning, the better you will be able to interact successfully with native speakers. This knowledge will also equip you with greater control over **your** language usage and the ability to act like a native speaker of your new language.

In this section of the book we look at some of the ways that social meaning is expressed in language. As we do this, it is important to keep in mind that the particular linguistic means by which social meaning is expressed in any language is **arbitrary.** We will see, for example, that politeness can be conveyed in a number of different ways. In some languages, words carry grammatical markers to denote differing degrees of politeness. Politeness can also be conveyed though the choice of sentence type, as in our example above: *May I have a coffee?* vs. *Give me a coffee!* Some languages may use both of these mechanisms, others may use only one, while still others may use an entirely different means of expressing politeness. The important points to remember then are first, the extent to which language is used to express social meaning depends on the language in question; and second, the particular aspect of language that is used to convey social meaning is arbitrary.

The notion of arbitrariness in language is not, of course, limited to the expression of social meaning. In our discussion of the combinations of sounds, for example, we saw that languages can differ in the number and type of sounds that can combine to form words. It is impossible to predict that language X will use one specific set of sounds, while language Y will use another. We also saw that the link between words and properties such as grammatical gender can be arbitrary, given that the word that refers to a particular type of thing can be masculine, feminine, or neuter depending on the language.

A particularly vivid illustration of the notion of arbitrariness can be seen by comparing the words used in languages to describe the sounds that animals make. When it comes to pigs, for instance, most native speakers of English would agree that a pig says *oink.* Yet in Estonian, a pig says *rui rui,* in Mandarin, it says *hulu hulu,* in Croatian *ruk ruk,* in French *groin groin,* in Japanese *buu buu,* in Korean *kkool kkool,* and in German *grunz grunz.* The fact that the sounds pigs make are described differently across languages is not, of course, an indication that pigs **speak** different languages or even make

English: *oink oink*
Croatian: *ruk ruk*
Mandarin Chinese: *hulu hulu*
French: *groin groin*
Japanese: *buu buu*
Korean: *kkool-kkool*
Estonian: *rui rui*
German: *grunz grunz*

different sounds in different parts of the world. Rather, it makes more sense to assume that the different words that people give to the sounds of animals are simply **arbitrary** labels determined by the speakers of a culture, constrained by the possible sound combinations in the language. The observation that animals "speak" differently around the world is then a simple illustration of how similar ideas are expressed in different ways across cultures.

In the following pages, we explore the link between language and culture, beginning with a look at the place of culture in language more generally. We consider some of the roles that language plays in social interaction and how these roles can differ from one culture to another. In the following chapters, we focus on two topics as a means of illustrating cultural differences in the expression of social meaning: politeness and swearing.

Exercise 1: Using Language in Different Contexts

It is not necessary to compare two different languages in order to see that language and culture are closely linked—it is apparent from the way we use different language varieties in different social settings.

Consider how you would (or at least could) ask each of the following people to repeat something that you did not understand: your kid brother or sister, your father or mother, your closest friend, the instructor in a class, and an armed law officer at a sobriety check.

What do you observe? Did you use different words, different sentence types? Which ones did you use in which context?

Language and Culture

As noted above, language is necessarily social, given its important functions in social interactions. We use language to influence the thoughts and actions of others, to request and obtain information, and to share our feelings. In general, we use language to communicate ideas and knowledge with others, and since communication involves more than one person, language is also social. The fact that social structure can differ from culture to culture and language to language makes learning a new language both fascinating and challenging.

Consider how people answer the phone, for example. English speakers might respond with "Hello," or in a business setting, a person might simply say her name, for example, [ring, ring] "Julia Roberts here." Dutch speakers, by contrast, commonly respond with *met* 'with,' for example, [ring, ring] "*met* Julia Roberts." While acceptable in The Netherlands, putting *with* before your name when answering the phone in an English culture, for example, American, Canadian, Australian, might seem very strange.

In this instance we see that a simple task such as answering the phone is accomplished in different ways in Dutch and various English cultures. Notice that for this illustration we have defined culture in terms of the specific languages that the individuals speak. Yet this is not the only or perhaps the best way to define this concept.

A **culture** can be defined more generally as a group of individuals with shared attitudes about what are acceptable and unacceptable ways of performing social tasks and accomplishing social goals. Our observation that people in The Netherlands and North America, for example, answer the phone differently indicates that there are different shared attitudes, or norms, involved in accomplishing this type of social task in each culture. In North American English culture, the norm is to say "hello," while in Dutch culture, the norm is to say 'with' followed by your name. Each culture has its own set of norms, and these norms may overlap to varying degrees with other cultures. Some social norms are encoded as laws, such as which side of the street to drive on. Other norms are unwritten yet nonetheless present in the culture. Some examples of unwritten social norms of English-speaking cultures in Europe, North America, Australia, New Zealand, and elsewhere refer to the direction to stand in an elevator (facing the door), the use of cell phones in theaters (frowned upon), and how to greet an acquaintance (extend your right hand to shake). In France, it is common for people to greet with a kiss on each cheek, while in The Netherlands, people kiss three times (right cheek—left cheek—right cheek). So even if we consider only how people greet each other, France, The Netherlands, and many English-speaking countries can be defined as different cultures.

Given that language is a social phenomenon, it should not be surprising that **language norms** also exist, that is, shared attitudes about what language form to use in a particular situation. Language norms can cover topics such as what form of address to use in a particular context (e.g., formal vs. informal), how politeness is expressed, what topics are considered taboo, how many people may talk at the same time in a conversation, how much you should talk during your turn in a conversation, how and when to end a conversation, and so on. Even though language norms may be unwritten, they constitute an integral part of the language and, consequently, are important for speakers to know if they want to be able to function as accepted members of the culture.

This then poses an interesting challenge to the language learner. Given that language norms are generally unstated and unwritten, how can a non-native speaker of the language learn what the norms of the culture are? Here are three approaches to consider. As you will see, some are more effective than others.

Perhaps the simplest way to learn about a language norm is to ask people explicitly. For example, if you are learning a language that has different forms of address for different situations, you might describe a particular scenario to a native speaker and ask her what would be the most appropriate form of address to use for that situation. Easy, right? In this particular case, perhaps, but it is probably not difficult to imagine the types of problems associated with this approach. For example, some norms may deal with sensitive or potentially embarrassing topics, and so actually asking about them may be violating a norm in and of itself! Also, asking explicitly about a norm has a tendency to elicit stereotypes rather than normal behavior. For example, if a foreign student were to ask a native English speaker about the polite way to greet someone in English, the student might be told to shake the right hand of the person and say "Hello, nice to meet you." However, were the foreign student to visit an American college campus, he might be surprised to see the stereotypical greeting replaced by a polite, though much less formal, greeting consisting of a nod of the head and the simple expression "Hey!"

An alternative means of learning whether something is a norm or not is to violate it and see what happens. The reaction of people around you will probably be a fairly good indication of whether the norm exists or not. Of course, the major drawback of violating a potential norm is that it may trigger discomfort, embarrassment, or any number of other negative reactions. Also, violating a norm does not in itself show how to **follow** the norm.

Probably the most effective way of learning about language norms, and norms in general, is simply to observe behavior. If you are visiting a foreign country, watch people when they greet each other. What do they say? How do they say it? Do adults greet each other the same way they greet children? Do women behave differently from men? Do older people behave differently from younger people? In short, become a keen observer of human behavior, and you will learn, just as every native speaker of the language you are learning has, what form of language to use in a particular situation.

Exercise 2: Hello, Good-bye

Investigate the different expressions that are used by native speakers of the language that you are studying (a) to greet someone and (b) to say goodbye. You can do this by observing native speakers interacting in person, in a film, or on TV. Or, if you are not living in a place where the new language is spoken, you can also ask your language instructor, watch films, look on the web, and so on.

Each time you observe someone using an expression to greet or leave, jot it down in a notebook. Next to it include details such as: Who used the expression? How old was the person? What sex is the person? In what context was the expression uttered?

As you gather more and more examples, review your notes to see if patterns are emerging. For example, is one expression more commonly used by young people, by women, at school, and so on?

What insights do your observations give you concerning your own use of the expressions for greeting and saying good-bye?

Language Varieties

In discussing language and culture, it is important to emphasize that a language need **not** define a single culture. Any one language can have many cultural groups associated with it. It may also be the case that the members of each of these cultures speak a different **variety** of the same language.

The term **language variety** refers to the language spoken by a group of people who belong to a particular social or cultural group, who communicate with other members of the community and who share common views about linguistic norms. A "variety" of language is simply a neutral term that can include more precise classifications like "language" and "dialect." Given this, we can say that **different languages** like English, Italian, French, and Swahili are also different language varieties.

A **single language** is also made up of many different varieties. English includes, among many others, British English, Cockney English, New Zealand English, Canadian English, and Southern American English. Notice that the term *language variety* can characterize the broad distinction between British English and American English, for example. Or the distinctions can be further refined in order to refer to smaller varieties of language such as Bostonian English, New York English, Southern American English, Valley Girl English, and so on.

Importantly, the observation that English has many different varieties is not a property just of English. All languages have multiple varieties. The French language includes Parisian French, Québécois French, and Moroccan French, among many others. In Spanish we can speak of, for example, Castilian Spanish, Puerto Rican Spanish, Chicano Spanish, and Florida/Cuban Spanish, while in Arabic we find Palestinian Arabic, Jordanian Arabic, Moroccan Arabic, and so on.

Different varieties of the same language are generally distinguished by pronunciation differences, the use of different words (e.g., *soda* vs. *pop*, *sack* vs. *bag*) or different grammatical structures (e.g., *he likes himself* vs. *he likes hisself*) to express the same idea. As stated in the definition of language variety above, however, speakers of different language varieties also share different norms about language usage.

Consider the norms surrounding the use of minimal responses by male and female speakers of American English (Coates 1998). The term *minimal response* refers to communication devices such as a nod or a small comment like "yes" or "mhm." A person listening to someone speak might insert a minimal response at various points in the conversation.

Research suggests that minimal responses can have different meanings for women and men in American culture. For women, inserting a minimal response in the conversation can be interpreted as "I'm listening to you, please continue." For many men, however, the meaning tends to be stronger: "I agree with what you are saying" or at least "I follow the argument so far." The finding that women use more minimal responses in conversation than men may be because women are listening or facilitating conversation more often than men are agreeing.

Yet these different language norms can lead to miscommunication and misunderstandings. For example, a man receiving repeated nods from a woman may interpret this as meaning that the woman agrees with everything he says; she does not have opinions of her own. A woman who is getting only occasional nods from a man may interpret this as saying that the man is not listening to her, not that he does not always agree. These different interpretations of minimal responses may explain two common complaints of men and women. The first comes from men who think that women are always agreeing with them and then conclude that it is impossible to tell what a woman really thinks. The second complaint comes from women who get upset with men who never seem to be listening (Coates 1998).

Each of these examples shows that how language is used in a community depends on the norms or rules decided upon by that specific culture. And, as pointed out earlier, in order to become a successful language learner, it is important to learn more than the sounds, words, and grammar of a language. Understanding the language norms of the community and how culture is expressed through the language will help you become a better language learner and, as a result, help you to both think and behave more successfully like a native speaker.

One explanation for these differences is based on the view that there are **cultural differences** between men and women (Maltz & Borker 1982). In this view, American men and women are seen as coming from different subcultures. In these subcultures, there are different norms concerning how friendly conversation is to be interpreted. There are also different rules for engaging in conversation and different rules for interpreting conversation. In other words, men and women have learned to do different things with words in a conversation, which at times can lead to miscommunication (Tannen 1990).

Language Attitudes

LANGUAGE AS A REFLECTION OF SOCIAL IDENTITY

Since language is so closely linked to culture, the language variety that a person speaks also brings with it a lot of information about that person's culture, **simply by association.** In this sense, language is a sign of social identity; it says (rightly or wrongly) who you are. A native speaker of one variety of English can usually determine, on the basis of listening to another speaker of English, where he is from at least in broad terms (e.g., Britain, Southern United States, Australia, Canada), her level of education, and social class.

The ability of speakers to make judgments about other speakers on the basis of their speech occurs in all cultures and with all languages. Whether these are actual characteristics of the person speaking or not is another issue. They may very well be stereotypes that we have learned to associate with a particular culture. Every variety carries with it a great deal of social meaning which generally reflects stereotypes about the group of people who usually speak the variety.

In studies of French varieties, for instance, Parisian French is generally considered more favorably than other varieties, particularly with respect to social status. Stereotypes are also reflected in the perception of personality traits of the speakers of these varieties. In fact, studies showed that French Canadians judged a speaker of French Canadian to be more intelligent and better educated when she spoke with a Parisian accent than when she spoke with her usual French Canadian accent. Of course, the subjects did not know that it was the same person speaking both varieties (see Hume, Lepicq, & Bourhis 1993 for related discussion).

A key point to remember is that the prestige and the perceived "beauty" of a language variety is determined by the cultural context in which the variety is spoken. In general, a standard variety is judged to be more prestigious and more aesthetically pleasing than nonstandard varieties of the same language. Speakers of the standard variety are typically looked upon as more intelligent, as having more self-confidence, and as speaking better. Speakers of nonstandard varieties are judged to be speaking a variety of language that is inferior to the standard.

It is important to emphasize that these are just stereotypes. **No variety is inherently better than any another.** All varieties are systematic and rule-governed. That is, they all have rules regardless of whether we are talking about English, French, Italian, Japanese, or any other language. We can see this clearly by comparing two varieties of English. Consider the formation of reflexive pronouns in standard American English and in Appalachian English, a nonstandard American variety.[1]

Standard English	**Appalachian English**
I like myself	I like myself
you like yourself	you like yourself
he likes himself	he likes hisself
she likes herself	she likes herself
we like ourselves	we like ourselves
you like yourselves	you like yourselves
they like themselves	they like theirselves

We can describe the rules for the making reflexives in the two varieties as shown in Table 16.1.

By comparing the two sets of rules, you should find it apparent that the nonstandard variety is not any less systematic than the standard one. In fact, we could say that it is **more** systematic since it has generalized the formation of the reflexive to all object pronouns. As a result, for the nonstandard variety there is simply one rule for the singular and one rule for the plural. On the other hand, to make reflexive pronouns in the standard variety, in some persons the suffix *-self/-selves* is added to the object pronoun, while in other persons it is added to the possessive pronoun. This means that two different rules are needed for the singular and two are needed for the plural.

1. Examples from Anouschka Bergmann, Kathleen Currie Hall, and Sharon Ross (Department of Linguistics, The Ohio State University), *Language Files,* 10th ed. (The Ohio State University Press, 2007), p. 412.

● **TABLE 16.1**

Rules for Making Reflexives

Standard	1st- and 2nd-person singular	add the reflexive suffix -*self* to **possessive** pronouns	(i.e., *my + self, your + self*)
	1st- and 2nd-person plural	add the reflexive suffix -*selves* to **possessive** pronouns	(i.e., *our + selves, your + selves*)
	3rd-person singular	add the reflexive suffix -*self* to **object** pronouns	(i.e., *him + self, her + self*)
	3rd-person plural	add the reflexive suffix -*selves* to **object** pronouns	(i.e., *them + selves*)
Nonstandard	1st-, 2nd-, 3rd-person singular	add the reflexive suffix -*self* to **possessive** pronouns	(i.e., *my + self, your + self, her + self, his + self*)
	1st-, 2nd-, 3rd-person plural	add the reflexive suffix -*selves* to **possessive** pronouns	(i.e., *our + selves, their + selves*)

The point of this example is simply to emphasize that how we perceive varieties of language is tied to our perception of the culture in question. It has nothing to do with any inherent quality of the structure of the language.

Yet if nonstandard varieties are perceived so negatively, you might be wondering why everyone doesn't speak the standard variety. There are several reasons for this. First of all, we learn the language that we are exposed to as children, and the longer we are exposed to it, the more ingrained it becomes (see chapter 1). Second, the variety of language that we use with family members, close friends, and in informal situations generally triggers feelings of solidarity, group loyalty, appreciation, and attraction. If you grew up speaking a nonstandard variety, you will probably have the feelings just noted toward that variety, even if it may be generally perceived as less prestigious than the standard language. On the other hand, studies have shown that people tend to evaluate someone who speaks a nonstandard variety more positively than a standard-variety speaker in terms of personality traits like friendliness and likeability.

Exercise 3: Standard and Nonstandard Varieties of Language

Take this opportunity to think about your own attitudes concerning varieties of English or other languages that you know well. Here is a simple exercise to help you do this.

Start by writing down the names of different varieties of English, starting with the one spoken by you and your family, for example, standard American English, African American English, Bostonian English, Cockney English, Jamaican English, Texan English, Queen Elizabeth's English, and so on.

Next to each variety, jot down words that come to mind to describe them. Do not read the rest of the exercise until you have finished this part.

• • •

Now, below your descriptions make two scales. The first corresponds to the **prestige** associated with a given variety, with low prestige at one end and high prestige at the other end. Prestige-related traits of the speakers include intelligent, sophisticated, aloof, stuffy, and so on. The second scale represents traits relating to your sense of **solidarity** with the variety and its speakers. Solidarity-related terms include friendly, kind, generous, fun-loving, down-to-earth, and so on. Locate high solidarity at one end of the scale and low solidarity at the other end.

Based on your descriptions, situate the varieties along the two scales. Now comes the hard part: try to think objectively about why you perceived some varieties as more or less prestigious than others and why some are associated with positive feelings of solidarity while others are not.

Typically, descriptions correspond not to the language itself but rather to the people who speak these varieties and the experiences that we or others have had with them and their culture. Remember, however, that there really is nothing inherently better about some varieties as opposed to others. Any negative or positive feelings that you associate with a variety is a learned reaction.

WHAT MAKES A LANGUAGE BE PERCEIVED AS MORE PRESTIGIOUS?

We know that all languages have different varieties: both standard and possibly many nonstandard varieties. We also know that the standard variety is generally associated with prestige. But what makes a language be perceived as prestigious? Some typical but **incorrect** answers given to this question are the following:

- The standard variety obeys all of the rules of grammar, while the nonstandard varieties lack certain rules. [This is **not** the correct answer!]

- The standard variety does not use slang, while the nonstandard varieties use a lot of slang. [This is **not** the correct answer!]
- The standard variety is more logical than the nonstandard varieties. [This is **not** the correct answer!]

The **correct** answer for why a language is perceived as prestigious is the following:

- The standard variety happens to be the variety spoken by people with greater power, wealth, or education, either now or in the past.

The relative prestige of a language is a historical accident. We are taught to view one variety as better than another. Think about British English, for example. Why do you think the standard variety (referred to as Received Pronunciation, or RP) is the prestige variety? It is because that is the variety spoken by those holding power: political power, social power, or economic power. It is no coincidence that the Queen of England speaks RP. If the seat of power had been established in Glasgow or Manchester or Liverpool, the prestige variety today would certainly correspond to the variety spoken in one of those areas.

Just as we develop attitudes about varieties of our own language, we do the same with foreign languages. In a small study conducted by the authors of this book over several years, American college students were asked to jot down what came to mind when they thought of the following languages: French, Russian, Italian, Arabic, German, and Maltese. Before reading further, you might also do this, and then compare what you wrote with what the students in the experiment wrote.

The results were as follows:

- Students generally used terms that were more positive to describe French and Italian, for example, romantic, smooth-sounding, harmonious, and so on.
- Students generally used more negative adjectives for Arabic, Russian, and German, for example, coarse, guttural, throaty, harsh, and so on.
- Students were not able to say anything about Maltese.

The perceptions of the first four languages, at least, probably reflect stereotypes that the students had acquired about these languages. French and Italian are commonly considered to be the languages of "romance" in the movies. Thinking of these languages may conjure up images of the Eiffel Tower, outdoor cafés, or a gondola on a canal in Venice. French and Italian, the languages of love!

Why are there negative adjectives associated with German, Russian, and Arabic? Again, these most likely reflect stereotypes that the students learned. Some views may have derived from the media which presented speakers of these languages in a negative light. Think, for example, about how many TV shows you have seen where the villain spoke with a Russian, German, or Arabic accent.

The results of this study showed that the degree to which each language was described as positive or negative reflected stereotypes about some aspects of the past or present **culture** associated with the language. It does not reflect the inherent beauty or lack thereof of the language. To underscore this point, it is interesting to note that some of the properties that were viewed negatively for one language were considered in a positive light for others.

For example, some respondents described Arabic using negative-sounding terms such as *coarse* or *guttural*. This quality may be because most Arabic languages have sounds made in the back of the mouth, like the pharyngeal [ʕ] and the uvular [q]. But English also has sounds made in the back of the mouth, such as the velar [k] which is quite similar to [q], as discussed in chapter 6. The French fricative 'r,' as in *rouge* 'red,' has the same place of articulation as the stop [q]. How can similar sounds lead to one language sounding coarse but another one sounding romantic?

What about Maltese? Maltese is an interesting language because the verb system and many of its sounds come from Arabic, but many of the words and other structures are related to Italian. Maltese then poses a serious problem for those who believe that one's perception of a language is tied to its inherent beauty or ugliness. If Maltese shares properties with both Arabic and Italian, does that make it inherently beautiful or ugly? This is clearly a problematic approach to viewing language. What we do know is that our attitudes toward a language variety, whether it be English or another language, are arbitrary and determined by the culture(s) that we are exposed to.

Relation to Language Learning

At this point you might be wondering why it is important to know about different varieties of language when you are learning a new language. There are several reasons. The first relates to the fact that the language variety taught in the classroom will almost certainly be the standard prestige variety. However, if you go to the country where the language is spoken, you may find that the variety used in the region you are visiting is not the standard variety. Before going abroad then, you may want to educate yourself about the variety of language spoken in that particular region and familiarize yourself with any cultural differences that may exist.

You do not have to go very far to encounter this. Suppose you have been studying French at an American university and then decide to take a trip to Quebec City in Canada to practice your French. It will probably be the case that the French that you have been exposed to in the classroom only approximates what you will hear in Quebec. Not only will it sound unfamiliar, but the words and phrases that you have learned to express a particular idea may be different. Knowing that differences exist can help you prepare and get the most out of your experiences.

Another area where knowing about different varieties of language can come in handy relates to using a dictionary (chapter 4). There are sometimes different dictionaries for different varieties of a given language. Because of this, it is a good idea to find out what language variety you are studying. You will also want to keep in mind that bilingual dictionaries (in book or online form) differ with respect to the variety of English being used. For example, a Mandarin/English dictionary that uses British English may be less helpful to you than one based on American English.

Finally and perhaps most importantly, being sensitive to cultural differences between speakers of different language varieties will make you a better person. Really! Knowing that attitudes toward language varieties are learned and arbitrary will help you to appreciate each variety for what it really is: a fascinating, complex, human phenomenon.

Exercise 4: Linguistic Heritage

What differences in the use of language have you noticed among the students in your classes that you would say correspond to their linguistic heritage, that is, the language of their parents or grandparents?

Have you noticed that people from different linguistic communities refer differently to (a) other people of the same and the opposite sex, (b) common everyday things, such as cars and foods, (c) themselves, (d) you, (e) their community, (f) the university?

Culture in Language

We turn now to consider some of the specific ways in which culture is manifested in communicating. There are many areas where we are likely to find differences across languages. We consider four of these areas throughout these remaining chapters.

- how men and women use language differently
- how people use gestures
- how people express formality or politeness in speech
- how people swear and insult each other

We introduced the first, how men and women use language differently, earlier in this chapter in the discussion of minimal responses. How people use gestures differently across cultures is outlined just below. The remaining topics make up the focus of the remaining chapters.

Gesture

GESTURE IN COMMUNICATION

We conclude this chapter on language and culture with some observations about the use of gesture in communication. Strictly speaking, gesture is not language. However, it is used at the same time as language is used in the course of communication. Moreover, just as we have to know something about the culture in order to use a language correctly in communication, it is useful to know something about the appropriate use of gestures.

Gesture is a huge part of communicating. Some researchers say that more than 50 percent of communication is done nonverbally. Gesture is especially important if you are trying to communicate in a culture where there is a language barrier for you; when you can't find the words you want to say, body language becomes even more important.

Gesture is used to communicate in all cultures, although it is used much more extensively in some cultures than in others. Brazilians and Italians, for example, are thought to use gestures more than Americans do. But even in American English culture, gesture is important.

Before considering other languages, we begin by thinking about our own use of gestures. Without uttering a word, here are some ways that we can express the following ideas using gesture in some varieties of English.

1. surprise	eyes wide open, raised eyebrows
2. ambivalence, indecision	shoulder shrug
3. gesturing to someone to come	arm outstretched, hand waving back and forth toward person doing the gesture
4. an angry mother beckoning her child	index finger curling toward her
5. hunger	holding or rubbing stomach
6. craziness	index finger circling around ear; index finger tapping one's temple
7. perfect, it's OK	thumb and index fingers making a circle

An interesting and very important part about learning to communicate in a different culture is that some of the same gestures that we use in our culture have very different meanings in others. The gesture that an angry mother might use toward her child is considered very rude in some Asian cultures. In some parts of Korea, for example, it is generally only used with animals.

But how do you learn the body language of a different culture? You can start by studying the gestures of your instructor or, if you are visiting the culture, study the people around you. There are also books available, such as Roger Axtell's *Gestures: The Do's and Taboos of Body Language around the World*. The Internet is also a rich resource. In the meantime, the important thing to remember is to be aware of the gestures that you use and **not** to assume that they mean the same thing in all cultures.

A simple example showing how gestures differ across cultures relates to greetings. When you meet someone for the first time in North America, you would probably shake the person's hand, especially if the situation is formal. If it is informal, you might just give an upward nod of the head (a sign of acknowledgment) or perhaps raise up your hand and give a small wave. What about in other cultures?

In Brazil, a handshake is quite common as well, although it is often accompanied by a touch on the elbow or forearm, or a pat on the back. More so than in North America, people in Brazil shake hands when departing as well as arriving.

Kissing is also a common way to greet people in many countries, as was noted earlier. In France, people may kiss on both cheeks when they meet. They can also kiss on both cheeks to say good-bye. In Greece, friends also greet by kissing each other on both cheeks, though they usually do this only if they have not seen each other for some time. In Holland, people kiss three times.

Bowing is also frequently used to greet people, especially in Asian culture. In China and Korea, a slight nod of the head can be sufficient.

Fukuda (1993:17) states:

The most common mistake non-Japanese make when bowing is to bend from the neck. While you may amuse your friends with your imitation of a goose, you're better off . . . if you bend from the waist. Another mistake, made by Japanese as well, is to bow more than necessary. Repeated bowing is appropriate when apologizing or making requests, but overly enthusiastic bowing . . . gives the impression of being unnecessarily servile.

In Japan, however, bowing is almost an art form! Basically, the deeper the bow, the more the respect, though there are quite a few rules governing how low you bow and who bows first. According to Fukuda (1993), the rules are basically as follows:

- the person of lower rank bows first and lowest.
- the higher the rank of the person facing you, the lower you bow.
- the lower the bow and the longer one holds the position, the stronger is the indication of respect, gratitude, humility, and so on.
- equals match bows.
- when unsure of status, the safest move is to bow a shade less low than the other person.

Notice that when bowing in Japan and other Asian cultures, you avoid direct eye contact. Prolonged eye contact also seems to be avoided in Puerto Rico and in some West Indian cultures. It can be considered rude, even intimidating, and may have sexual overtones.

As this illustration shows, the same meaning, in this case a greeting, can be expressed in many different ways across cultures. We will see additional examples in the next few pages, but we start with a look at cases where the same gesture is used to mean different things.

SAME GESTURE, DIFFERENT MEANING

In this section we present some cases where the gesture used in another culture is similar to one in North American culture, but where the meaning is quite different.

One such gesture involves the way that people indicate 'yes' and 'no.' In North American culture, we nod our head to say 'yes' and shake our head to say 'no.' In Sri Lanka you would be in trouble with these gestures since in that culture you move your head from side to side to say 'yes,' and you nod your head up and down to say 'no.' The gestures used by Greeks and Turks also differ. To say 'yes,' a sharp downward nod is used. To say 'no,' you raise your chin and simultaneously click your tongue. If you shake your head in those cultures, you are saying that you do not understand.

Turkish culture also seems to differ from North American culture in terms of the amount of smiling that people do. Turks seem to interpret too much smiling as a lack of sincerity or even a degree of deception. On the other hand, North Americans should not think that just because Turks do not smile, they are unhappy!

Some other gestures involving the hands that we use in this country include snapping, making the OK sign, and making a V for victory or peace. In Spain, snapping a few times is used for applauding. As for the V sign, it is a gesture to avoid if you are visiting England, especially if you have your palm facing toward your face since this makes an obscene gesture.

The gesture used in North American culture to denote OK takes on many different meanings around the world. In France, it means 'zero' or worthless, while in Japan you use it to ask for money or change in coins. In Brazil, Turkey, and Germany, it is an obscene gesture. In Brazil, for example, it is an obscene way of telling someone to get lost. And in Turkey, the symbol indicates that you are calling someone a homosexual and can be interpreted as very offensive. Obviously, it is important to know what is appropriate and inappropriate in the culture of the language that you are learning. This is especially so if you plan to visit the country where your new language is spoken. Think about the reaction that a Brazilian might have if you used the OK gesture to say that the directions they just gave you were perfect. This stranger might not be quite as forgiving as your language instructor!

One more gesture that we have in American culture but that receives a different meaning elsewhere is the movement of rubbing your palms together back and forth. While in North America it can mean that you are being devious or up to something. In Italian, it is a positive gesture, meaning something like 'how wonderful!,' 'good!,' 'that's nice.'

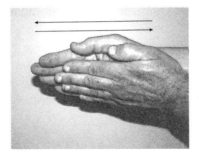

Exercise 5: Observing Gestures

Watch people who you cannot hear interact with one another. What do you notice about their gestures? Do they coordinate with one another, or take turns? Do they favor one hand over another? Do they coordinate the movements of their arms and hands with the expressions on their faces? Do you find the same gestures across a range of different speakers?

VARIATIONS IN GESTURES

We have seen that cultures can assign quite a different meaning to a similar gesture. Of course, most cultures also have a range of gestures that we do not use at all. A sampling of these is given below.

You may be interested to learn that in some cultures, mouths are used to point. In the Philippines, for example, people may shift their eyes toward the object they want to point to, or purse their lips and point with their mouth. Similar gestures are used in parts of Vietnam.

To show appreciation or admiration in Turkey, you can hold up your hand with the palm up and slowly bring your fingers toward the thumb to mean that something is good. Some French speakers also use a hand signal to indicate that something is terrific: one stretches out an arm, makes a thumbs-up sign then brings the thumb down a notch. Brazilians also have an interesting way of showing how much they like something such as food: a person pinches his earlobe between thumb and forefinger, and to dramatize it further, he will reach behind his head and grasp the opposite earlobe.

As for an Italian, if something is perfect you might see him pull across an imaginary line or string with his thumb and index finger.

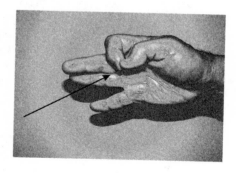

Clearly, Latin culture is rich in body language. Here are a few more fun gestures from Brazilian culture. To indicate that someone is stingy, tap your left elbow with your right hand. Spaniards also use this gesture. If you rub your hand under your elbow in Brazil instead of tapping it, you are calling someone jealous. Perhaps not surprisingly, the Brazilians and some French speakers have a gesture to show disbelief: pull down the skin under your eye with your index finger. In English, by contrast, we might simply say a sarcastic "yeah, right!" In Brazil, if you hold your palm upwards and spread your fingers, you are letting someone know that you think they are stupid.

In Italy, the gesture for stupidity involves moving your hand back and forth in front of your forehead, as shown here.

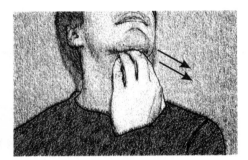

The chin is also a good source for body language in Italian. For example, if you want to express indifference, that you do not care, take the back of your hand and brush it up and away from your chin.

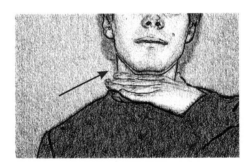

Or, if you take the side of your hand and move it against your neck, you are saying that you just cannot stand something.

The various gestures presented above are, of course, just a sampling of the vast number of gestures used in cultures around the world to communicate. Nonetheless they provide a good illustration of the ways in which languages can differ and also of the idea that how a particular idea is expressed in a given language is arbitrary, determined by the speakers of that language and codified as a written or unwritten norm of the culture.

In the next two chapters we continue our look at the role of culture in language and focus on two different means of expressing social meaning: at one end of the spectrum, politeness, and at the other end, taboos and swearing. Both provide striking examples of how much culture impacts the way that we use language.

References

Axtell, Roger. 1993. *Gestures: The do's and taboos of body language around the world.* New York: Wiley.

Coates, Jennifer. 1998. *Language and gender: A reader.* Oxford, UK; Malden, MA: Blackwell.

Department of Linguistics, The Ohio State University. *Language files,* 10th edition. 2007. Ed. Anouschka Bergmann; Kathleen Currie Hall; & Sharon Ross. Columbus: The Ohio State University.

Fukuda, H. 1993. *Flip, slither, & bang: Japanese sound and action words.* Tokyo: Kodansha International.

Hume, Elizabeth; Dominique Lepicq; & Richard Bourhis. 1993. L'influence de l'accent dans l'enseignement/l'apprentissage du français, langue seconde. *Canadian Modern Language Review* 49(2).209–35.

Maltz, D. N., & R. A. Borker. 1982. A cultural approach to male-female miscommunication. *Communication, language and social identity,* ed. J. J. Gumperz. Cambridge: Cambridge University Press. 196–216.

Tannen, Deborah. 1990. *You just don't understand: Women and men in conversation.* New York: William Morrow and Co.

Politeness

Introduction

*P*art of knowing your language is to know the rules about how to use your language, which naturally includes knowing about politeness (and rudeness). Sometimes it is very important to be polite, such as when you want to request something of someone or make a good impression on a first date, in a job interview, and so on. Politeness is useful in these kinds of situations because, among other things, it smoothes social interactions, it helps to avoid confrontational situations, it shows respect for the other person, and it can enable us to get what we want without the other person's feeling as if we have imposed upon them.

Not surprisingly, knowing about politeness is also important for the language learner. As discussed in the previous chapter, the norms underlying social phenomena like politeness are determined by a given culture, based on assumptions about what it means to be polite in that society. This means that the way people express politeness can differ from culture to culture. Part of mastering another language and knowing how to use it requires being able to understand the cultural differences between your own culture and that of the language you are learning. This necessarily means that understanding the rules governing politeness is very important.

In fact, research suggests that native speakers are generally quite tolerant of mistakes in the speech of foreigners relating to pronunciation, word formation, and word order. But when foreigners violate norms relating to language usage, such as politeness, native speakers tend to interpret the behavior as bad manners. Here's an illustration from English and Greek. In English, politeness is closely tied to formality, while in Greek this is not the case. One result of the differences may be that since Greeks are not as formal in their social interactions, an English speaker might be led to view the Greek speaker as impolite. By contrast, Greeks might judge an English speaker as too formal and distant rather than polite.

To restate a familiar point: learning a language involves more than learning sounds, words, and sentences. It is also important to learn the rules of language usage. When it comes to politeness, you can learn to show respect and cooperation for the person you are interacting with, or you can insult the person, even unintentionally. At least if you know the rules, you can actually choose how you want to treat people!

In this chapter we will start by getting a better understanding of how politeness is expressed in English. The degree to which a particular politeness strategy is used can differ from one English-speaking culture to another, so consider how closely the observations discussed here parallel your own situation. We will also look at some non-English-speaking cultures and see how they differ in terms of the nature of politeness and the strategies used to express it.

Solidarity and Deference

One way of looking at politeness is to consider its functions in a culture. According to Brown & Levinson (1987), the functions of politeness generally fall into one of two categories: **positive politeness** and **negative politeness.** In positive politeness, the speaker tries to treat the listener as a friend or at least to include him or her in the conversation. Positive politeness is used as a way of emphasizing **solidarity** with another person. Compliments are an example of this type of politeness. Another example of positive politeness is to go beyond a simple 'Hi' when you meet people. You may ask them about their family, about a recent trip they took, or about some other subject that they are interested in. A goal of this type of politeness is to make the person feel closer to you, that is, to emphasize solidarity between the two of you.

While positive politeness encourages **solidarity,** negative politeness emphasizes **deference.** By deference we are referring to a type of courteous respect, or the act of yielding to the opinion of another person. We might want to do this to preserve the other person's self-respect or to avoid making them feel bad. Suppose a friend asks you if you like her new shirt. You may tell her that you do, even though you think the shirt is completely hideous. This is a type of negative politeness since you are being polite so as not to hurt the other person's feelings, for example. Another reason to use negative politeness might be to show respect. Responding to a dinner invitation by saying *I would be honored to come to dinner* rather than *I'll come to dinner* is showing negative politeness. Negative politeness is also used in situations to give the impression of not imposing upon the other person too much, for example, *If it is not too much trouble. . . .* Or, you might use negative politeness to create or maintain distance between you and the person you are talking to. Impersonal expressions are commonly used to achieve this goal. For example, a salesclerk, trying to be polite to a pushy customer, might say the following: *Sir, customers need to line up to the right of the counter.*

In general, politeness strategies in a language fall on a continuum with solidarity at one end and deference at the other.

Expressing Politeness in English

Many different strategies are used in the English language to express politeness. These include the use of questions, modal verbs, tag questions, and past tense, among others. These strategies generally have the effect of making the request less direct, a characteristic of conveying politeness in English. The extent to which a given community uses these grammatical devices is culturally determined. Speakers of Canadian English, for example, tend to use indirectness more than New Yorkers do, resulting in the stereotype of Canadians as being more polite than New Yorkers.

Compare the sentences in (1). Most English speakers would probably perceive sentence in (1b) as more polite than sentence (1a), and there are a couple of grammatical mechanisms being used to achieve this relating to sentence type and verb structure. The first sentence is in the imperative while the second is interrogative. Framing a request in the form of a question in English tends to create indirectness and, as a result, softens the impact of the request.

(1) a. Give me $35 for the football tickets.
     b. Can you give me $35 for the football tickets?

Making use of the **modal verb** *can* in sentence (1b) is also contributing to the politeness. Other modal verbs include *would, could, might,* and *must* and can also add politeness to a sentence.

A small question added to the end of a sentence, called a **tag question,** is an additional device used to convey politeness, as in the examples in (2).

(2) Leave it here, will you?   (vs. Leave it here.)
     You can do it, can't you? (vs. You can do it.)

Another way to soften the impact of a sentence is to use a **hedge.** Examples include *I was sort of wondering if . . . , maybe if . . . , I think that . . . , would you mind if. . . .* These expressions add indirectness to a request or command; such utterances are generally perceived by English speakers as more polite than a direct utterance.

Indirectness can also be achieved by prefacing a sentence with an **apology,** for example, *Excuse me, but I was wondering if . . . , Sorry to trouble you but. . . .* **Diminutives** such as *little, small amount of, tiny,* and so on can also soften the impact of a request or command. See some examples in (3).

(3) Could you give me a <u>little</u> milk?
     I need <u>a few</u> minutes of your time to help me with something.

The expression *real quick* is an expression used by speakers in some varieties of American English, especially young adults. It too can be interpreted as a type of diminutive, intended to attenuate or downplay the imposition that the request may have on the person being asked.

(4) Can you give me that <u>real quick</u>?

The choice of **verb tense** is also used to convey politeness in English, contributing once again a sense of indirectness to the sentence. Some speakers would likely judge the sentence in (5a) with the past tense verb *were* as more polite than the one in (5b) with the present tense *are*.

(5) a. <u>Were</u> you looking for something?
     b. <u>Are</u> you looking for something?

A final strategy worth mentioning is the use of **pre-statements,** again adding indirectness to a phrase as shown in the examples in (6). In (6a) the request is softened by the pre-statement (or pre-request), while in (6b), a pre-invitation is used before the actual invitation. One of the functions of a pre-statement seems to be to give the person being addressed an easy way to say no while at the same time preserving the self-respect of both the addressee and the person making the pre-statement. Pre-statements are then examples of negative politeness.

(6) a. You (pre-request):   Do you have a minute?
         Response: Sure, what's up?
         You (actual request):   Would you read over my homework for me?

     b. You (pre-invitation):   Are you going to be in town this weekend?
         Response: Yup.
         You (actual invitation): Do you want to go out to dinner?

If you are a speaker of English and were able to judge a particular sentence as more polite than another, this means that you have learned the rules of politeness in your culture as well as the different strategies used to convey politeness.

In addition to the particular device used to express politeness, many factors need to be taken into account in order to know when politeness is in order. Age, for example, is a common consideration. Is the person you are addressing older than you or younger than you? The social distance between you and the other person, the context in which the interaction occurs, and your familiarity with the other person may all be relevant. In addition, the urgency of the message also factors in. For example, the command *Get away from there!* would probably not be interpreted as rude and offensive when yelled by a firefighter trying to keep you away from a car that is about to explode than it would be in some less urgent situation.

If you are able to determine, based on these kinds of factors, how polite you would need to be in a given situation, you have been successful in acquiring an amazing amount of information regarding the use of English in social interactions. Let's now consider how other cultures may differ in expressing politeness.

Example 1: Politeness

Think of ten or more ways to get someone to turn down loud music. Rank them in order of decreasing politeness. What factors seem to make the more polite versions more polite, and the ruder versions ruder?

Politeness across Cultures

In this section we focus on three ways that languages differ from English in expressing politeness. The first involves situations in which the same type of politeness strategy is used, but the responses to the strategy differ in the two cultures. In the second, the same type of politeness is conveyed in different ways among different language varieties. And finally, we touch upon cases in which politeness has become an integral part of the language's grammar.

SIMILAR STRATEGY, DIFFERENT RESPONSE

The use of compliments and requests are fruitful areas of study to discover differences among cultures. Comparative studies of politeness between Chinese and American speakers, and Japanese and American speakers, have shown that while each culture uses negative and positive politeness strategies, their responses to compliments and requests are quite different. In each culture, compliments are recognized as compliments and requests are recognized as requests. What differs is the way that speakers are expected to respond.

Chen (1993), for example, found that Chinese speakers frequently responded to compliments either by rejecting the compliment completely or by thanking the speaker and then denigrating or putting themselves down, as shown in (7). You can see that Americans accepted a compliment given to them about 39 percent of the time. Compare this to 1 percent for the Chinese participants. Americans were also more likely to return a compliment than Chinese. While the Chinese speakers thanked the person for the compliment and then put themselves down about 3 percent of the time, their overwhelming response was to completely reject the compliment.

(7) Differences in American English Speakers and Chinese Speakers (Chen 1993)

	American	Chinese
Accepting the compliment	Yes (39.3%)	Yes (1.0%)
Returning the compliment	Yes (18.5%)	No
Thanking and denigrating	No	Yes (3.4%)
Deflecting	Yes (29.5%)	No
Rejecting the compliment	Yes (12.7%)	Yes (95.7%)

To illustrate, consider the example where someone says, "Wow, you look great in that outfit!" A typical American response might be along the lines of "Thanks" (39.3 percent), "You look good too!" (18.5 percent); or "Really? I think it makes me look fat" (12.7 percent). For Chinese, by contrast, the first two responses would be either nonexistent or very rare. Rather, while they might say something like "Thanks, I really do not deserve to wear such nice clothes" (3.4 percent), a response such as "Really? I think it makes me look fat" would occur an astonishing 95.7 percent of the time. This difference appears to be related to social value differences between the two cultures, particularly in their respective beliefs regarding what constitutes self-image (Hondo & Goodman 2001).

Japanese speakers respond in a similar fashion as the Chinese. In a study by Daikuhara (1986), it was found that 95 percent of Japanese responses to compliments were "self-praise avoidance"; only 5 percent showed appreciation. By contrast, "thank you" was the most frequent response for Americans. It is interesting that Daikuhara also found that Japanese speakers rarely compliment their own family, while it is not uncommon for an American to do so. Hondo and Goodman (2001) suggest that this could be an indication of the function of downgrading oneself in Japanese culture, since in Japan the family is often considered to be a part of oneself.

It is not hard to imagine how miscommunications could arise because a speaker of one language is not familiar with the ways in which compliments are interpreted in the other language. Here are a few examples from Hondo and Goodman (2001). The first one involves an American speaker giving a compliment to a Japanese speaker. The American says, "Your child is one smart girl," by which she means exactly what she says: the girl is smart. The Japanese speaker replies, "Oh, no, she is not." She says this because she has learned in her culture that it is not good to praise one's own child too much. The result is that the American is left thinking that the Japanese woman does not think her own child is very smart.

In the second scenario, a Japanese woman gives a compliment to an American. She says, "Your presentation last week was excellent," and she means it. The American does not really think her presentation was that great but does not want to argue so she says, "Why, thank you." Since in Japanese culture accepting a compliment is considered inappropriate, the Japanese speaker is left thinking that the American is full of herself; according to Japanese culture, the American should have said something like "No, it really wasn't very good."

These two examples show just how important it is to understand the rules of conversation of another language. Both miscommunications could have been avoided had the speakers been aware of and sensitive to cultural differences in their language usage.

Example 2: Giving a Compliment

In some English-speaking cultures, people tend to be very aware of how they look, and want others to think that they look good. What sort of relationship might you and another person have in order for each of the following to be appropriate?

a.   You look nice.
b.   You are very nice-looking.
c.   You look great—have you lost weight?
d.   That hat looks great on you!
e.   I've never seen you looking so good.
f.   You look hot!

What determines what you would say to someone else?

THE NATURE OF THE COMPLIMENT

We continue our look at compliments, turning to the nature of the compliment and some additional ways in which languages express politeness differently from English.

Interestingly, the **focus and content of a compliment** can differ from culture to culture. Egyptians, for example, tend to offer compliments about a person's appearance and personal traits but not about what the person does or has (Nelson, Bakary, & Batal 1993). This is done apparently to avoid harm caused by the "evil eye"; when seeing something attractive and beautiful belonging to someone else, one must say "God preserve you from the evil eye." If not, something bad might happen to the owner of the beautiful object. The "evil eye" could be viewed as similar to the "knock on wood" superstition used in some English-speaking cultures.

Elsewhere in the Middle East, Persian speakers use other culture-specific devices to express politeness (Akbari 2002). Many speakers, mostly older or uneducated ones, use positive politeness strategies that are rooted in religious beliefs, such as "if God wishes." Referring to God when making a request is based on the belief that if they are talking about doing something in the future, they must say "if God wishes"; otherwise, they might not be able to do it when they intend to.

The study also found that "prayers" are used by a speaker to encourage the listener to do something for him/her. Akbari (2002) gives the following example of a mother asking her daughter to do her a favor: "My dear daughter, may your life be blessed. Would you please hang these clothes up upstairs? My legs hurt and I cannot go up the stairs."

While compliments are strongly influenced by religion in Arab cultures, at least one type of compliment in Hispanic culture is influenced by romance and art. These compliments, called *piropos*, are considered by many Spanish speakers to be a type of verbal artistry. According to Moore (1996:116), *piropos* are commonly used by a young man toward a young woman. Some examples from Moore's study are given in table 17.1, with the cultural meanings added by Hondo and Goodman (2001).

● **TABLE 17.1**

Examples of *piropos*

Spanish Form:	¡Vaya usted con Dios y su hija conmigo!
(Direct Translation:)	('May you go with God and your daughter with me!')
Cultural Meaning:	*You have a beautiful daughter.*
Spanish Form:	¡Dios mío! Tantas curvas y yo sin freno!
(Direct Translation:)	('My God! So many curves, and me without brakes!')
Cultural Meaning:	*You are sexy.*
Spanish Form:	Dejaran el cielo abierto y se voló un angelito.
(Direct Translation:)	('Heaven was left open, and out flew an angel.')
Cultural Meaning:	*You are beautiful.*

Moore (1996) and Hondo & Goodman (2001)

In many English-speaking cultures, there is a good chance that *piropos* would be interpreted not as compliments but instead as sexist, or maybe even as harassment. In Hispanic cultures, however, there is good reason to believe that they are intended to be compliments, since they can be said to children as well as adults. As Hondo and Goodman (2001) point out:

> One Spanish speaker consulted in this regard pointed out that the phrase, "¡Vaya usted con Dios y su hija conmigo!" "(May you) go with God, and your daughter (go) with me" may be uttered to a little child. . . . In that context, the statement is no more an invitation to sex than the American English expression to a child "he's so cute I could just eat him up" is a display of cannibalistic tendencies.

The appropriate **number of compliments** can also differ from culture to culture. Egyptians tend to offer fewer compliments than Americans, and the reason is, of course, cultural, related to the Arab belief in the "evil eye": too many compliments can bring bad luck (Nelson, Bakary, & Batal 1993).

DIFFERENT RESPONSES TO REQUESTS

Languages also differ in the types of sentences used to express politeness. As we saw for English, questions are more polite than declaratives. This is not the case in all cultures. An interesting example comes from Wes Collins, an expert on the Mam language of Guatemala. There are approximately 500,000 Mam speakers spanning five major dialects. While Wes was learning to speak Mam, he also learned about how his American culture differed from Mam culture, sometimes unintentionally. For example, when Wes was working in a Mam village, he asked his language consultant, in what he thought was a polite manner, "Would you like some coffee?" Every time he asked this, the language consultant just looked embarrassed and never quite knew what to say. When she did finally answer, she said, "Perhaps, yes."

The reason for the Mam speaker's hesitation is that Wes's request was interpreted as "Is it possible that you might want some coffee at some point in the future?" This is because any reference to the future in Mam is cast in **dubitative** aspect, which associates doubt with a sentence. This reflects the belief in Mam culture that the future is unknowable. So if an English speaker asks a Mam speaker if she would like some coffee, she interprets it as meaning "at some point in the future." How would she know how to answer such a question? As a result, the response is usually a simple, "Perhaps, yes." Since, for a Mam speaker, the future is in such doubt, it would be presumptuous to know the future and to assume that there would be coffee at some point in the future. Consequently, while Wes was using politeness strategies that he had learned in English, he was actually being rude. What Wes should have said was, "Here, have some coffee." It is inconceivable that a Mam would be offered a cup of coffee and not accept it.

Greek and American cultures also differ in how one makes a request. In Greek society, imperative constructions, or commands, are appropriate forms for making a request in many more contexts than in American culture. In American culture, making a command is generally perceived as impolite. As a result, an American might interpret Greeks as "impolite" or "bossy."

The Expression of Politeness in Grammar

In this section we look at additional examples where politeness has been encoded into the grammar. In these languages different words are used to express degrees of politeness.

Many languages use different pronouns to express differences in respect. These include French, Greek, Spanish, Italian, Russian, and German, to name a few. In French, for example, there are different forms of the second-person pronoun 'you,' as shown in (8). In very general terms, the singular pronoun *tu* is used when talking with someone you know, to someone who is younger than you, and in casual speech. The plural pronoun *vous* is used if addressing someone you do not know, a superior, or if the situation is rather formal. The *vous* form is also used when referring to more than one person, regardless of how well you know the people or how formal the situation is.

(8)   **French 'you'**

Singular, informal:	Tu vas au cinéma?	'Are you going to the movies?'
Plural; formal singular:	Vous allez au cinéma?	'Are you going to the movies?'

What happens if you use the wrong form? For instance, what if you are meeting your new girlfriend's or boyfriend's mother for the first time and you use the *tu* form? Let's just say that you probably would not make a very good first impression. In fact, you would probably be thought of as rude.

There is also a flip side to this. In some cultures, people do not really expect foreigners to master their language, so they are more sympathetic to the blunders that a non-native speaker might make. This apparently is the case with Russian. According to Offord (1996:179),

> there are particular advantages for the foreign student of Russian in deploying the correct formulae in a given situation. . . . Russians are aware of the difficulty of their language for the foreign student and have little expectation that a foreigner will speak it well, let alone that a foreigner would be sympathetic to their customs. . . . They therefore tend to be more impressed by and favourably disposed toward the foreigner who has mastered the intricacies of their language and is prepared to observe at least their linguistic customs than are perhaps the French toward foreign French-speakers.

For the language learner, it can then be a win-win situation to learn to use the appropriate forms in a given context. You will not be misperceived as rude, and you might even impress the people you are speaking to!

It is therefore useful to know what the appropriate form is for a given situation. However, it is also important to keep in mind that the choice of which form is used to express familiarity or formality is arbitrary and can differ from culture to culture. We saw in French, for example, that the second-person singular is the familiar form, while the second-person plural is formal. In Italian, by contrast, the polite form is the third person, not the second person. So instead of saying "How do you do?" you would say "How does he do?" But both sentences would still be interpreted as meaning "How do you do?"

As seen above, English also uses grammatical devices to express politeness; the past tense sometimes can be perceived as more polite than the present tense. Some additional examples are given in (9).

(9)

More polite?	**Less polite?**
Did you want something?	Do you want something?
I was thinking of borrowing your car.	I am thinking of borrowing your car.
I didn't understand what you were saying.	I do not understand what you are saying.

The differences between the sentences in (9) are very subtle, and not all speakers will have the same judgments. If, on the other hand, the difference between the two tenses were systematic and all instances of the past tense were always interpreted as more polite, we would say that politeness is an integral part of a particular word or phrase. In this sense, it has been **grammaticalized,** such as the *tu* vs. *vous* forms in French. That is, it is part of the rules governing the form and structure of words and sentences in the language. This is not the case in English. Instead, our strategies for expressing politeness are rules of language **usage.**

In some languages, however, the grammaticalization of politeness has been raised to an art form. This is the case in languages like Korean and Japanese, where forms of language called **honorifics** are used to express different degrees of politeness and respect. An honorific is a type of prefix or suffix that is added to a word to show respect for the person that you are talking to. Here is an example of the same sentence in Japanese, first without an honorific and then with an honorific (Bonvillain 2002).

(10) **Without honorific**

Yamada ga	musuko to	syokuzi o	tanosinda.
Yamada	son	dinner	enjoyed

'Yamada enjoyed dinner with his son.'

With honorific

Yamada-san ga	musuko-san to	o-syokuzi o	tanosim-are-ta.
yamada-HON	son-HON	HON-dinner	enjoyed-HON

'Yamada enjoyed dinner with his son.'

In Japanese, there are different types of honorifics, and the one that you use depends on a number of different factors, including the social relationship between you and the person you are talking with, where the conversation is taking place, the activity involved, and so on. According to Shibatani (1990:380), the honorific system "functions to indicate the relative social and psychological distance" between the speaker and the addressee. Every person has an "intuitive personal sphere," and politeness is a way of managing the positions of other individuals with respect to this sphere.

We can illustrate how this distance can vary through the use of spheres. As illustrated in figure 17.1, the size of the sphere indicates the social status of the two people, where a bigger sphere means higher social status and the smaller, lower status. Note that age is a very important factor determining status: the older you are, the more status you have and the more respect you should be shown.

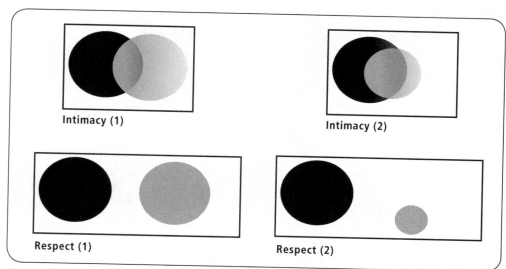

Figure 17.1

Showing intimacy indicates your belief that the other person is within your sphere (and that you are in his or hers), while showing respect indicates your beliefs about the distance between the spheres, as well as your social levels relative to one another.

As shown in figure 17.2, one class of honorifics, or *keigo* as they are called in Japanese, is called *sonkeigo*. This literally means 'respect language' and is used to raise the relative level of the person that you are talking to. Another one, called *kenjōgo*, means 'humble language.' This lowers the level of the speaker so that it makes the person talking seem more humble. A third type is called *teineigo* which generally means 'polite language.' This is used to raise the level of the speech as a whole (Hendry 1993).

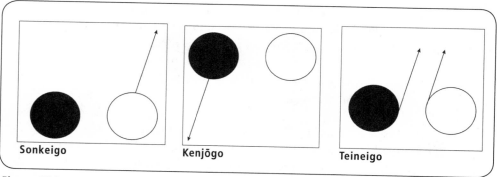

Figure 17.2

The level of speech used is controlled in large part by the formality of the situation. Polite language is always used in formal situations. If a situation is informal, honorifics might not be used, but again it depends on the social relationship between the speaker and addressee, the topic under discussion, and so on. Just because a situation is informal does not mean that an honorific is not used!

We provide an example from Shibatani's book (1990:377–78), illustrating many different levels of politeness.

(11) a. **Vulgar**

Ore	aitu	ni	au	yo.
I	that fellow	to	meet	

'I'll see that fellow.'

b. **Plain, informal**

Boku	kare	ni	au	yo.
I	he	to	meet	

'I'll see him.'

c. **Polite, informal**

Boku	kare	ni	ai-masu	yo.
I	he	to	meet-POLITE	

'I'll see him.'

d. **Polite, formal**

Watakusi	kare	ni	ai-masu.
I	he	to	meet-POLITE

'I'll see him.'

e. **Polite, formal, object honorific**

Watakusi	kare	ni	o-ai-si-masu.
I	he	to	HON-meet-POLITE

'I'll see him.'

f. **Polite, formal, object honorific, honorified 'he'**

Watakusi	ano	kata	ni	o-ai-si-masu.
I	that	person	to	HON-meet-POLITE

'I'll see that person.' (lit. 'yonder')

g. **Polite, formal, super object honorific, super-honorified 'he'**

Watakusi	ano	o-kata	ni	o-me	ni	kakari-masu.
I	that	HON-person	to	HON-eye	to	involve-POLITE

'I'll see that person.' (lit. 'I'll be humbly involved in the eye's (seeing) that honorable yonder.')

The first expression in (11) might be said by some drunken working-class men. The final particle *yo* means something like 'all right?' and adds to the informality of the sentence. The second sentence is also informal. The difference is that it is not vulgar. Note that although there are only two informal examples, there are at least five different levels of politeness. The level of respect and formality increases through the addition of politeness endings like -*masu* and honorifics like the prefix *o-*. The final super respectful sentence is especially interesting. Literally, it means 'I'll be humbly involved in the eye's (seeing) that honorable yonder,' though the actual translation is just an extremely polite and respectful way of saying "I'll see that person."

Summary

From this brief discussion of politeness across cultures we hope that you can appreciate that how a particular culture shows respect and politeness is arbitrary. The norms are defined on a culture-to-culture basis. Note again that we say *culture* not *language*. This, of course, is because different varieties of the same language can have different rules about politeness. In French Canada, for example, it is quite common for college students to refer to each other with the singular *tu* 'you' form even if they do not know each other. In Paris, however, a higher degree of formality is maintained and *vous* 'you' is more commonly used for someone you do not know, even if that person is the same age and social class as you are.

References

Akbari, Zahra. 2002. The realization of politeness principles in Persian. Isfahan, Iran: Department of Foreign Languages, Isfahan University, ms. Online: http://www3.telus .net/linguisticsissues/persian.pdf.

Bonvillain, Nancy. 2002. *Language, culture, and communication: The meaning of messages,* 4th edition. London: Prentice Hall.

Brown, P., & S. Levinson. 1987. *Politeness: Some universals in language usage.* New York: Cambridge University Press.

Chen, R. 1993. Responding to compliments: A contrastive study of politeness strategies between American English and Chinese speakers. *Journal of Pragmatics* 20(1).49–75.

Daikuhara, M. 1986. A study of compliments from a cross-cultural perspective: Japanese vs. American English. *Working Papers in Educational Linguistics* 2(2).103–34.

Hendry, J. 1993. *Wrapping culture.* Oxford: Clarendon Press.

Hondo, Junko, & Bridget Goodman. 2001. Cross cultural varieties of politeness. *Texas Papers in Foreign Language Education: Selected Proceedings from The Texas Foreign Language Education Conference 2001.* Austin: University of Texas at Austin

Moore, Z. 1996. Teaching culture: A study of *piropos. Hispania* 79(1).113–20.

Nelson, G., W. Bakary, & M. Batal. 1993. Egyptian and American compliments: A cross-cultural study. *International Journal of International Relations* 17.293–313.

Offord, D. 1996. *Using Russian: A guide to contemporary usage.* Cambridge: Cambridge University Press.

Shibatani, Masayoshi. 1990. *The languages of Japan.* Cambridge: Cambridge University Press.

Swearing, Insults, and Taboos

Introduction

*J*ust as languages can differ in terms of their rules of politeness, it is perhaps not surprising that they can also differ when it comes to the specific terms and topics that form the basis of swearing and insults. In this chapter you will be introduced to some of the ways in which languages differ in this regard. You will learn how cultural views **influence** swearing and insults in a given language. To begin, however, let's consider why one might swear in the first place. In other words, what is the function of swearing?

As you are well aware, swearing is generally used as a means of expressing frustration, anger, excitement, pleasure, or some other strong emotion, whether it be positive or negative. For example, when seeing an old college roommate at a party ten years after graduation, a man might exclaim, "Hey, how the *hell* are you! What the *f*** are you doing in town?" In a situation like this, swear words can be used in conversation among friends without a negative or confrontational meaning. Swearing is a way of signaling in-group membership, friendship, and solidarity. By contrast, it is not hard to imagine a situation where these same swear words would be used to express anger or some other negative emotion.

As Andersson and Trudgill (1990) point out in their book *Bad Language,* swear words are not intended to be taken literally. So, for example, if a person yells "This paper is full of shit!" she probably was not literally referring to human excrement.

Swearing is also used to denigrate someone or something. Referring to a person as an animal, such as *bitch, cow, pig,* is a good example. This is because in English-speaking and many other cultures, humans are more highly valued than animals given their higher position on the evolutionary scale, greater intelligence, and so on. As a result, referring to a person as an animal, that is, a lower life-form, is interpreted as an insult. Denigration thus involves associating someone or something with a lower position on some scale as defined by a given culture. Other common scales used in English-speaking cultures for the basis of denigration include manliness (strength, virility), chastity (for women), sexuality, social status, and so on.

For each of the cases of swearing and insults mentioned above, the words used can have a very strong impact, particularly if used in a negative context. But what gives them such power? The answer is that they refer to taboos. Taboos are topics governed by written or unwritten rules about what is or is not appropriate to talk about in a given context. Taboos are not necessarily prohibited topics; rather, they are topics associated with social norms relating to appropriate and inappropriate usage. In English, these include topics such as bodily functions, body parts, sex, mothers, animals, religion, race, and ethnicity. There is nothing inappropriate, for example, about discussing bodily functions in a university biology course, though the same discussion could be considered taboo if discussed in most other contexts, even though these are important functions needed to live. This is also illustrated by the use of euphemisms in some English-speaking cultures to refer to the room used for these functions. There is the term *restroom,* though one rarely "rests" in the room, and the *bathroom,* even if it doesn't have a "bath." In Canada, it is called a *washroom,* evidently because it is more polite to talk about "washing" than about bodily functions, and in England it can be referred to as the *WC* or the *loo.* New Zealanders are more direct with their use of the term *toilet.* This directness can be surprising to North American visitors used to more euphemistic references!

The key point about swearing for our purposes, and illustrated by many of the examples above, is that what defines swearing can differ from culture to culture. This is because the topics forming the basis for swearing directly reflect the attitudes and social structure of a particular community. If a society is not religious, then using a religious term in an inappropriate context will not provoke a reaction. Similarly, if the particular scale used as the basis for denigrating someone is not understood by the members of a community, it will not be an effective basis for swearing. In other words, the word used for swearing will have no power.

Swearing, Insults, and Language Learning

Just as learning about politeness is important when you're learning another language, so too is learning about the nature of swearing and insults. Since swearing (and insults) is so tightly intertwined with the values of a particular culture, it can pose a problem for you if you do not know the rules. This is also the case if you are using a swear word from a foreign language. The word will most likely not arouse the same strong emotions for you as it would for a native speaker. For this reason, use swear words in a foreign language with care (even if you're interjecting them in your own language)! In Canadian French, for example, almost any religious term can be made into a swear word. However, the

• • • • • • • • • • • • • • • •

term *fucké,* meaning 'broken, screwed up,' is considerably less strong than it is in some English-speaking cultures, even though it was borrowed from English.

Knowing when, how, where, and why to use swear words (or not to use them!) gives you more power over your interactions with native speakers.

So how can you find out what the swear words are in Spanish or Mandarin or Swahili or whatever the language is that you're learning? Obviously, one place to look would be in a dictionary (see chapter 4). You can always look up a swear word in English and see what the translation is. For example, if you were to look up *shit* in a French, German, Swedish, or Spanish dictionary, you'd probably be given the terms *merde* (French), *Scheisse* (German), *skit* (Swedish), and *mierda* (Spanish).

That is a good start, but unless you are using a **good** dictionary, it may not tell you how vulgar the term is in that particular language. Is it all right to use *merde* with your friends as well as with your mother or your professor? Using a dictionary is a start, but be sure that it is up-to-date. This is crucial because it reflects the current state of the language better than older versions do. Taboos, like swear words that violate them, change over time. We can see this with regard to religion as a basis for swearing in English-speaking cultures in, for example, North America, New Zealand, and Australia. The shock value of religious swear words is less severe than it was even a few decades ago due to the rise in secularization. *Damn* and *hell* are now considered fairly mild, while most of the blasphemies used by Shakespeare—exclamations like *Zounds!* (God's wounds) and *marry!* (by the Virgin Mary)—disappeared long ago.

Another source for swear words is obviously your language instructor, if he or she feels comfortable talking about taboo words and topics. Some language grammars also include sections on swearing. For example, the textbook *Using Russian: A Guide to Contemporary Usage* by Derek Offord includes a section on profanity in Russian.

The Internet of course is also a rich resource for swearing terms in foreign languages. By typing "swearing" or "curses" or "profanity" in most search engines, you'll come up with more links that you'll probably ever have time to look at!

Common Bases for Swearing and Insults across Cultures

As we stated above, swearing mirrors the values of society, and since social values vary from culture to culture, so do swear words and insults. This affects the topics used as well as who uses them. In some cultures, men and women both use swear words, while in others, such as Russian, it is considered more shocking for a woman to use vulgarities. In this section we review some of the common bases for swearing and insults in languages.

SEX

In many languages, English included, one of the main topics of swearing has to do with sex. For English, the sexual taboos of Victorian English are to blame, though they became even more severe in North America. Hollywood played a big role in this. In 1934, the film industry enacted a code of ethics that laid out what was and was not appropriate behavior on-screen. Inappropriate behavior included behaviors such as lustful kissing, lustful embracing, and suggestive postures and gestures. Profane language and expressions were also censored, and, as a result, words like *God, Lord, Jesus,* and *Christ* were strictly prohibited unless used for religious purposes.

The situation has clearly changed. Between the 1950s and 1970s there was a dramatic shift in attitudes and, consequently, the increased use of vocabulary that had previously been considered profane. Media outlets were partly responsible for this change—in particular, competition between the movie industry and TV. As a way of attracting viewers away from TV, which was more family-oriented and sanitized than the movies, film studios incorporated riskier and more risqué language and behavior into movies.

The 1960s also contributed a great deal to the change in attitudes. This was a time of social division and sexual liberation, and a strong, sexual vocabulary became linked to the movement. Many of the protest movements that developed at this time exploited this language to get attention and stress their radical nature, such as Berkeley students' "Filthy Speech Movement" (Hughes 1991). Many other influences can be noted as well, including the publicity surrounding comedian George Carlin and his shocking discourse monologue. His famous "Seven Words That You Can't Say on Television" and other monologues that he gave on his "Filthy Words" radio program led to charges against him which were ultimately upheld by the Supreme Court.

Of course, nowadays, even television shows billed as family entertainment contain words and phrases that would have been completely banned by Hollywood's earlier code of ethics. In fact, the use of profanity on TV is increasing every year. According to Bauder (2002), during four weeks of viewing in 1989, Parents Television Council researchers counted 108 uses of *hell* and *damn*. By 1999, there were 518.

RELIGION

In other cultures, some of the most common types of words used for swearing have to do with religion. These include languages like Italian, Spanish, French, and Catalan.

Consider Catalan (Vinyoles 1983), a Romance language related to Spanish and Provençal spoken by about 6 million speakers mostly in the northeast region of Spain. The most common and severe swear words in the language relate to God, Christ, the body parts of God (e.g., the head of God, the heart of God, the liver of God, etc.), the Virgin Mary and the saints, the body parts of Mary, other biblical persons, and liturgical objects (unleavened bread, host).

Québec French is similar. Josh Freed and Jon Kalina (1983) present a comical look at swearing in Québec in their book, *The Anglo Guide to Survival in Québec*. We provide a sampling of examples from Freed & Kalina's book in table 18.1. It provides a rich assortment of religious terms that share a single idea in English: *sun-uv-a-gun* or, usually, a stronger version of this.

● **TABLE 18.1**
Québec French Swear Words

Québec French	Literal Translation	Meaning
hostie	host; small delicate water representing the body of Christ	son-of-a-bitch!
calvaire	Calvary, the place where Christ was crucified	son-of-a-bitch!
sacrifice	holy sacrifice	son-of-a-bitch!
esprit	the Holy Spirit	son-uv-a-gun

Freed & Kalina 1983

Table 18.2 gives an interesting look at how swear words are attenuated in both Québec French and English. On the left we find different variations of the word *tabernacle*. Looking down the list of English translations on the right, you can see the impact of the swear word also decreasing, with *shit* (or something stronger) at the top and the innocent term *shucks* at the bottom. An English parallel would be the use of the euphemisms *jeez, jeepers,* and *sheesh* for the name *Jesus*.

● **TABLE 18.2**
Attenuation of the Québec French Swear Word *Tabernacle*

Québec French	Literal Translation	Meaning
tabernacle	tabernacle; altar	shit!
taberouette	tabernacle; altar	shoot!
tabernouche	tabernacle; altar	sugar!
taberslaque	tabernacle; altar	shucks!

Freed & Kalina 1983

Religious terms are so commonly used for swearing in these cultures because the Catholic Church has traditionally been a very strong presence. For any culture that places importance on religion, a powerful insult involves referring to aspects of the religious belief in a negative manner. While sexual terms still figure into swearing in French,

Spanish, and other traditionally Catholic societies, they are generally less common and typically less powerful than religious terms.

MOTHERS

Reverence toward motherhood as the basis for swearing is not uncommon cross-culturally. For example, in Macedonian and Serbian, referring to someone's mother in an inappropriate manner, for example, in sexual terms, can be considered one of the worst types of profanity.

Using motherhood as a basis for swearing is considered by some scholars to reflect cultural views regarding the categorization of women as, on the one hand, angelic objects to revere and worship like the Virgin Mary and, on the other hand, the wild temptress such as Eve. This is often referred to in the literature as the angel vs. whore dichotomy (Hughes 1991).

Hughes suggests that this has traditionally been reflected in English through the use of terms of praise and abuse when referring to females:

- abuse: slut, whore, hussy, broad, bitch, hag, witch
- praise: honey, sweetheart, darling, dear, angel, baby, sweetie

There have traditionally been few neutral terms that refer to women besides *woman*. Even seemingly neutral terms like *lady* and *girl* can have strong negative connotations depending on the context and culture. In fact, most terms used for women have strong connotations in either moral or emotional terms. For men, by contrast, there have (at least in the past) been a larger number of neutral terms, for example, *guy, bud, fellow, man, mate, dude, dog.*

SOCIAL STATUS

Cultures with strong social hierarchies regarding, for example, class, gender, sex, race, and ethnicity, frequently base insults and swearing on these scales.

In many Asian cultures, great emphasis is placed on hierarchical social relations, as between male vs. female, older vs. younger, superior vs. subordinate, learned vs. illiterate, and so on. Not surprisingly, there are strict norms governing appropriate behavior in each of these relations. Deviating from this behavior through either words or actions is a serious offense and the focus of many insults and swear words. In Chinese culture, one's elders and those who went before are held in high regard, so any negative reference to them is considered derogatory. One such insult translates as "forgotten origin" which would be used to refer to a person who has forgotten his or her own ancestry.

Hierarchical relations based on sex are also common themes for swearing in cultures where one sex is less highly valued than the other. We see this in American English where women have traditionally been considered to have lower social status than men. Most women runners would not be offended were someone to tell them that they "run like a man"; in fact, it may even be taken as a compliment. However, telling a man that he "runs like a woman" would be less well received by most men. Differences in the use of positive and negative terms for men and women noted just above can be viewed as a reflection of these differing roles in society. The lower status of women in traditional China and other cultures where men typically occupy a higher social level than women is similarly reflected in swearing where there are more negative terms focusing on the behavior of women than of men.

ANIMALS

Finally, as we noted at the beginning, reference to animals is used in some cultures as a basis for swearing. In traditional Chinese culture, for example, the division between humans and animals is very clear-cut, and to move over this line is a way of degrading a person. Some insults include *bald donkey* 'a bald man who looks like a donkey'; and *well-bottom frog* 'a person who has narrow views regarding some things, like a frog who sits at the bottom of a well; an ignorant or arrogant person.'

Summary

It should be clear that the terms people use for swearing and insults reflect the values of that culture. Learning a new language means more than learning to say words and sentences. It also means learning how to use the language and how not to use it if you choose.

Learning about politeness or swearing in another language is important because it gives you power. If you know when, how, where, and why to use rude or polite terms, you will have more power over your interactions with native speakers and, as a result, be closer to acting like a native speaker.

References

Andersson, Lars-Gunnar, & Peter Trudgill. 1990. *Bad language*. London: Penguin.
Bauder, David. 2002. A red-letter day for TV swearing. Monday, March 11, 2002. *The Associated Press*.
Freed, Josh, & Jon Kalina. 1983 *The Anglo guide to survival in Québec*. Montreal: Eden Press.

Hughes, Geoffrey. 1991. *Swearing: A social history of foul language, oaths and profanity in English*. Cambridge, MA: Basil Blackwell.

Offord, Derek. *Using Russian: A guide to contemporary usage*. 1996. Cambridge: Cambridge University Press.

Vinyoles, J. J. 1983. Catalan blasphemies. *Maledicta* 7.99–107.

Conclusion

*L*et us review where we have been and what we have learned.

Language Is a Human Phenomenon

Young children are remarkably successful in acquiring language. The human mind is uniquely adapted for this purpose. Children are able to identify the general properties of the language or languages that they are exposed to and use this knowledge to speak and understand. For various reasons, this capacity is gradually lost as children grow older and acquire their first language.

Language Is a Skill and Practice Is Essential

A child learning a first language has ample opportunities for practice. The speech directed to children is generally very simple; the concepts are basic; the sentences are short; and there is considerable repetition and feedback. The child gets to practice this very fundamental skill all day long from a very early age.

The task for the adult learner is similar to the task for the child, but there are some important differences. The main similarity is that it is a skill for the adult just as it is a skill for the child. The key to success for both is practice, practice, practice.

But the differences are significant.

- The child's 'universe of discourse' is very limited and simple; the adult's is very broad and often complex.
- The child gets to practice the same things over and over again for most of its waking day; the adult has other things to do, the time for practice is limited, and practice may become boring.
- Practice for the child is mixed in with learning to do other things, such as playing, eating, and interacting with other people; for the adult learner, language practice is often an activity that is distinct from other activities.
- The first language that a child learns is not competing with another language; a second language that an adult learns is competing with a first language that has been very well learned and intensely practice for many years. The linguistic habits associated with the first language often interfere with the capacity to perform flexibly and spontaneously in the second language, especially in the early stages of learning.
- An adult learner is able to reflect on the structure of his or her own language and that of the language to be learned.

There Is a Social Aspect to Language

When we learn a language, we must learn not only what to say and how to say it but also when to say it. The 'when' has to do with the social situation and what is appropriate in a given situation. Appropriateness has to do with choice of words, use of particular grammatical constructions, and even accent.

Children learning a first language are usually very good at identifying the social aspects of languages and figuring out what is appropriate in a range of situations. However, the task is a complex one, and the rules are sometimes difficult to figure out, even given ample evidence.

For the adult learner there are cultural differences that have to be understood and internalized in order to use a language properly in social contexts. These differences are usually difficult to describe in concrete terms. While it is sometimes possible to state clearly the linguistic differences between two languages (e.g., in terms of the sounds or the order of words), the cultural differences can be very subtle and often not understood consciously by native speakers. Nevertheless, sensitivity to the existence of these differences is an important part of learning another language.

Look at Your Own Language

Adult learners typically do not have the time that young children have to focus on the problem of language learning. This, and the fact that the first language interferes with the second language, suggests that adult learners need to adopt certain strategies to make their task more manageable and increase the likelihood of success. One is to understand as well as possible the differences between the two languages. For some people, a conscious recognition of the differences is an important step toward isolating where problems lie and for dealing with them.

The main areas that we have looked where there are significant differences among languages are the following:

- *Word order*: Different languages order the main verb and other important words differently with respect to other parts of the sentence than English does.
- *Word forms*: Some languages mark the function of words and phrases using inflection (such as case, tense, and aspect), while for the most part English does not.
- *Sounds*: The sound inventories of languages can differ dramatically, as can their phonotactics.
- *Getting people to do things*: What counts as a polite request in one language sounds rude in another language and doesn't sound like a request at all in yet another language.

How to Use This Knowledge

Observations such as these can be used to structure your learning to make the best use of your available time and energy. Here are some of the strategies we have suggested in this book.

- **Keep it simple.** Don't try to master something complex until you've mastered the parts.
- **Structure matters.** Language has structure. It is possible to take advantage of the structure to understand the differences between languages more effectively and focus on what needs to be learned and practiced.
- **Play the odds.** The best strategy is to focus your time and energy on those aspects of the language that are most frequent. This includes the words, the forms, the structures, and the set phrases.[1]
- **Practice, practice, practice.** Learning a language is like any skilled activity that requires physical and mental coordination—practice makes perfect.

---

1. We do not recommend this strategy if you are going to be tested on a large number of relatively infrequent items.

Subject Index

Language Index

African American Vernacular English. *See* English, African American Vernacular

Algonquian language. *See* Ojibwa

Amharic, 125

Ancient Greek. *See* Greek, Ancient

Appalachian English. *See* English, Appalachian

Arabic, 67, 68, 85, 94, 125, 188–89, 212, 217–18; Egyptian, 232–33

Bantu language. *See* Swahili

Bella Coola, 70

Berber, 70, 125

Boumaa. *See* Fijian

British English. *See* English, Received Pronunciation

Bulgarian, 84, 111, 121–22, 125, 140, 141, 149–50

Burmese, 125

Canadian French. *See* French, Canadian

Cantonese, 125. *See also* Chinese

Catalan, 243

Cebuano, 125

Chinese, 57, 61, 82, 116, 129, 141, 149–50, 157, 186, 196, 230–31, 245. *See also* Mandarin

Chipewyan, 70

Croatian, 84, 208

Cubeo, 125

Czech, 56, 110

Dravidian language. *See* Malayalam

Dutch, 84, 160–61, 209–10

Egyptian Arabic. *See* Arabic, Egyptian

English: African American Vernacular, 57; Appalachian, 214–15; New Zealand, 107; Received Pronunciation, 96, 217

Eskimo, Siberian. *See* Siberian Eskimo

Estonian, 125, 208

Ewe, 85, 111

Fijian, 94

Finnish, 42, 57, 125

French, 5, 37, 39–41, 43, 53, 56, 61, 66, 67, 84, 85, 86–87, 100–101, 102, 104, 105, 111, 116, 125, 133, 135–36, 138, 141–42, 147, 149–50, 155–56, 169, 182, 196–97, 198, 208, 212, 217–18, 234–35, 242; Canadian, 214–15, 239, 241–42, 243–44; Parisian, 214–15, 239

Gaelic (Scots), 125

International Phonetic Association

The International Phonetic Association webpage provides the full chart of consonant and vowel symbols as well as IPA fonts: https://www.internationalphoneticassociation.org/.

Consonants of Standard American English

The consonants of Standard North American English, in IPA, classified by voicing, place of articulation, and manner of articulation:

		Place of Articulation													
		Bilabial		Labio-dental		Inter-dental		Alveolar		Retroflex		Palatal		Velar		Glottal	
Plosive		p	b					t	d					k	g		
Nasal			m						n						ŋ		
Flap									ɾ								
Fricative				f	v	θ	ð	s	z			ʃ	ʒ			h	
Affricate												tʃ	dʒ				
Approximant			w								ɹ		j				
Lateral approximant									l								

(Manner of Articulation — row labels on left)

State of the Glottis: | Voiceless | Voiced |

Vowels of Standard American English

The vowels of Standard American English, in IPA, presented using the traditional American classification system:

Monophthongs:

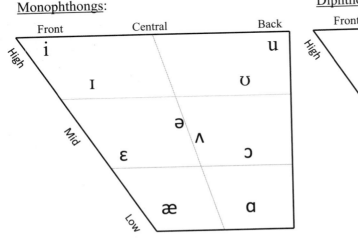

Diphthongs:

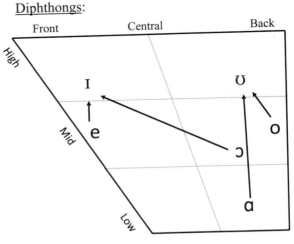